DEFLECTING IMMIGRATION

DEFLECTING IMMIGRATION
NETWORKS, MARKETS, AND REGULATION IN LOS ANGELES

Ivan Light

Russell Sage Foundation • New York

The Russell Sage Foundation

The Russell Sage Foundation, one of the oldest of America's general purpose foundations, was established in 1907 by Mrs. Margaret Olivia Sage for "the improvement of social and living conditions in the United States." The Foundation seeks to fulfill this mandate by fostering the development and dissemination of knowledge about the country's political, social, and economic problems. While the Foundation endeavors to assure the accuracy and objectivity of each book it publishes, the conclusions and interpretations in Russell Sage Foundation publications are those of the authors and not of the Foundation, its Trustees, or its staff. Publication by Russell Sage, therefore, does not imply Foundation endorsement.

Library of Congress Cataloging-in-Publication Data

Light, Ivan Hubert.
 Deflecting immigration : networks, markets, and regulation in Los Angeles / Ivan Light.
  p. cm.
 Includes bibliographical references.
 Contents: Globalization and migration networks—Regional dispersion of Mexicans—When is migration demand-driven?—Hard times in the barrios—How the garment industry expanded—Why the garment industry contracted—Asian place entrepreneurs—Deflecting Latinos from suburbs—Racism or poverty intolerance?—Sequential absorption and deflection.
 ISBN 0-87154-538-1
  1. Los Angeles (Calif.)—Emigration and immigration—Economic aspects. 2. Immigrants—California—Los Angeles. I. Title.

JV6926.L67L54 2006
304.8'79494—dc22

2005057776

The paper used in this publication meets the minimum requirements of American National Standard for Information Sciences—Permanence of Paper for Printed Library Materials. ANSI Z39.48-1992.

Text design by Suzanne Nichols.

RUSSELL SAGE FOUNDATION
112 East 64th Street, New York, New York 10021
10 9 8 7 6 5 4 3 2 1

For Jerome I. Hyman and Louis W. Pitt
with thanks long overdue

"The law in its majestic equality, forbids the rich as well as the poor to sleep under bridges, to beg in the streets, and to steal bread."

—Anatole France

— Contents —

=== About the Author ===

Ivan Light is professor of sociology at the University of California, Los Angeles.

= Preface =

THIS BOOK emerged as a result of a decade's reflection on globalization theory, which I read, and Los Angeles, where I live. The fit was poor. Globalization was expected to send as many immigrants as world cities could house and employ. As the years passed, however, Los Angeles had become the default destination for a mass migration of Mexican and Central American immigrants that was quasi-independent of the job supply and the housing supply. Worthy, courageous, and deserving people, these impecunious migrants were so numerous that the Los Angeles metropolitan area could not properly house nor employ all of them without undermining the region's livability. The inability was ultimately the result of a migratory influx that exceeded the region's growth capacity, but that is old news, and not the subject of this book.

The subject of this book is what Los Angeles and, by inference, other first-reception cities of the First World did and do in self-defense when inundated by sustained, high-volume migration of poor people. The scenario is common in the twenty-first century. There is a simple answer to it. The cities deflect some immigrants elsewhere by enforcing municipal, regional and state ordinances and laws that prohibit slums, sweatshops, and an impoverished life style. Deflection reduces the burden of immigrant integration by transferring it somewhere else. Deflected immigrants become someone else's concern. This transfer does not reduce the volume of immigration to the destination country. Immigrants come in the same numbers as before, but fewer come to the deflecting locality, whose absorption burden is thereby eased. Sequential absorption and deflection from first-reception cities to second-reception cities to third-reception cities becomes national immigration policy by default when national governments cannot or will not constrain immigrant influx to manageable levels, support first-reception areas with targeted relief for their exceptional burdens, or effect long-term immigration's equal dispersion over the national terrain.

What I describe in these pages as Los Angeles's evolution toward a poverty-intolerant growth regime summarizes three decades during which the city and the region searched for solutions to ever-intensifying problems that arose from the influx of low-wage Latinos from Mexico and Central America The English call this method of problem solving "muddling through." The region's de facto solution brought together four linked but independent contributors: home owners, social justice movements, housing and labor markets, and local governments. First, selfish homeowners were partly successful in defending Los Angeles's suburbs against affordable housing. Second, the actions of caring and humane citizens of the Los Angeles region reduced the supply of slum housing and sweatshop jobs. Third, in conjunction with housing and labor markets, immigrants' social networks effectively relayed the bad news to new immigrants still in Mexico, thus discouraging their intention to settle in Los Angeles. Finally, Los Angeles regional governments became increasingly intolerant of immigrant poverty, and so began to enforce previously ignored laws and ordinances that restricted the ability of poor people to live in the area.

Deflecting Immigration is not a heart-warming story. In general, the native-born residents of the Los Angeles metropolitan region clung to their automobile-dependent, decentralized, wasteful, but beloved and internationally coveted style of life against an unexpected threat, the mass migration of poor people from Mexico and Central America. Integrating these immigrants would have required Los Angeles to reduce its livability as not only its citizens defined it, but also as many urban experts do. Facing a self-propagating mass migration, projected to continue for sixty years, Los Angeles confronted the unexpected and novel problem of how to apportion the region's, California's, and the nation's responsibility to integrate impoverished newcomers and how to equalize among the states the social and economic burdens that integration required. The unofficial policy of poverty intolerance that finally prevailed, broadly interpreted, permitted Los Angeles to deflect approximately one million immigrants who would otherwise have made Los Angeles their home during the 1990s. Instead, this million went elsewhere in the United States. Deflection protected suburban homeowners from neighborhood changes they disapproved of, but permitted thousands of immigrants already vested in the Los Angeles region to enjoy better housing, better health, better wages, and better life quality than they otherwise would have done. This improvement was a victory for the many social justice movements that took up the cudgels for immigrant rights in the 1980s and 1990s. However, like it or not, deflection was the policy Los Angeles actually followed.

Sources

Five chapters in this book were originally conceived as independent articles and appeared in journals and edited collections. They were edited to promote coherence and readability and to add documentation. No chapter is as it originally appeared. All coauthors of the original articles were graduate students at the University of California, Los Angeles. Chapters 1, 2, 3, 9, and 10 are completely new, and were written expressly for this volume.

In an early form, chapter 2 was presented at the Annual Meeting of the American Sociological Association in San Francisco on August 17, 2004. My coauthor was Michael Francis Johnston, who was then a post-doctoral scholar at UCLA.

An earlier version of chapter 3 was published as Ivan Light, Rebecca Kim, and Connie Hum (2002), "Globalization Effects on Employment in Southern California, 1970–1990," in *Globalization and the New City*, edited by Malcolm Cross and Robert Moore, New York: Palgrave.

An earlier version of chapter 4 was Ivan Light, Richard Bernard, and Rebecca Kim, 1999, "Immigrant Incorporation in the Garment Industry of Southern California." *International Migration Review* 33: 5–25. Additional methodological and empirical details appear in that paper.

An earlier version of chapter 5 was published as Ivan Light and Victoria Ojeda, 2002, "Wearing out Their Welcome," in *Unravelling the Rag Trade*, edited by Jan Rath, Oxford: Berg.

Chapter 6 was originally published as Ivan Light, 2002, "Immigrant Place Entrepreneurs in Los Angeles, 1970–1999." *International Journal of Urban and Regional Research* 26: 215–228.

Chapter 7 was first published as Ivan Light (2003), "Immigration and Housing Shortage in Los Angeles, 1970–2000," in *Host Societies and the Reception of Immigrants*, edited by Jeffrey G. Reitz, San Diego: Center for Comparative Immigration Studies of the University of California.

Acknowledgments

M Y INTELLECTUAL and practical debts are many. First, I had graduate student collaborators on several chapters in this book that, although edited additionally for this publication, originally appeared elsewhere. I thank in this connection Richard B. Bernard, Connie Hum, Michael Francis Johnston, Rebecca Kim, Victoria Ojeda, and Elsa von Scheven. Additionally, two undergraduate work-study student assistants, Angie Yi and Neerada Garcia, sweated over the text, the notes, the excel files, and the other, endless tasks that every book requires. Anthony Alvarez also proofed text and tables, and assembled polling data on regional attitudes toward immigration. I thank them all for their tireless and careful work. Several undergraduate students at UCLA were sufficiently interested in and enthusiastic about this book that they took photographs for it. Their photographs appear along with a few of my own, I thank Maria Benitez, Marissa Manalo, Mayra Marentes, Rachel Sarabia, Lizabeth Suon, and Antonio Vallejo Jr. for their contributed photographs. I thank Elizabeth Tirado for her archival research.

I also thank the Research Committee of the University of California Academic Senate that supported five of these chapters with small research grants. The University of California's Institute for Mexico and the United States provided a small grant that permitted me to expand the data analysis in chapter 2 during the summer of 2005. During the spring of 2002, I enjoyed a three month fellowship at the Hanse-Wissenschaftskolleg in Delmenhorst, Germany, where the earliest version of chapter 1 was presented at a colloquium. The Rockefeller Foundation also gave me the benefit of thirty peaceful days at their Bellagio Study Center, a valuable gift of time. Several colleagues took the time to read and critically evaluate my chapters. I thank especially Edna Bonacich, Rubén Hernández-León, Robert Kloosterman, Jan Rath, and Jeffrey Reitz. Anonymous reviewers of the book manuscript offered some excellent advice. Naturally, despite these liberal and generous helpers, I bear exclusive responsibility for errors of fact, interpretation, or method.

Finally, as ever, I owe my physical survival to my practical wife, Leah, who never hesitated to remind me that, however parlous the state of the world, our garbage cans needed to be curbside Wednesday mornings.

Ivan Light

= Chapter 1 =

Globalization and Migration Networks

NTIL RECENTLY, globalization theorists claimed that Third World immigration to the world's large cities was simply a product of the changing income structure in the countries receiving those immigrants, especially in the largest cities.[1] This change in income distribution had produced a large and growing effective demand for cheap labor to which the Third World immigrants responded.[2] At the top of the income distribution, so the globalization argument proceeded, newly rich dual earner households need cleaners, gardeners, roofers, and childcare providers.[3] Immigrants from poor countries took these low-wage jobs and unemployed native workers declined them.[4] The immigrant workers received no social security benefits and no employer-paid health care. Their wages were not reported to tax officials, and their job tenure was casual. Immigrant employees of rich households therefore could not afford the mainstream products and services that require a mainstream income. Like their newly downsized native-born counterparts, immigrant workers looked for discounted goods produced and sold in the informal sector. Like the rich, the immigrant poor bought clothing manufactured in the informal sector. Unlike the rich, who bought clothing in fancy boutiques, the workers in the informal sector bought garments from street-corner vendors and swap meets. Their housing was cheap, dilapidated, and overcrowded.

The flow-chart in figure 1.1 shows how the leading theorist of demand-driven immigration, Saskia Sassen, explained Third World immigration and informalization.[5] Sassen's explanation was linear.[6] First, global restructuring changes the income structure of the advanced countries, on the one hand increasing the number of the wealthy and their share of total income, and on the other increasing the number of the poor but decreasing their share of the income. The hourglass income distribution creates demand for low-priced goods the poor can afford, and for the personal services the rich want. Responding to the new demand for personal services and informal

1

Figure 1.1   Global Restructuring and Informalization

Global Restructuring	$\longrightarrow$	Demand for Cheap Labor	$\longrightarrow$	Immigration from Third World	$\longrightarrow$	Informalization

Source: Author's compilation.

production workers, immigrants from poor countries swarm into the great cities of the developed world where they fill both needs. Much of this employment is informal. Whether they work for wealthy households or for industrial sweatshops, the immigrant poor receive substandard pay and benefits, often in cash. However, in this view, globalization-induced changes in demand completely explain immigration and informalization. In a nutshell, restructuring theory maintained that globalization emanates from world cities whose income structures "create a strong demand for immigrant labor."[7]

By the millennium year, both immigration and informalization had increased in the large cities of the developed world,[8] just as expected, but a strict demand-driven explanation seemed less convincing than it had earlier.[9] Its major proponent had even modified it in the face of criticism.[10] Insisting that "the recent growth of an informal economy in the large cities of the core countries" still required explanation, Saskia Sassen claimed only that "a good share of the informal economy" was attributable to demand-driven immigration.[11] This modification invites the conclusion that another, and equally good, share was the product of "immigrant survival strategies" imported from sending countries. If so, Sassen belatedly acknowledged that immigration was partially supply-driven after all. Sassen's theoretical revision addressed and incorporated criticism of her earlier demand-driven theory.[12] Critics agreed that changes in income structure in the 1970s, the alleged globalization effect, had triggered the Third World migration to the most developed countries. However, once under way, it was argued, Third World migration soon saturated the original demand, and then began to propagate itself through migration networks independently of labor demand. In this argument, critics advanced a two-stage model of immigration of which the second stage was supply-driven, and the first demand-driven. That is, whatever may originally have initiated it, Third World immigration to the developed world's biggest cities later derived from what Douglas Massey, George Durand, and Nolan Malone called "cumulative causation"[13] rather than, or in addition to, the original causes.[14] Cumulative causation means that, once begun, migrations build momentum independent of the initiating conditions. Thereafter, they no longer depend upon the initiating condition for continuation. There is ample historical precedent for such "spillover" migration.[15]

Urbanization or Overurbanization?

Moreover, a two-stage theory is more compatible with historical studies of Third World migration to Third World cities. Addressing such cities, mid-twentieth-century research uniformly stressed supply-driven migration, not demand-driven. In the three decades immediately after World War II, urbanization studies focused upon the puzzling tendency of internal migration into Third World cities such as Nairobi or Mexico City to expand faster than the cities' employment bases.[16] Economists declared that this migration was based upon irrational optimism about employment chances.[17] Other scholars dubbed this tendency "overurbanization" in deference to the belief, then widely shared, that real urbanization could expand only to the limit permitted by the job supply, and that, notwithstanding Henry Mayhew's account of London's ubiquitous street hustlers,[18] the nineteenth-century urbanization of Europe had observed this decent constraint.[19] Hence, migration-driven urbanization beyond that limit in the twentieth century had to be overurbanization, not simply urbanization.

This conclusion conferred troubling paradoxes. The term overurbanization denied contemporary Third World urbanization on the basis of prior First World experience, thus consecrating the past as the infallible model of the present. Moreover, the term overurbanization denied Third World urbanization on logical grounds, rejecting facts in the name of theory. Keith Hart's discovery of the urban informal economy in 1973 broke this conceptual barrier.[20] The urban informal economy consisted of workers outside the purview of government regulation and recognition. Petty vendors, repairmen, unlicensed taxicabs, service personnel, and the like plied their trades in Third World cities without the knowledge of government tax or statistical agencies.[21] Paralleling the informal occupational sector was an informal housing sector. The urban informal housing sector consists of colorful self-built squatter shanties in hillside communities called favelas or bidonvilles.[22] Scholars who relied exclusively on government-supplied statistics could not see the hidden occupations that supported overurbanization because official statistics did not report them. This blind spot created an illusion of frantic urbanization that had outstripped employment growth, leaving large urban populations without support. Overurbanization was the name of that illusion.[23] In reality, we now realize, migration-driven urbanization had outstripped only the growth of the mainstream or formal employment sectors reported in government statistics. It had not outstripped the urban informal sector, which expanded invisibly to support the huge population of ex-peasants.[24]

Contemporary migration to major cities of the developed world resembles the overurbanization that an earlier generation of scholars observed in great cities of the Third World.[25] In both cases, international migrants

Table 1.1   U.S. Population by Nativity and Metropolitan Residence, 2000 (Percentages)

	Total	Native	Foreign-Born
Total population, of which:	100	100	100
Metropolitan areas	81	79	95
In central cities	29	28	45
Outside central cities	52	52	50
Five million or more population	30	27	54
In central cities	11	9	27
Outside central cities	19	18	27
One million or more population	55	52	78
In central cities	19	17	37
Outside central cities	16	17	14

Source: Schmidley (2001).

showed initial preference for the largest cities. In the United States of America, 54 percent of immigrants lived in cities with populations of five million or more in 2000, but only 27 percent of the native born did so (table 1.1), and immigrants showed a comparable preference for big cities in Europe.[26] Similarly, as in the Third World, immigrants to those large cities first saturated the mainstream urban labor markets that governments supervised, regulated, and counted, and only then poured into informal sectors, which expanded to accommodate them. As in the Third World, this process created a two-tier economy of a regulated mainstream and an unregulated informal sector. Western capitals like Washington, Paris, and London now have the same dual occupational structure as Dakar and Lagos. In effect, great cities of the First World are now attached to the "overurbanization" that, two generations ago, had only affected the great cities of the Third World. Overurbanization's leap across international boundaries and oceans reflects three decades of globalization in the interim.[27] Globalization links regions that previously were not linked, opening labor flows where none previously occurred, and widening those that had existed. Thanks to globalization, London, Paris, and Los Angeles now connect to labor-exporting hinterlands whose uttermost reach once terminated in Lagos, Algiers, and Mexico City. In this sense, globalization remains part of the explanation for informalization in great cities of the developed world even when the one-stage, demand-driven hypothesis is abandoned: One finds additional evidence of globalization in the supply-driven migration of Third World people to large cities of the developed world.

The pace of migration to the developed countries quickened in the late twentieth century. According to Douglas Massey and Edward Taylor, "the world's population of immigrants has increased at a rate exceeding world population growth and the potential for future growth in international migration is . . . staggering"[28] according to the International Organization for Migration,[29] the world contained 84 million international migrants in 1975; by 2000, there were 175 million international migrants in the world. About 2.3 million persons emigrated every year from the developing to the developed world. In Europe, 7.7 percent of population were international migrants in 2000; in North America, 13 percent; in Australasia, 19.1 percent. But in Asia and Latin America only 1 percent of the population were, and in Africa only 2 percent. Except for globalization, there would be more international migrants in Latin America, Africa, and Asia, and fewer in North America, Europe, and Australia.

Systemic Limits to International Migration

The questions addressed here are how far network-driven migration can continue in big cities of the developed world before it engenders and encounters systemic resistance, and what form will this resistance take— political, economic, or both?[30] The underlying assumption is that, thanks to globalization, the supply of immigrants in the world has become unlimited, organized by migration networks, cumulative, self-propagating, and connected to the large cities of Europe, Australia, and North America.[31] If so, left to itself, Third World immigration into the developed countries will continue until it encounters systemic resistance—or until everyone who could migrate has done so.[32] Systemic resistance unfolds from the migration process itself rather than from adventitious or conjunctural causes such as droughts, hurricanes, or even wars. In this sense, systemic resistance is a spontaneous and predictable countermobilization capable of slowing or stopping additional immigration to a destination. The form of the resistance means just that: is it political resistance, or economic, or some combination of the two?

Of great practical importance to immigration control, this question is also of theoretical significance in immigration studies, which seek to understand the natural history of migrations. This history starts with processes that initiate migrations and continues to those that slow and stop them. Migrations have a beginning, middle, and an end.[33] They do not continue indefinitely because something stops them. Underlying this inquiry is the expectation that, once under way, cumulatively caused migrations end in predictable ways. Hence, as David Heer has declared, the processes that terminate migrations are as worthy of investigation as the causes that begin them.[34]

Neoclassical economic theory already explains both how migrations end and how they start. Economists propose that as migrations mature, international markets gradually equalize labor costs in the destination and sending countries. The slow equalization of labor costs tends to slow the migration, which ends when labor costs are identical at destination and origin. Here is a systemic theory of why migrations end, but the focus is markets, not social networks. Social science lacks a systemic theory of migration comparable to what economists utilize. Lacking it, social science research routinely addresses the inception of migrations, and their maturation, but not their termination. Addressing the termination entails examining the political and economic constraints on immigration in the expectation that, as cumulative migrations mature, the constraints on them increase and eventually stop the migration altogether. If we find a difference between the political and the economic limit, the narrower limit defines the boundary of the possible. That is, migrations cannot persist past either their political or economic limit.

International Migrants' Economic Options

Once abroad, migrants must earn livelihoods, or receive transfer payments, or both. Legal migrants entering developed countries enjoy access to government-mandated welfare benefits, such as income support, free education, subsidized housing and transport, and tax-supported medical care. Illegal migrants can even claim some welfare benefits. Comparable benefits for migrants are not present in Third World cities, nor were they during the industrial urbanization of the nineteenth century. Transfer payments therefore did not then support unemployed immigrants at their destination, though they do now. Particularly in the European welfare states—the world's most generous—transfer payments and welfare benefits remain substantial. Welfare states support unemployed immigrants more generously than do the migrants' countries of origin. In Third World cities, today as in the past, immigrants must find employment to live. The task is not so easy there either. Josef Gugler reminds us that underemployed rural-urban migrants place substantial burdens on the infrastructure of Third World cities. In 2005, as if to signal his agreement with Gugler, President Robert Mugabe torched Zimbabwe's urban shantytowns in an effort to force rural-urban migrants back to the countryside.[35] Even in welfare states that tap economies of abundance, political constraints limit the extent to which international migrants can rely upon welfare benefits and transfer payments. After all, transfer payments to unemployed immigrants impose a burden upon host economies, diverting resources to the subsistence of immigrants that might have gone to other useful purposes. Although immigrants do not receive more transfer or welfare benefits than their counterparts, immigrants are generally poorer.[36] Therefore, as a group, immigrants receive more transfer payments and welfare benefits, and are more often poor in both Europe and North America.[37]

Intergroup differences are large. Immigrant families were 7.5 percent of families in Norway in 2001, but the immigrant families obtained 66 percent of total social assistance payments and 16 percent of unemployment payments.[38] Additionally, the ratio of transfer payments to immigrants relative to nonimmigrants has steadily grown less favorable to immigrants and more burdensome to state treasuries.[39]

The economic limit allowable for immigrant welfare is 100 percent of the national domestic product, leaving nothing for any other purpose. The political limit is the largest share of domestic product that host governments will allocate to the welfare of immigrants. Obviously, political limitations on transfer and welfare payments begin well before the economic limit is reached. In that sense, the support limit of welfare assistance must be political, not economic. Naturally, more generous and immigrant-friendly political parties will compete with less generous counterparts, leading to internal political debate in reception countries about how generous to be. This debate is under way now in Europe and the United States, and has been stiffening resistance to immigration for a generation. Setting a specific limit on how many immigrants to support must, ultimately, be a political decision. Welfare states run out of the will to support immigrants before they run out of the capacity. Boeri declares that nonmigrants in Europe "oppose migration because they perceive it as a tax."[40] Indeed, a political backlash against welfare benefits for immigrants has been under way for three decades in all the developed countries,[41] slashing transfer payments and welfare benefits, and limiting immigrants' access to both.[42] Supply-driven migration into the developed welfare states therefore cannot depend on infinitely expanding welfare state benefits to support new immigrants. The political limit on immigration, however, has not yet been defined in either Europe or North America.

Transfer payments aside, employment is the principal economic support for immigrants in destination countries. Employment is also usually instead of transfer payments and welfare benefits, but may be in addition to them. Immigrants bring hands to work, not just mouths to feed, and they earn their way. Seeking work, immigrants find employment in the mainstream or the ethnic economy, the latter including the informal sector.[43] The mainstream economy offers wage and salary employment fully subject to official regulation and enumeration. Here immigrants work as employees for wage and benefits packages comparable to what nonimmigrants receive and within legal standards governing their occupation and industry. Employment discrimination against immigrants is illegal in all developed countries. European welfare states have tried to restrict immigrant employment to this mainstream sector, constraining self-employment and the informal economy, while guaranteeing immigrants wage parity with nonimmigrants, and using transfer payments and welfare benefits to support the unemployed.[44] They have been partly successful, but immigrant self-employment has increased regardless.[45] Moreover, the cost of suppression has been high unemployment among immigrants, especially in northern Europe, where government policy deliberately stunted ethnic economies.[46] Even outside Europe, the mainstream economy is everywhere the principal way immigrants support themselves, far exceeding all the alternatives (welfare and transfer payments, ethnic economy) in terms of enrollment.

Expansion of Employment Buffers

Immigrants look to two other sectors for income, however. The first is the ethnic economy, which includes both the ethnic ownership economy and the informal sector. Ethnic ownership economies consist of business firms owned and managed by immigrants as well as the coethnics they employ.[47] Immigrants can start and operate businesses; they need not always be employees. The firms of the ethnic ownership economy have addresses, telephone and fax numbers, and business licenses. They pay taxes. Firms in the ethnic ownership economy are known to governments, which subject them to regulation with appreciable if not entire success. True, this regulation is lax, but because it exists, wages and working conditions in ethnic economies cannot lag too far behind those in the mainstream. The second source of immigrant income outside the mainstream economy is the informal sector of the ethnic economy. In informal sectors, immigrants work for unusually low wages in inferior working conditions. They often obtain employment from other immigrants, who need not be coethnics. Thus conceived, subway musicians are self-employed in the informal sector. Each busker owns a firm with one employee, herself. Governments do not count subway buskers as firms, nor do they regulate their wages or working conditions. The informal sector is a genuine free market. As a result, wages and working conditions trail those in the administered mainstream, and even the ethnic economy. There is no economic limit on the possible deterioration of working, safety, and health conditions in politically unregulated economic activities. In the informal sector, there is no wage too low, no job too dangerous or too dirty, and no right to health care.

As long as the mainstream economy has an abundance of jobs to offer immigrants, immigration enjoys smooth sailing. Foreign workers were welcome in Europe during the 1950s and 1960s, when they helped rebuild the war-devastated continent.[48] Immigration's stormy ride begins when the mainstream labor market cannot employ all who seek work, but fresh immigrants nonetheless arrive.[49] At that saturation point, other and more troublesome means of support must expand. Failing that, the immigration simply stops. Immigrations that continue after mainstream labor markets, or their resolute political interdiction, result in unemployed or underemployed immigrants, increased utilization of welfare benefits and transfer payments, expanded ethnic ownership economies, and expanded informal sectors. These expansions support the surplus immigrant workers.[50] Of course, welfare states, ethnic economies, and informal sectors do not arise abruptly as a result of and following upon the saturation of the mainstream economy. Subsequent immigration expands them, but does not cause them. Moreover, welfare states serve nonimmigrants as well as immigrants and normally nonimmigrants are more numerous than the immigrants. Nonimmigrants also work in informal sectors, and are usually the largest group in them. Nonetheless, continuing immigration into labor markets of Europe and North America required and led to the expansion of the ethnic economy and informal sector.[51] This expansion offered migrants income above and beyond what they earned in the mainstream economy or might obtain as transfer payments, and as an alternative to under- or unemployment. Ethnic ownership economies and urban informal sectors expand to absorb those who cannot find employment in the mainstream economy.[52] Expanding in response to need, the informal sector and the ethnic economy buffer the interdiction of destination economies that would arise from the unavailability of mainstream employment and transfer payments. When immigration is protracted, the expansion of ethnic economies signals declining well being of immigrants.[53] Thanks to strong and generous welfare states, immigrant self-employment was initially constrained in Europe, but has increased there despite the constraints.[54] In North America, where freer markets predominated and welfare benefits were more limited, ethnic ownership economies and informal sectors were initially stronger than in Europe, but both have continued to expand in the last generation as well.

The ethnic ownership economy and informal sector form an employment buffer. In effect, the employment buffer (informal sectors and ethnic ownership economies) expands the carrying capacity otherwise imposed by mainstream employment, welfare benefits, and transfer payments.[55] In Third World countries, 40 to 90 percent of urban workers find employment in buffer sectors; an estimated half of Mexico's workers work in the informal sector.[56] In cities of the developed world, the numbers are more modest, rarely exceeding 20 percent.[57] Nonetheless, 20 percent appreciably expands a world city's immigrant absorption capacity over what the mainstream alone could support. One might suppose that, though they slightly expand the carrying capacity of destination cities, informal sectors and ethnic economies cannot expand it indefinitely. After all, if high-volume migratory influx continues, destination cities finally experience saturation in the ethnic economy and informal sector just as they earlier experienced it in the mainstream economy. Ultimately even the buffers reach saturation, thus signaling the economic limit of immigration.

That plausible expectation is mistaken. In reality, ethnic economies and informal sectors enjoy a virtually unlimited expansion capacity in response to the self-propagating, cumulatively caused migration of the impoverished.[58] There really is no economic limit to the capability of First World cities to support impoverished migration from the Third World. That is, no matter how many migrants are dropped into world cities, and no matter how abruptly they arrive, those cities have the economic resources to assure the immigrants' bare survival. To be sure, if abruptly and generously introduced, additional migrants would experience sharply declining standards of living even in the world's wealthiest cities. When they crowd into already crowded cities, they reduce their average wages and housing quality.[59] Confronting unlimited new immigration, migrants' earnings, housing, food, and health care decline in quality and quantity as local resources are stretched ever farther. In overcrowded labor markets, new arrivals drive wages of earlier immigrants down, and those earning low wages require cheap housing.[60] In the extreme case, immigrants simply cannot afford rent, and must manufacture their own housing from cast-off building materials. In principle, the immense migrant shantytowns that ring Lagos, Rio de Janeiro, and Mexico City could equally well be constructed around Paris, London, New York, and Los Angeles by migrants from Lagos, Rio, or Mexico City, thus permitting Paris, London, New York, and Los Angeles to support many more impoverished immigrants than they currently do.

This denouement has not already happened in world cities because it is politically impermissible, not economically impossible.[61] Well before impoverished migrants starve, metropolitan police intervene to demolish their shantytowns, impound their wares, and eject them from the vicinity.[62] "Inhabitants of shantytowns" step outside the law "from the moment they acquire land and start the protracted building process."[63] World cities are politically unwilling to tolerate the slums that surround the primate cities of the Third World, but, except for this political intolerance, there is no economic reason Third World slums could not arise outside London, Paris, New York, and Los Angeles right now. Political intolerance of immigrant poverty is expressed as political refusal to permit the degraded economic activities that the immigrants' survivalist lifestyle requires.[64] These activities include sweatshops where low-paid work violates wages, health, and safety regulations and slums that violate municipal housing ordinances. In world cities, the political willingness to tolerate immigrant poverty is weaker than the economic capacity to do so.[65] In this sense, the systemic limit to sustained, high-volume immigration of the impoverished is political, not economic.[66]

Political Control of Unwanted Immigration

From the perspective of reception localities, immigrants are unwanted when their numbers exceed the employment capacity of the mainstream economy, and thereby expand slums and sweatshops, both economic buffers. Immigrants are also unwanted when their numbers add significant costs to the local welfare bill, including prisons, education, and health. When immigrants' tax payments flow to the national government, but their added costs fall to local and state governments, as happens in the United States, the resulting "fiscal mismatch" imposes financial hardships in the provinces that are invisible in the capital.[67] The economic burden of immigration on localities does not consist only of illegal immigrants, although these are politically most vulnerable. It also includes legally authorized but impoverished immigrants whose number imposes significant added costs on state and local treasuries. Indeed, impoverished but legal immigrants are harder for states and localities to accommodate than illegal immigrants because legal immigrants have full and unquestionable rights to state welfare benefits. From a local perspective, the blameworthy failure of national immigration policy does not lie solely in the national government's inability to exclude illegal immigration, but also in the national immigration laws that admit more lawful immigrants than localities can comfortably house and employ.

Only national governments have the legal authority to make immigration policy and control immigration. Quite inconveniently, national governments cannot fulfill their responsibilities, and impacted localities cannot take up the political slack.[68] Thus, the U.S. Constitution provides no role for states to regulate borders or legislate immigration. The result is political deadlock: those who can will not, and those who will cannot regulate migration. In illustration, consider California's unsuccessful suit against the federal government in 1994. Because the federal government had exclusive responsibility for immigration, Governor Pete Wilson demanded that Washington compensate California for costs of imprisoning illegal immigrants. These costs, he claimed, California had wrongfully been compelled to assume because the federal government failed in its constitutional responsibility to exclude illegal immigrants. Federal courts rejected California's petition for relief, but the federal government failed thereafter to prevent illegal immigration to California.

National governments are not entirely ineffective. National immigration policies and border enforcement have reduced unwanted immigration below the unregulated level—but they have not stopped it in either the United States or in Europe. As a result, since 1970 the population of unwanted immigrants and illegal immigrants continued to grow in all the First World reception areas of the preceding generation.[69] Between 1970 and 1998, the foreign population of sixteen European countries increased by eight million, and their share of the European population from 3.6 percent to 5.3 percent.[70] In approximately the same period, the foreign-born population of the United States increased by fifteen million, and their share of the total United States population from 4.7 to 9.2 percent.[71] Thanks in significant part to illegal migration—itself a response to stricter border controls—border controls alone cannot stop cumulatively caused migration.[72] For the same reason, political controls at national borders slow but do not stop the buffer expansion that attends saturation of mainstream labor markets and retraction of welfare state benefits, including health and education, and of transfer payments. A nation's impacted cities attract the lawful migrants whom immigration law cheerfully admits as well as those illegal migrants whom porous borders fail to exclude.

This situation will not change soon. Experts do not consider national states capable of controlling international immigration.[73] Neither, however, do they consider localities to have such power. Peterson says that municipalities are powerless to exclude immigrants because they "cannot issue passports or forbid outsiders from entering their territory."[74] This judgment still holds sway among immigration scholars, who regard it as unassailable, but dissenters increasingly ask whether Peterson's judgment underestimates the ability of localities to manage immigration.[75] As Jeannette Money[76] emphasizes, the national state's immigration control is simply the primary control on immigration, not the sole one. Municipalities have long assumed practical responsibility for receiving and managing the overly numerous immigrants they receive as a result of the partly failed immigration policy and border enforcement of their national states. That part is well understood.[77] But, contrary to the accepted wisdom, in so doing, cities also assume a de facto role in national immigration policy.[78] They are not supposed to do so: it is supposedly the job of the national state.[79] They make the policy anyway.

Taking an orthodox perspective, which entirely deprives impacted cities of political agency, economists' remedy for failed border controls is stricter national legislation, which in turn is intended to penalize employers of unwanted immigrants.[80] However, also taking the orthodox view, political scientists point out that this legislation will not materialize. Impacted municipalities cannot expect relief from national governments until they can change a national election. That electoral success will require decades to achieve. Meanwhile, impacted areas can do nothing. Sociologists declare that effective national employment controls could end migration, but these are politically impossible—so nothing can be done.[81] Development economists declare long-term economic development in the sending countries the only way to shut down the unwanted migration. This conclusion, however, also imposes a long wait upon cities.[82] "There is no quick fix."[83] All these recommendations require long-term changes before impacted cities experience any relief from immigration. No one asks how the cities cope in the intervening decades of waiting. After all, they must somehow cope. While they wait, they perforce assume migration control responsibilities that complement national migration policy. Indeed, as nation states wait for migrations to run their natural course in the coming century, the ultimate political control over unwanted migration lies at the municipal, not the national, level.

Municipalities assume this policymaking role willy-nilly when they individually and independently decide how much local immigrant poverty to tolerate. To tolerate poverty means to accept socioeconomic conditions that violate subjective and legal standards of human decency.[84] Municipal toleration of immigrant poverty permits cumulative migration to continue to deteriorate economic conditions.[85] That is, the immigrants flood into expanding ethnic economies and informal sectors; as they do so, wages and working conditions decline, poverty increases, and slums expand. Lacking income, the immigrants cannot purchase adequate housing, so take up residence in slums, the most affordable housing. The result is an elongated socioeconomic hierarchy in which the distance from the top to the bottom has increased, sometimes dramatically. The elongation of this hierarchy spells painfully increased economic and social inequality in impacted municipalities.[86] When municipalities tolerate this change, the immigrant influx continues. When they enforce laws against slums and sweatshops, the local influx slows.

Municipal political controls on migration take multiple forms. This control has not, however, involved the municipalities' enforcement of federal law at the local level.[87] Sometimes municipalities actively restrict or restrain unwanted migration, a policy that exceeds their legal authority.[88] Most commonly, and of interest here, municipalities simply enforce existing industrial and housing regulations that were not originally intended to restrict unwanted migration, but have that effect.[89] These controls arise from active and aggressive municipal enforcement of state and local laws and ordinances that govern housing quality, driver's licenses, taxi licenses, health care, minimum wages, and employment conditions.[90] Intended to support minimal standards of human decency, these regulations establish a statutory floor below which social and economic conditions are not lawfully permitted to sink. Thanks to the network-driven influx of Third World immigrants, and the consequent degradation of housing, medical care, and employment conditions, migrants' conditions soon fall below the minimally acceptable legal and subjective standard of decency. In the world's advanced cities, it is illegal to earn poverty wages, to work in unsafe conditions, to peddle trinkets on the street, or to live in self-built shanties; municipal police can enforce those laws. The more generous the minimal standards of human decency, the sooner the network-driven immigration collides with them. Deteriorated and overcrowded immigrant housing is illegal, not just unsightly. Similarly, wages below the legal minimum and unsafe working conditions are not just deplorable, but illegal. In many welfare states, but not in the United States, which tolerates medical indigence, inadequate health care is illegal, not just inhumane. Once expanded by network-driven migration, employment and housing buffers require systematic violation of welfare regulations and laws because they cannot otherwise squeeze everyone into their lifeboat. Violation of housing and industrial codes is therefore an implicit condition of the supply-driven immigrants' ability to work in the ethnic and informal sectors and to live in slums, and hence a condition of their ability to stay in town. Enforcement of sanitary, health, housing, and labor standards regulations destroys economic buffers, effectively driving out the unwanted immigrants.[91]

For this reason, the aggregate of a nation's local and regional governments and law enforcement agencies becomes the last resort arbiter of the size of immigrant population the entire nation will accept. In so doing, local law enforcers are compelled to choose between opposing arguments that plumb the limit of their discretionary authority. On the one hand, local police often feel sympathy with impoverished immigrants whose economic circumstances compel them to labor and live under illegally and subjectively squalid conditions. When immigrants and their citizen co-ethnics have local political influence, as they certainly did in Los Angeles, their political influence reinforces this message.[92] Additionally, mayors, city councilors, and police understand that shutting down the slums and sweatshops would strip many immigrants of their wretched livelihood and dilapidated lodgings, leaving an unhoused, unemployed immigrant population in destitution instead of an inadequately housed, underemployed one in poverty. Finally, owners of substandard factories (dubbed sweatshops) use political influence to neutralize enforcement of health and safety legislation. Law enforcement threatens the sweatshop owners' livelihood because their businesses cannot survive if they must pay statutory minimum wages and maintain minimally legal sanitary, health, and safety conditions. Sweatshops exist because they evade these legal minima. Sweatshop employers supplement political influence, where essential, with bribery of law enforcement. For all these reasons, local police are reluctant to enforce housing and working standards and conditions.[93] Political toleration permits the informal sector to exist and even to grow in impacted municipalities.

On the other hand, as local economic and housing conditions deteriorate, thanks to the unrelenting influx of supply-driven migrants, migrant poverty worsens. Shameful and degrading social conditions arise, bringing with them the political pressure to enforce wage, sanitary, housing, and safety laws more effectively. This political pressure may emanate from frankly anti-immigrant political movements, but it need not. Immigrant protection movements also decrease immigration to a locality. In the name of fairness, social solidarity, and human decency, immigrant protection movements object to low-wage exploitation of immigrant workers and to the redolent slums they inhabit, and demand instead enforcement of existing working, health, sanitary, and housing standards.[94] At some point, this countervailing political pressure, which comes from the left as well as from the right, compels reluctant mayors and police chiefs to strengthen enforcement of housing, occupational, and industrial legislation. Enforcement renders a world city less hospitable to additional migration. Because, thanks to the augmented enforcement, there are fewer slums or sweatshops or, at least, no more can be created, there are fewer jobs and less housing for new, low-wage immigrants. The least successful local migrants depart for more hospitable municipalities elsewhere. Fewer replacements arrive, and local immigrants' housing, employment, and health conditions actually improve—without reducing the flow of impoverished immigration into the destination country. Municipalities improve the life circumstances of their resident immigrants by deflecting the rest, and it is in their long-run self-interest to do so.

The Case of Amsterdam

The best evidence in the existing archive derives from an international study of the garment manufacturing industry in seven cities that Jan Rath and colleagues undertook.[95] This study coordinated research on the garment industry in Paris, London, the West Midlands, Amsterdam, New York, Miami, and Los Angeles. In each of these metropolitan areas, immigrant entrepreneurs controlled the garment manufacturing industry[96] in which immigrant workers, many or most of them illegal, provided the labor supply. The survival of the garment industry depended everywhere on evading the laws regulating hours of labor, wages, sanitary conditions, industrial homework, taxation, health care, and social contributions. In each of these cities, garment factory owners neither paid employees for all the hours they worked, nor maintained legally required sanitary and safety conditions in their plants. The immigrant entrepreneurs also imposed illegal homework, evaded income taxation, and did not make legally mandated social security contributions.[97] Although frequently subject to journalistic exposés, garment sweatshops rarely attracted regulation by authorities, who tolerated industrial lawlessness. Bribery was sometimes involved, but a policy of implicit toleration was more important. To keep the immigrants' jobs in town, police and politicians tolerated the garment manufacturers' ubiquitous violations of industrial regulations. The police and the politicians considered toleration of immigrant poverty a humane, liberal, and pro-immigrant policy, as indeed it was.

Amsterdam provides the decisive case.[98] Probably because the Netherlands is among the most corporatist of Europe's corporatist economies, but also because a powerful anti-immigrant political backlash was under way there, Amsterdam authorities finally enforced the industrial code.[99] Amsterdam's police raided immigrant-owned garment factories and seized their books. Courts fined and shut down immigrant entrepreneurs who were out of compliance with wages, health and safety, or sanitary regulations. As a result, Amsterdam's scofflaw sweatshops simply closed down. Within three years, strict law enforcement had closed 90 percent of Amsterdam's garment factories.[100] (Many immigrant-owned garment firms relocated to Poland, where cheaper labor and lower labor standards provided a haven.) Successful law enforcement left Amsterdam with additional unemployed immigrants, leaving open the possibility that strict enforcement of industrial regulations had not been in the city's economic interest much less in that of its immigrants. Of the six large cities that Rath and his colleagues studied, Amsterdam was the only one in which police enforced existing industrial laws. Nonetheless, the others had the option too, and Amsterdam's experience displays the policymaking choice that inescapably resides with municipal authorities.

If every municipality in the Netherlands had, in tandem with Amsterdam, simultaneously enforced identical housing and work standards legislation, the instant result would have been uniform national curtailment of local informal and ethnic economies that buffered network-driven immigration. In effect, the national immigration policy, enforced at the national border, would be reinforced locally by independent poverty-intolerant urban regimes. This is a purely hypothetical illustration. Nothing of the sort happened. Imagining simultaneous enforcement simply highlights the role that urban regimes have in determining national immigration control. By enforcing existing welfare legislation, poverty-intolerant municipalities deflect immigrants into municipalities that do not enforce them.[101] In those, the process of labor market saturation and buffer expansion repeats until at last there, too, municipal authorities intervene to enforce existing wage, sanitary, safety, health, and housing laws. In this way, intolerant municipalities gradually nationalize immigration that had been local as they reduce the local scale of immigrant poverty.[102]

Conversely, when the national state declares a restrictive immigration policy at the border, but municipalities tolerate illegal housing, health, and employment conditions among illegal immigrants, the political system sends a mixed signal to potential immigrants, not a negative one. Having passed the border, an immigrant is ensured economic toleration somewhere within the reception state. Local tolerance of unlimited immigrant poverty invites illegal immigration, and contradicts the national state's closed border policy.[103] Poverty-tolerant municipalities attract immigrants whose deteriorating economic condition eventually makes those municipalities intolerant. In turn, intolerance of poverty nationalizes immigration awareness until national and municipal intolerance coincide. At that point, a systemic response against unwanted immigration is finally in place. To illegal immigrants, the national state's border policy says, "no illegal immigration," and the nation's cities all say, "no sweatshops or slums permitted here." True, to legal but impoverished immigrants, the national state's border policy still says "welcome." At the same time, however, all the municipalities now say, "no sweatshops or slums," which means, "you cannot earn a living or find an affordable residence anywhere in this country even if you gain lawful access." This massive and universal negative by municipalities trumps the national state's generous immigration policy, ending the unwanted migration even without a change in national legislation. The process is driven to this by the self-interest of municipalities, including their humane interest in decent living conditions among their immigrants.

The Cycle: From Demand- to Supply-Driven Migration

Because networks channel low-wage immigration, impoverished immigrants initially cluster in a few, poverty-tolerant municipalities. The clustering focuses and intensifies their local impact. Regional and metropolitan clustering intensifies the pressure on labor and housing markets, driving wages down and rents up. Ultimately, when civil society's minimal standard of human decency is breached, the immigrants' deplorably substandard housing and employment conditions encourage enhanced municipal enforcement of health, housing, and working standards. Law enforcement restricts the employment and housing buffers that permit the unwanted migration to continue. Municipal code enforcement is objectively anti-immigrant even should it proceed in the name of fairness and humane treatment of immigrants.

Second, and rather paradoxically, when municipalities enforce housing and labor codes, they indirectly benefit the immigrants they strip of housing and jobs. After all, when declining local economic conditions and police intolerance coincide, a city's immigrants experience incentives to identify new localities where wages are higher, housing is cheaper and less overcrowded, and police are still tolerant of poverty. In effect, the converging structural pressures, both economic and political, communicate to impoverished immigrants an incentive to divert the network-driven influx to greener pastures elsewhere, if any remain. This powerful convergence deflects a migration network from saturated and newly intolerant municipalities to others, still unsaturated and still tolerant of poverty. Hence, individual municipal closures cannot terminate the network-driven migration into their country, but can deflect the migration to other municipalities.[104] In new settlement cities, mainstream employment and housing opportunities are still available.[105] In them, the buffers can still expand to accommodate new migration. Suppose immigrants to a world city like Los Angeles have reached the limit of political toleration. The alternatives are either to discontinue the migration altogether or to colonize new localities in the United States. Once these new settlements are fully colonized, the continuing migration repeats the process, which consists of network restructuring, mainstream saturation, buffer expansion, buffer saturation, poverty intolerance, and deflection. The migration process thus breaks out of its initial encapsulation in the biggest cities and expands across the entire territory of the destination country.[106]

If so, the relationship of globalization and migration is appreciably more complex than existing theory acknowledges. Even if we agree that migrations begin in the income distribution of great cities, as globalization theorists proclaim, the migrations need not end there. The network-driven migration initially heads toward the biggest cities in the destination country because, thanks to their advanced economies, these cities offer the most attractive employment options. However, as the network-driven immigration saturates the initial demand for immigrant labor in the initial destinations, the housing and employment buffers expand. Expanded informal and ethnic economies provide employment buffers; expanded slums provide the housing buffers. Expansion of the buffers signals the transition from a demand-driven to a supply-driven migration. Ultimately, as time passes, working and housing conditions decline in the buffers, after which local political toleration of immigrant poverty also declines. These structural changes confer incentives for the migration network to identify and colonize new localities in the destination country. As these are located, newly colonized areas undergo—in sequence—influx, saturation of the mainstream, buffer expansion, buffer saturation, political intolerance, and deflection. The speed of this process, like the rate of influx, depends heavily upon urban regimes, which decide how much flouting of economic and housing laws and regulation they will tolerate. Municipal intolerance of illegal economic conditions sets the political limit on economic saturation, and occasions the dispersal of immigrants into new destinations within the reception country, a process well under way now in the United States.[107]

Why Investigate Los Angeles?

The devolution of migration policy and management to municipalities refocuses research attention onto municipalities and away from national states.[108] To address this need, the balance of this book addresses the city and county of Los Angeles and southern California, its encompassing region. One minor reason is Los Angeles's much vaunted status as "the paradigmatic case of the post-Fordist metropolis."[109] However, its main advantage to those interested in forecasting the post-Fordist future is its massive overall and massive immigrant populations. The second largest city in the United States, and the nation's largest reception center for international migration, Los Angeles is not a representative or average American city (figure 1.2). Rather, it is a representative world city with an immense immigrant population born of three decades of continuous and heavy influx. Cities of this sort occupy a special place in the world cities literature, which celebrates the case for demand-driven immigration to them. Hence, the

Figure 1.2   Metropolitan Areas with Foreign-Born Population of
One Million or More in 2000

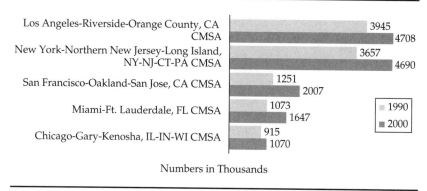

Los Angeles-Riverside-Orange County, CA
CMSA
New York-Northern New Jersey-Long Island,
NY-NJ-CT-PA CMSA

San Francisco-Oakland-San Jose, CA CMSA

Miami-Ft. Lauderdale, FL CMSA

Chicago-Gary-Kenosha, IL-IN-WI CMSA

3945
4708
3657
4690
1251
2007
1073
1647
915
1070

1990
2000

Numbers in Thousands

Source: Schmidley (2001, figure 5.1).

supply-driven immigration to Los Angeles is of special theoretical rele-
vance to that world cities literature.

The value of a case study of Los Angeles is also enhanced when juxtaposed to a demographic literature that cannot look inside the cities whose
population changes it tracks. First stimulated by the research of William
Frey, a now substantial demographic literature addresses the dispersion
of immigrants within the United States from traditional settlement destinations to new ones.[110] This internal relocation of population began in the
1980s and gained momentum in the 1990s. This demographic research
alerted social science to events of substantive and theoretical moment.
But demography cannot open metropolitan areas to examine their internal social, political, and economic dynamics. Such is the task of this non-
demographic book. It argues that network-driven immigrant influx
generates intra-metropolitan dynamics, which actually caused the geographical dispersion of immigrants that demographers observed but
could not explain. To make that case, it is essential to access the internal
dynamics by means, at least initially, of a case study. In this respect, thanks
to its location in California, a traditional settlement state, Los Angeles
offers as good a site as any, and better than most.

Finally, the experience of Los Angeles offers an opportunity to evaluate
the theoretical expectation just sketched. Network-driven migrations
should generate consequences. Hence, if in response to network-driven
immigration from Mexico and Central America, buffers did not expand in
Los Angeles between 1970 and 2000, then buffers probably do not expand
elsewhere either. If the immigration-driven expansion of buffer economies
in Los Angeles did not pose increasingly thorny legal and political issues

there, then they probably do not pose them elsewhere either. Finally, if emerging legal and political issues did not decrease tolerance for immigrant poverty in Los Angeles, then they probably do not have this effect elsewhere either. In this sense, a case study design subjects new theoretical ideas to the possibility of falsification right then and there.

Conversely, if these ideas successfully illuminate Los Angeles, then additional warrant exists for additional research in other places and using other methods is merited. The logic of testing is not the logic of discovery, but social science needs both. Moreover, especially in social science, where problems are vast and resources scanty, the research community has to eschew the old-fashioned idea that null hypotheses are rejected once and for all on the strength of a single result. Rather, they are accepted on the strength of the total literature. For individual research projects, especially those that introduce rather than test ideas, an interstitial category serves very well: the plausible. Plausibility exists when a community of researchers finds ideas likely but proof still falls short of definitive. The plausible defines the area in which research makes most sense. If a project is not plausible, we should not bother; if it has been proved, we need not bother. Social research enters the realm of the plausible when theoretical ideas make sense in the light of existing research literature and when authors introduce additional and focused evidence in support. Although plausibility does not constitute proof, it does legitimate additional research, which may lead to proof. Plausibility is what this book claims for its results, but that is a lot.

A Brief Road Map

Each chapter advances the argument in a different way, and together the ten make the full case. Chapter 2 compares the residential settlements of immigrants from Mexico and from India between 1980 and 2000. Using a data set comparing metropolitan areas, chapter 2 shows that immigrant influx in the 1980s increased the rent-to-wage ratio of both groups by 1990, but that this increase was dramatic for low-wage Mexicans and modest for Asian Indians, a much more affluent group. During the 1990s, metropolitan regions with high rent-to-wage ratios became less attractive to Mexican settlement than they had been in the 1980s. This evidence suggests that migration networks initially undermine the economic conditions of immigrants in high-volume destinations, thus tending later to redirect the migrant networks toward initially lower-volume destinations that are still unsaturated. This is the main evidence presented that directly supports the presumptive generalizability of the Los Angeles results to other metropolitan areas in the United States.

Chapters 3 and 4 form a conceptual unit. Chapter 3 spells out the theoretical implication of demand-driven migration theory. In essence, demand-driven migrations can continue forever without depreciating migrants' economic conditions in impacted destinations. Conversely, when migrations have become supply-driven, immigrant economic welfare in destinations declines as the migration continues. Chapter 4 then shows empirically that thirty years of migration from Mexico and Central America to Los Angeles resulted in ever-declining economic welfare among the newer migrants. This result is not what one would expect from demand-driven migration, but it is exactly what a supply-driven migration should deliver.

Chapters 5 and 6 also form a conceptual unit. Both deal with the garment industry of Los Angeles, the city's largest immigrant industry, and a large industry by any standard. Chapter 5 asks how and how much the garment industry expanded between 1970 and 1996. Because it was mostly informal, its growth represented the kind of buffer expansion that accompanies supply-driven immigrations. There was, however, a technical issue in the expansion because, as the chapter shows, the buffer expansion was beyond the capability of the ethnic economies to accomplish by themselves. The chapter introduces a new conceptual tool, the immigrant economy, that is essential to explain how buffer expansion actually worked.

In chapter 6, the theme is the contraction of the Los Angeles garment industry by one-third between 1996 and 2000. Although this change owed much to NAFTA and to Chinese competition, the chapter shows that increased industrial law enforcement played a part as well. Increasingly subject to police surveillance, sweatshops closed and their immigrant employees lost their jobs. Losing their jobs, some left Los Angeles. This result strengthens the claim that buffer expansion generates poverty intolerance that then deflects immigration to other destinations.

Chapters 7 and 8 address the residential integration of immigrant Latinos and Asians. Chapter 7, again introducing the Asian comparison case, offers a foil for the Latino case, which chapter 8 introduces. Thanks to the entrepreneurship of coethnic property developers and real estate agents, immigrant Koreans and Chinese enjoyed simple, prompt, and uncontested access to desirable and appropriate housing. They had all the excellent housing they needed. The chapter shows that Asian immigrant entrepreneurs joined Los Angeles growth machine in the late twentieth century.

In contrast, as chapter 8 shows, immigrant Mexicans had to struggle against regulatory barriers that raised the price of housing in suburban cities beyond what these working-class people could afford. Mexican immigration required relaxation of suburban housing codes, but the opposite materialized in the Los Angeles region. Enforcement of suburban housing codes limited Mexican access to affordable housing in the metropolitan region and thus accelerated their deflection from the region.

Chapter 9 defensively addresses the possibility that racism and ethnocentrism, not poverty intolerance, deflected Mexicans from Los Angeles. Citing evidence that contradicts this possibility, the chapter strengthens the inference that it was growing poverty intolerance that actually deflected Mexicans away from Los Angeles. The chapter does not claim, much less prove, that racism did not exist in Los Angeles, but only that it does not explain why Latinos went to new settlement states where racism was worse or, at least, just as bad.

Last, chapter 10 makes the dramatic claim that sequential absorption and deflection really amount to America's unstated and tacit immigrant policy. It then sketches the consequences of this policy. The basic four-step sequence—absorption, saturation, intolerance, deflection—pushes poor migrants around the nation's cities, subjecting them to sequential invasions of their civil rights en route. Police harassment is a routine and regular part of deflection, which is the nation's de facto immigrant policy. Harassment is not a mistake. On the positive side, a policy of absorption and deflection gradually opens all of a nation's cities to immigration, equalizing the burden of immigrant absorption on the regions, and even opening new economic opportunities to immigrants as old ones are saturated.

═ Chapter 2 ═

Regional Dispersion of Mexicans

MIGRATION NETWORKS connect immigrants abroad with friends, neighbors, and relatives at home. When favorable information about a destination reaches them, the friends, neighbors and relatives acquire both the desire and the ability to migrate. The desire comes when migrants abroad point out the advantages that migration has afforded them. The ability comes when migrants explain how they coped in a strange land, and offer to assist them to do the same. The new migrants then settle where friends, former neighbors, or relations have already most advantageously settled. Their choices of destination create nodes of settlement abroad linked to specific points of origin in the homeland.

The Cumulative Causation of Migration

Migration networks have been reliable and recurrent features of internal as well as international migrations in the past, and even in antiquity.[1] Once called "chain migration," migration networks are not newcomers in the social science literature.[2] Nonetheless, as both proponents and critics acknowledge, since Douglas Massey and his colleagues refocused the theoretical debate around them, migration networks have been the central theoretical preoccupation in the sociology of migration.[3] The reason is the self-reinforcing character of the networks.[4] Although they had borrowed the idea of "cumulative causation" from Gunnar Myrdal, Massey and his colleagues were the first to apply it to migration networks.[5] Since then, the research literature has demonstrated the ability of networks to organize the immigrants' settlement process by continuously reducing the emotional, social, and financial costs of migration.[6] The emotional cost of migration is reduced because networked migrants live and travel with friends, family, and coethnics, thus avoiding social isolation and loneliness, painful accompaniments to solo migration. The social cost of migration is reduced because migrants maintain their homeland social ties after leaving. Old friends are kept, not lost. The financial cost is reduced because migrants obtain help and information from earlier migrants, thus avoiding the financial mistakes greenhorns make. These initial advantages grow as the migration network matures because mature networks transmit more information about more possible destinations. Thanks to these serious advantages, once international networks have formed, migration becomes cumulative and self-causing. That is, once underway, a migration network self-levitates above the economic and social conditions that caused the migration, and protracts the migration by reenacting itself.[7] This transition arises when and because it has become easier and more attractive for network participants still in the homeland to migrate rather than not to migrate.

Massey and his colleagues understood that migration networks must mature to reenact themselves.[8] Subsequent scholarship has explored the maturation itself, seeking to identify what changes as networks mature. Results support the multidimensional salience of network maturity to network effects and effectiveness. Jacqueline Hagan reported that, unlike incipient networks, mature networks conferred more economic opportunities on male migrants than on female migrants.[9] Ivan Light and numerous colleagues have shown that mature migration networks do not only facilitate migrants' search for economic resources, but also expand migrants' economic opportunities, thus permitting more people to migrate.[10] William Kandel and Douglas Massey observed cultural changes in favor of migration in long-term sending communities.[11] David Heer pointed out that mature migrations sometimes exhaust the local resources abroad that support them.[12] Elizabeth Fussell addressed the start-up conditions in Mexican localities such that some incipient migrations become cumulative whereas others do not reach a self-sustaining phase.[13]

The export of network awareness to economics brought migration networks into productive juxtaposition with research on markets.[14] Anne Bartel found that immigrants settle in American cities where many coethnics live rather than in those that objectively appeared to offer the greatest economic opportunities.[15] Bartel and Marianne Koch reported that immigrants were less likely to move when they lived in cities with many coethnics, and that Asians were less mobile than Hispanics.[16] James Rauch and Gary Hamilton recommended that economists could benefit from "a deeper understanding of the sociological approach to networks"[17] Unfortunately, they did not explain just how network migrations connected to economists' traditional priority, markets. Economists study markets, not networks. Nonetheless, economists observed migration network effects in their data, and acknowledged that both markets and migration networks "explain variation" in migration volume.[18] This conclusion permitted economists to maintain their professional focus on factor price equalization and acknowledged the exogenous role of migration networks, but this acknowledgment did not achieve a closer theoretical integration of networks and markets, which is one goal of this chapter.

That integration progressed, however, thanks to economists' research on the local wage impacts of migration. After two decades of efforts to measure any effect of immigration on the wages of native-born workers, economists reached a virtually unanimous conclusion: Immigrants do not depress the wages of nonimmigrants very much. Because this issue has been uppermost in public attention, the result circulated widely, and was widely, if erroneously, interpreted to mean that immigration did not affect anyone's wages. Ignored was the research regarding the impact of immigration on the wages of earlier immigrants: sustained immigration reduces the wages of earlier migrants, especially coethnic immigrants, but does not much reduce the wages of nonimmigrants. The explanation is simple. Immigrants affect those most like them in the labor market, who are precisely earlier coethnic immigrants in the same localities.

Although the recent research literature on immigrants' rents is undeveloped relative to research on their wages, Albert Saiz (2003) has recently shown the immigration raised short-term rents on moderate-priced housing in reception cities. Moreover, a long tradition of research on housing still applies. Since the Chicago School of the 1920s, we have known that sustained immigration increases rents most in heavily immigrant regions and neighborhoods, and least or not at all in nonimmigrant areas and neighborhoods.[19] Immigrant influx raises rents most in ethnic neighborhoods where earlier arriving coethnics already reside. Indeed, precisely this concentration of immigrants in ethnic neighborhoods of the central city, with its upward pressure on neighborhood rents, drives residential succession, which is the master process whereby urban morphology adapts to population influx.[20] When they settle next to earlier coethnic immigrants, as they usually do, new immigrants drive up rents in the ethnic neighborhoods in which their numbers are the greatest. They do not equally affect rents in neighborhoods where they do not live. True, ramifying displacement waves later affect entire metropolitan areas, changing their urban morphology after a lag. According to Ernest Burgess and Donald Bogue, vintage authorities of the Chicago School of urban sociology, the driving force behind morphological change in American cities of the early to mid-twentieth century was sustained immigration to city centers by low-wage migrants.[21] In the early twentieth century, these low-income immigrants were southern and eastern Europeans; now they are Mexicans and Central Americans. The rest is very similar. Low-income immigrants still cluster in the center of America's biggest cities. As residential densities rise in city centers, residential pressures rise after a lag on concentric peripheries, causing metropolitan areas to expand radially and to reallocate internal land uses. This expansion finally corrects the initial upward impact of immigration on inner city rentals, returning rents to earlier levels, but this restoration is possible only because metropolitan areas expanded radially from the center in response to immigrant influx in the center.[22]

Two Hypotheses

Taken together, these research findings yield two basic hypotheses. The first is that, when sustained over time, network-driven migrations gradually drive down immigrants' wages and drive up their rents in highly frequented network destinations. If immigrants dispersed randomly over the entire terrain of the destination country, their arrival would not deteriorate the local ratio of rents to wages because their impact would be diffused. A product of the migration network, the initial clustering of immigrants focuses the immigrants' economic impact, causing deterioration of their own economic welfare in major network destinations. As the migration network matures, and new cohorts of immigrants settle where predecessors had already settled, the ratio of immigrant rents to immigrants' wages becomes less favorable. Admittedly, some migrants move up the social ladder, then relocate into the suburbs, making access for new migrants in the central city. Mexican entrepreneurship still speeds this self-repair process just as the entrepreneurship of European immigrants did a century ago.[23] With this help from ethnic entrepreneurs, reception areas can continue longer to integrate newcomers without deleterious wage or housing effects. But a high-volume, protracted, migratory influx overwhelms this partial self-repair. Despite the forty-year moratorium on migration caused by the Immigration Act of 1924, European immigrants took three generations to climb out of America's socioeconomic basement.[24] In the twenty-first century, without the benefit of any moratorium, Mexicans and Central Americans face harder conditions for effectuating this climb, but they are nonetheless moving in that direction.

After a lag, self-correction begins when economic deterioration in the most frequented destinations compels the migration network to reorganize its station list, sending newer migrants to previously low-ranking destinations while reducing the number selecting traditional destinations. As David Heer once put it, external economic opportunity "counters the effect of migration networks."[25] Therefore, as they mature, migration networks should routinely disperse immigrant populations from top-ranking destinations to initially lesser-ranked destinations. Dispersal is a normal and predictable long-range result of sustained, high-volume, network migration. In effect, when following migration networks, large-scale, protracted immigrations disperse immigrants from traditional settlements to what Micah Bump, Lindsay Lowell, and Silje Pettersen called "new settlement states."[26] This generalization is my second hypothesis for which confirmatory evidence is sought below in the comparative analysis of the regional dispersion of immigrant Mexicans and Asian Indians between 1980 and 2000.

Table 2.1   Foreign-Born Mexicans by State and Year of Entry, 2000

States	Total	Entered 1990 to 2000	Entered 1980 to 1989	Entered Before 1980
California, Texas, Illinois	6,425,898	2,714,727	1,934,108	1,777,063
(Percentage)	(70%)	(61%)	(75%)	(83%)
Other forty-seven states	2,754,288	1,730,338	655,321	368,629
(Percentage)	(30%)	(39%)	(25%)	(17%)
Total, United States	9,180,186	4,445,065	2,589,429	2,145,692

Source: U.S. Census Bureau (2000c).

Regional Dispersion of Migrants, 1980 to 2000

Regional clustering characterized immigration to the United States in the historic past, and still does.[27] European immigrants clustered by national origin in the eighteenth and nineteenth centuries, and in the early twentieth. Nonetheless, since the 1980s, but especially in the 1990s, the foreign-born population of the United States has tended to disperse from the six states of traditional immigrant settlement to new settlement states.[28] This dispersal has somewhat reduced the regional clustering of immigrant population, but dispersion has not equally affected the entire United States. On the contrary, nineteen new settlement states, mostly located in the South and West, experienced more than 100 percent growth of their foreign-born populations in the 1990s.[29] In the other twenty-six states, where moderate growth prevailed, the population of foreign-born persons grew by less than 100 percent in the 1990s. As of 2000, the six traditional states still housed 69 percent of the entire foreign-born population of the United States. Nonetheless, the dispersion of foreign-born population during the 1990s had partially nationalized what had been a regional problem—and, in the process, relieved the heavy immigrant concentration in the six traditional states of settlement.

By far the largest migrant group entering the United States, Mexicans began to disperse from traditional destinations in the 1980s and 1990s, especially the latter. In contrast, the relocation of native whites from California was greater in the 1980s than in the 1990s, and owed much to the sale of high-priced houses that the whites replaced inexpensively in other regions.[30] Three big states (California, Texas, and Illinois) had housed 83 percent of the immigrant Mexican population of the United States in or before 1980 (table 2.1). In 2000, these three states housed only 70 percent of the total Mexican immigrant population.[31] Because of this population shift,

1,193,656 foreign-born Mexicans, who would otherwise have resided in the big three, lived in forty-seven nontraditional states in 2000. Growth of population in those forty-seven reduced the immigrant population of the three traditional states below what it would have been without dispersion. This dispersion was partially a product of relocation of settled immigrants, who moved from traditional to nontraditional settlement destinations. However, the dispersion mainly reflected shifting settlement choices among Mexicans still outside the United States.[32] By deciding to enter non-traditional states during the 1990s, Mexican immigrants inside and outside the United States reduced the share of the total Mexico-born population in California, Texas, and Illinois in 2000.

Substituting metropolitan area data for state data permits a more refined analysis of the dispersion of the Mexican-origin population between 1980 and 2000 and highlights concealed variation in local economic conditions.[33] The 1980, 1990, and 2000 public-use samples of the U.S. census permitted an evaluation of the extent to which population dispersion had occurred among 100 metropolitan areas. This analysis uses the 5 percent public use samples of the 1980, 1990, and 2000 U.S. censuses.[34] The key variable is "metropolitan area"—a county, or combination of counties, centered on a large urban core. The analysis eliminated areas for which data were not available in 1980, 1990, and 2000.

Michael Francis Johnston (personal communication) created four data-sets from the three decennial censuses. The first contains 225 metropolitan areas. It examines the economic situation of foreign-born Mexicans (FBM) and foreign-born Asian Indians (FBAI). The second contains only those thirty-five metropolitan areas in which five or more FBM and five or more FBAI reported earning income, and five or more FBM and five or more ($5 \times 20 = 100$ residents) FBAI reported paying rent. It compares FBM and FBAI in particular metropolitan areas. The third dataset contains only the eighty-five metropolitan areas with five or more FBM who reported earning income and five or more who paid rent. The fourth dataset contains only the forty-seven metropolitan areas with five or more FBAI who reported earning any income and five or more who paid rent. It scrutinizes the economic situation of FBAI.

The datasets also permit a comparison of foreign-born Mexicans and foreign-born Asian Indians with respect to their dispersion from metropolitan areas in the 1980s and 1990s. Because Asian Indians were the most educated foreign-born population in the United States in 2000, and earned correspondingly more than other immigrants, comparing them with foreign-born Mexicans, a low-wage population, exposes any differences in propensity to disperse that might be attributable to socioeconomic status or income.[35] Table 2.2 displays the census population estimates for these two immigrant groups in 1980, 1990, and 2000 as well as the number of metropolitan areas in which both national-origin groups were represented

Table 2.2   Foreign-Born in U.S. Metropolitan Areas

	1980	1990	2000
Foreign-born Mexicans			
People	1,821,440	3,479,620	7,194,560
Metro areas	214	238	269
Foreign-born Asian Indians			
People	178,700	376,320	847,180
Metro areas	215	238	265

Source: U.S. Census Bureau (2000a), 5 percent PUMS.

above trace levels. The fourth largest immigrant group in 2000, Asian Indians, was only one-eighth as numerous as the Mexican group.

The first task is to identify the top one hundred metropolitan areas in which Mexicans and Asian Indians lived in 1980. These one hundred were grouped into five deciles, each of which consisted of ten metropolitan areas ranked according to the number of foreign-born Asian Indians or Mexicans each contained. As table 2.3 indicates, of immigrants who lived in the one hundred largest metropolitan areas of the United States, 67.1 percent of foreign-born Mexicans and 74.8 percent of foreign-born Asian Indians lived in the top fifty in 1980. Between 1980 and 2000, both groups reduced their populations in the single largest settlement. Among foreign-born Mexicans, drop was from 49.2 percent in Los Angeles to 37.3 percent. Among foreign-born Asian Indians, it was from 51.3 percent in San Jose to 38.8 percent.[36] Beyond this top-ranked metropolitan area, Mexicans dispersed down the urban hierarchy more than Indians did. In 2000, Indians clustered as heavily in the largest fifty metropolitan regions as they had in 1980, whereas Mexicans had shifted 6 percent of their urban population to the smaller fifty metropolitan regions. The intermetropolitan dispersion of Mexican immigrants tended slightly to nationalize the awareness of Mexican immigration, but it greatly simplified the problem of immigrant integration among the top ten immigrant-reception regions. Small potatoes for the United States, the relocation was immensely consequential in first-reception metropolitan areas.

Why Did Mexicans Disperse?

Demographers have abundantly documented the dispersion of the Mexican population, but only David Heer tried to explain it.[37] Heer noticed that Hispanic immigrants had dispersed from traditional settlement states during the 1990s.[38] To explain this dispersion, Heer proposed that large Hispanic communities saturated coethnics' economic opportunities, thus

Table 2.3   Dispersion of Foreign-Born Among Hundred Biggest Metropolitan Areas

Decile	Cities	Total Population	FBM	Percentage FBM	FBAI	Percentage FBAI
1980						
1	1 to 10	477717	11087	49.2	1412	51.3
2	11 to 20	211978	1911	8.5	307	11.1
3	21 to 30	149287	1324	5.9	193	7.0
4	31 to 40	111758	696	3.1	90	3.3
5	41 to 50	86310	88	0.4	57	2.1
Total				67.1		74.8
2000						
1	1 to 10	478920	33580	37.3	4894	38.8
2	11 to 20	247546	10696	11.9	1711	13.6
3	21 to 30	172650	4082	4.5	1347	10.7
4	31 to 40	128988	4948	5.5	687	5.4
5	41 to 50	102000	1563	1.7	792	6.3
Total				60.9		74.8

Source: U.S. Census Bureau (2000a), 5 percent PUMS.

compelling newcomers to seek greener pastures elsewhere. Although he conjectured that the cause of the dispersion was differential "economic opportunity," he did not directly examine the effects of either wages or rents on Hispanic dispersion. Instead, he inferred economic opportunity in a locality from the relative size of Hispanic populations in each. The more Hispanics in a state, the fewer their presumed economic opportunities. As predicted, Heer found that the "percentage increase" of Hispanic migrants during the 1990s was higher in states with smaller Hispanic populations in 1990.[39] "The results . . . strongly support the idea that relatively unfavorable job opportunity can counter a positive spiral causing continual increase in immigration into a particular locality"[40]

Did IRCA Cause the Dispersion of Mexicans?

However, Heer's is not the most visible explanation. Taking quite a different approach, Massey, Durand, and Malone proposed a political-legal explanation. They suggested that new federal laws and new federal migration-control strategies diverted Mexican immigration from traditional destinations because the federal remedies lowered the wages of Mexican immigrants.[41] Their principal proof is the shift of illegal immigrants' entry points eastward after 1993, an approximate coincidence in time of federal remedies and the initiation of the regional dispersion of Mexican immigrants. The coincidence implies that federal laws and policies caused the Mexican dispersion.[42]

It is certainly true that changes in federal laws preceded the dispersion as the authors claim, but reviewers have already declared their political-legal explanation simplistic and one-dimensional.[43] Massey, Durand, and Malone's explanation of wage declines among Mexicans focuses on the federal level, overlooking state and local policies that might also have affected wage levels. Chapters 3 though 7 in this volume show that state and local laws did affect the Mexican wage levels, rents, and dispersion. Moreover, even if federal policies affected the dispersion, as Massey, Durand, and Malone aver, federal laws did not single-handedly cause it. A large and international literature had already documented the economic causes of the long-term decline of Mexican immigrant wages in the United States.[44] Among those identified, globalization and the focused impact of network migration on local wages predominated.[45] Ignoring this literature, Massey, Durand, and Malone complain that "a perverse consequence" of the 1986 Immigration Control and Reform Act (IRCA), which expanded employer sanctions, was "to lower the wages and undermine the working conditions" of Mexican immigrants, legal and illegal alike because of its cost incentives.[46] Although they mention and credit the proliferation of inexpensive and bogus immigration documents that occurred in the aftermath of IRCA, they do not agree that bogus documents entirely subverted IRCA's intended economic effect, which was to interdict the employability of illegal immigrants. They claim that employers deducted the costs of the extra paperwork IRCA necessitated from the wages they paid immigrants.[47] The result was lower immigrant wages. Employers also learned to favor subcontracting over hiring in order to evade IRCA's punishment for knowingly hiring illegal immigrants. This tactic enhanced the trend toward informalization. The result was again lower wages for Mexican immigrant workers. In effect, according to these authors, IRCA lowered Mexican immigrant wages—but did not structurally change the economy or the operation of migration networks.

Mexican immigrant wages did fall, and informalization of Mexican economic activity did increase after IRCA as Massey and his colleagues claim. The facts are clear.[48] However, it is not clear that these authors correctly identified the real causes. First, Mexicans' wages began to decline before IRCA became law, which would not have happened if IRCA alone caused the declines.[49] Also, Mexicans were not the only immigrants to suffer wage decline in the 1980s and 1990s.[50] Wage declines would not have been so general had IRCA caused them. Third, IRCA was a national law, nationally enforced. If it caused declining wages among Mexicans, then the decline should have been nationally proportional among all states: wages should have declined as much in Nebraska or Maryland as in

Table 2.4   Hourly Wages of Foreign-Born by Native Decile:
Percentage in Lowest Decile, 1990

	Native	Foreign-Born	Foreign-Born Arrival		
			1985 to 1990	1980 to 1984	Before 1980
Six high-immigration states	10	17.7	27.5	21.8	13.7
California	10	22.7	37.0	27.1	17.0
Los Angeles	10	29.5	44.5	35.9	22.4

Source: Reprinted with permission from Smith and Edmonston (1997, 180). © the National Academy of Sciences, courtesy of the National Academies Press, Washington, D.C.

Texas, California, or Illinois. However, this was not the case: wages of all immigrants were lower wherever immigrants were most concentrated (table 2.4).

Most strikingly, in both 1990 and 2000, the incomes of immigrant Mexicans were lower where they were most concentrated and their gross rents were higher. Assisting on this project, Elsa von Scheven assembled evidence, presented in table 2.5, about Mexican immigrant incomes and rents in 1990 and 2000.[51] She arranged both distributions in descending order of Mexican concentration. Los Angeles County led the array, followed by California, Texas, and Illinois. All these are traditional destinations and home many Mexicans. Next came eight new settlement states, which saw heavy Mexican influx in the 1990s, and after them the thirty-nine other American states.[52] The economic conditions of Mexicans improved in both 1990 and 2000 as they moved to lower-density Mexican settlements. For example, in 2000, immigrant Mexicans reported average annual incomes of $8,469 in Los Angeles, $8,898 in California, $9,337 in Texas and Illinois. The figure was $10,090 in the eight new settlement states and $10,919 everywhere else. Mexicans' gross rents displayed the opposite tendency, higher in traditional settlements and lower elsewhere. This patterning is compatible with the hypothesis that migration networks reduced Mexican immigrants' earnings and increased their rents. The IRCA hypothesis cannot explain these results.

Massey, Durand, and Malone also claim that IRCA actually hurt legal immigrant wages more than illegal immigrant wages.[53] Of course, Congress intended IRCA to reduce only the wages of illegal immigrants. IRCA's reduction of the wages of legal immigrants the authors declare a counterproductive result of badly framed federal legislation. There is a simpler way to explain why the wages of legal as well as illegal Mexicans immigrants fell in the aftermath of IRCA: low-wage immigration reduces the wages of earlier coethnic arrivals, legal and illegal alike.[54] That is, continuing immigrant influx (not IRCA) saturated prime network labor markets,

Table 2.5   Rents and Wages of Mexican Immigrants Eighteen or Older

	Los Angeles County	California	Three Traditional States	Eight New Settlement States	Other States
1990					
Yearly income	$5,805	$5,998	$5,843	$6,183	$7,099
Gross rent	$529	$507	$445	$271	$366
2000					
Yearly income	$8,469	$8,898	$9,337	$10,090	$10,919
Gross rent	$618	$634	$562	$498	$540
1990, N	12,200	27,373	36,199	3,828	4,093
2000, N	15,600	27,685	49,793	18,201	19,901

Source: U.S. Census Bureau (2000a); U.S. Bureau of the Census (1990), 5 percent PUMS.

and pulled down the wages of all Mexican immigrants. Desperate for work, legal and illegal immigrants turned to the informal economy, which expanded in consequence, lowering wages additionally as it did. These results would have occurred even if IRCA had never passed.

One issue remains: what consequences for immigrant settlement followed from declining immigrant wages and living conditions and from expanded informalization? Massey, Durand, and Malone declare that IRCA and border enforcement did not "deter many migrants," their stated objective.[55] If so, IRCA did not disrupt the flow of immigrant labor. Had IRCA disrupted the flow, causing fewer immigrants to enter the United States, immigrant wages would have fallen more slowly in the late 1980s, undermining the likelihood that labor market saturation caused the Mexican dispersion of the 1990s. However, IRCA did not reduce immigration influx and so did nothing to diminish the force of the saturation argument.

Having claimed that IRCA caused wage declines among Mexican immigrants, Massey, Durand, and Malone never investigated the subsequent impact that wage declines had on the regional dispersion of Mexicans. Therefore, even conceding for the sake of argument that IRCA caused declining wages, the declining wages then caused the dispersion of Mexican immigration. In that case, the political explanation would only be half right.

However, the critique does not end here. The proliferation of bogus documents that followed IRCA reduced and possibly even eliminated IRCA's economic impact. With bogus immigration documents available everywhere for a day's pay, illegal immigrants did not need to lose their jobs because of IRCA.[56] Spanish-language newspapers told readers where bogus documents were for sale, and how much they cost.[57] On this ground, one can minimize IRCA's contribution to the adverse economic changes that affected Mexicans in the 1990s. If bogus documents subverted the economic effects of IRCA, rendering the act ineffective, then why did immigrant wages fall in the 1990s? Something else must have done it if IRCA did not.

What about high rents? Already, beginning in the 1980s, rising rents in traditional reception centers, such as Los Angeles and California, put additional economic pressure on Mexican migrants, legal and illegal alike.[58] Of course, rents all over the United States rose in the 1990s for reasons unrelated to immigration, but in the immigrant neighborhoods, they also rose because of immigration. Rising rents reduced immigrant well-being as surely as did declining wages. In the 1990s, Mexican migrants were whipsawed by declining wages and rising rents, a hardship that encouraged them to prefer new settlement states over traditional states. However, neither IRCA nor Operation Gatekeeper raised rents even supposing they lowered wages.

Massey, Durand, and Malone's explanation of Mexican dispersion is incomplete at best, and wrong at worst. Even if IRCA did lower Mexican immigrant wages and increase their informalization, as the authors contend, then these economic effects, not IRCA, were immediate causes of the diversion of Mexican immigration from traditional to new settlement areas. Additionally, because of bogus documents, IRCA probably did not reduce wages very much, if at all. Third, we must acknowledge the probability that the sustained, focused migration of Mexicans drove down Mexican wages in affected labor markets by increasing the supply of unskilled labor. Focused economic impacts are frequent themes in the immigration literature.[59] Finally, IRCA did not raise rents anywhere; but network migration did. In sum, IRCA does not offer a convincing explanation of Mexican dispersion.

Did Mexicans Really Use Migration Networks?

The case for a network-derived explanation of Mexican dispersion rests on what Aristide Zolberg has identified as the "strongest correlate of current U.S. migration," the regional distribution of the foreign born.[60] Network-driven migration directs new immigrants exactly where previous coethnic immigrants have already settled, a self-reproduction attributable to the initial ability of the networks to overwhelm market forces. The overwhelming power of migration networks is manifest in their sustained ability to send newly arriving immigrants to the same metropolitan regions and states regardless of rents and wages. Because of this tendency, newcomers gravitate to settlement destinations in exact proportion to the prior settlement of coethnics in every destination. That is, if 10 percent of their

Table 2.6   **Foreign-Born Population for Fifty States and Puerto Rico: Pearsonian Correlation**

Foreign-Born Mexican Population	Foreign-Born Mexicans Entered	
	1980 to 1989	1990 to 2000
1970	.995	.968
1980	.993	.959

Source: U.S. Census Bureau (2000a; 2000c); U.S. Bureau of the Census (1980a, 291–96; 1983).

coethnics resided in a Los Angeles twenty years ago, then, thanks to network migration, 10 percent of immigrant newcomers still settle there. Even if the aggregate number of immigrants rises or falls in the intervening time, the proportion of newcomers settling in places tends to remain the same over very long periods of time because of self-reproducing migration networks.

Networks themselves are usually measured directly, as Massey and his colleagues have already done. Their method shows that Mexican migrants had friends, neighbors, or kin in the destination they selected when they arrived in their destination. However, the attractive power of migration networks is measurable without actually measuring the networks themselves in this way. The alternative method is much simpler to accomplish too, and has not yet been done. One may infer the existence of migration networks from their measurable effects just as, in 1796, astronomers inferred the existence of Pluto, then invisible to telescopes, from Pluto's measurable effects on visible planets. Taking a comparable approach, table 2.6 shows the correlation coefficients that connected fifty states' prior population of foreign-born Mexicans with the number of foreign-born Mexicans resident there later, but who had entered the United States well after the initial measurement. The correlation coefficients reach a magnitude rarely found in social research. Thus, when we correlate—by their state of residence in 2000—the number of foreign-born Mexicans who lived in the fifty states and Puerto Rico in 1970 with the number of those who had entered the United States between 1990 and 2000, the coefficient is an astounding .968. In other words, the entry population of foreign-born Mexicans in the decade 1990 to 2000 fanned out among fifty states in virtually perfect correspondence to the coethnic population of those states twenty to thirty years earlier. These newly arriving immigrants from Mexico could have gone to any of the fifty American states or Puerto Rico, but instead selected states for residence in exact proportion to the 1970 and 1980 Mexican population of the states they chose. Here is indirect quantitative evidence of the power of Mexicans' migration networks.

A harder test assesses the correspondence between new immigrants' metropolitan residence in 2000, and the metropolitan residence of coethnics

Table 2.7   **Pearsonian Correlation Coefficients on
Metropolitan Area Residence**

	New Arrivals, 1995 to 2000	
	Foreign-Born Mexican	Foreign-Born Asian Indian
Foreign-born Mexicans		
1980	.82	.32
1990	.83	.30
Foreign-born Asian Indians		
1980	.50	.80
1990	.58	.86

Source: U.S. Census Bureau (2000a), 5 percent PUMS.

in 1980 and 1990. This test is harder because in 2000, there were 269 metropolitan areas that contained immigrant Mexicans and 265 that contained immigrant Asian Indians. There are only fifty states. Additionally, because most immigrants cluster in six immigrant reception states and the metropolitan areas within them, any correspondence between old settlers and new immigrant coethnics might be inflated by the tendency of all immigrants to prefer the six traditional immigrant reception states.

To obviate this problem, table 2.7 compares the residence in 2000 of newly arrived immigrant Mexicans and Asian Indians with the metropolitan residence profile of coethnics and non-coethnics in 1980 and 1990. It displays the coincidence between the residence choices of Asian Indians in 1980 and 1990, of newly arrived coethnics in 2000, and of newly arrived immigrant Mexicans in 2000. Conversely, the residence choices of newly arrived Asian Indians in 2000 were predicted from the residence profile of immigrant Mexicans. This exercise establishes an empirical baseline that identifies an expected agreement between any two immigrant nationalities and the augmented level of agreement that migration networks afford. These results show that the 1980 and 1990 residential distribution of immigrant Mexicans offered a surprisingly accurate prediction ($r = .32, .30$) of where newly arrived Asian Indians would live in 2000, and vice versa. After all, most immigrants go to the same six immigrant-friendly states. However, the residential distribution of foreign-born Mexicans in 1980 and 1990 offered a much more accurate prediction of where newly arrived immigrant Mexicans would live in 2000. The same was true of foreign-born Asian Indians whose 1980 and 1990 residential distribution among 265 metropolitan areas corresponded much better to that of the newly arrived coethnics in 2000 than it did to newly arrived immigrant Mexicans in that year. The disparity offers indirect proof of the migration network's attractive power.

Why should new immigrants slavishly repeat prior coethnics' settlement choices even decades later? The migration network is the invisible but presumptive answer. If social networks connect every destination to sending communities, then every American state in 1970 and 1980 aggregated network ties with Mexico and India in exact proportion to the number of Mexicans or Asian Indians already living there. The durability of the network tie is measured by the tendency of newly arrived coethnics in 2000 to select for residence the same metropolitan areas or states in which coethnics had settled decades earlier. The reproduction of immigrant population among destinations corroborates the massive qualitative evidence that two generations of social and economic research has already gathered about migration networks.[61]

Cities Deflect Immigrants Too

The impact of immigrants on recipient localities is already well understood. Immigrant influx changes urban morphologies as nonimmigrants move toward the periphery under pressure from new immigrants in the urban core.[62] Here the cities absorb the immigrants and are changed by the process. What escaped scholarly attention is the counterimpact of cities on immigration. Immigrants do not just change the cities they enter; they also bounce out of saturated cities. Because individual cities encapsulate local labor and rental housing markets, a nation's labor market or a nation's rental housing market aggregates thousands of local markets. As migrants settle in network-linked termini, impacted destinations become less congenial for continued settlement. Having absorbed as many immigrants as they could or, more accurately, as they wished, reception cities then deflect newcomers to other localities. Deflection means adopting policies that discourage settlement. Therefore, the initial stage of absorption is followed by a second stage of deflection.

As wages drop and rents rise in prime network destinations, the bad news travels back to homeland staging areas. New migrants increasingly substitute non-prime destinations for prime. Non-prime destinations are little used network-serviced termini. They were low-growth destinations in the period of initial settlement. As migrants switch to non-prime destinations, the growth of immigrant populations in the destination country begins to favor places with more favorable rent-to-wage ratios. Market pressures thus constrain and restrict the growth of prime network destinations in favor of non-prime destinations once the network has matured.

Absorption and Deflection of
Mexicans and Asian Indians

The actual migration of Asian Indians and Mexicans into American cities closely follows this two-stage sequence of absorption followed by

**Figure 2.1   Mean Rent-to-Wage Ratio of Mexicans in 1980
and Metropolitan Growth Rates in 1980s**

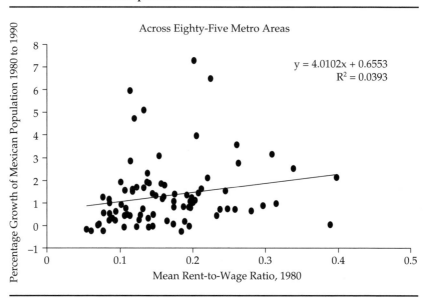

Source: U.S. Bureau of the Census (1980a, 1990, 2000a).

dispersion. Turning first to Mexicans, figure 2.1 shows that their rent-to-wage ratio was quite favorable in 1980. This measure is the relation of the mean rent of any group in a metropolitan area to the group's mean wage. When an immigrant group's rent-to-wage ratio exceeds .30, the immigrants are paying on average more than a third of their wages in rent. The housing literature considers one-third of wages the threshold of overpayment on rent, and one-half of wages the threshold of serious overpayment.[63] Overpayment constitutes economic hardship. In 1980, Mexican immigrants paid less than 30 percent of their wages in rent in virtually every American locality. Given this favorable circumstance, the rent-to-wage ratio did not disperse Mexicans in the 1980s from the network's prime destinations. During the 1980s, growth of Mexican-born population was more rapid in those metropolitan areas whose ratio had been initially most unfavorable.

Now we turn to the impact of Mexican population growth on the rent-to-wage ratio, the reverse relationship. High growth of the Mexican immigrant population in the 1980s produced unfavorable ratios in 1990. That is, where Mexican-born people had settled most heavily in the 1980s, causing rapid population growth, the ratio was most unfavorable in 1990. This result is evidence that rapid growth of the immigrant population in the 1980s drove Mexican rents up and their wages down (figure 2.2). Comparing

Figure 2.2   **Metropolitan Growth Rates in 1980s and Mean Rent-to-Wage Ratio of Mexican Population, 1990**

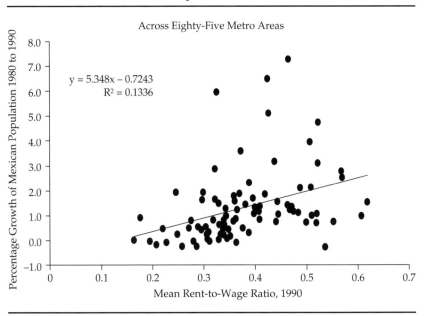

Across Eighty-Five Metro Areas

$y = 5.348x - 0.7243$
$R^2 = 0.1336$

Percentage Growth of Mexican Population 1980 to 1990

Mean Rent-to-Wage Ratio, 1990

Source: U.S. Bureau of the Census (1980a, 1990, 2000a).

figures 2.1 and 2.2, one notes as well the dramatic worsening of the Mexican rent-to-wage ratio in the 1980s. In 1980, Mexican rents were below the hardship threshold in about 90 percent of cases. By 1990, however, they were above that threshold to the same degree. In other words, by 1990, the rent-to-wage ratio of Mexicans had moved into hardship territory, and in many cases extreme hardship. Hardship in the 1990s was the consequence of riding the migration network in the 1980s.

Now attention turns to the impact of high rent-to-wage ratios in 1990 on Mexican population growth during the decade that followed. This impact measures the reciprocal effect of economically unfavorable localities on migration networks. Growth of Mexican population in the 1990s, unlike that in the 1980s, was greatest in metropolitan areas whose rent-to-wage ratio had been more favorable in 1990. These were places with low rent-to-wage ratios. As figure 2.3 shows, the rent-to-wage equation changed direction in the 1990s, going from positive to negative. True, the change did not lower the average ratio of the Mexican immigrant population, which remained unfavorable. But, thanks to augmented growth in the more advantageous metropolitan regions, the average ratio (for Mexicans) did not deteriorate further during the 1990s despite a huge influx of new Mexican migrants in that decade. In the 1990s, Mexican immigrants began to take

Figure 2.3   Mean Rent-to-Wage Ratio of Mexicans in 1990
and Metropolitan Growth Rates in 1990s

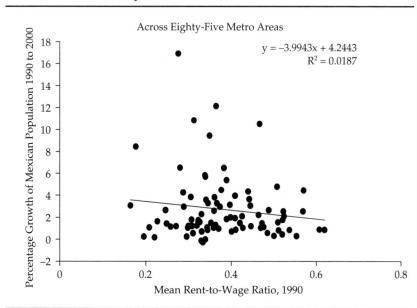

Across Eighty-Five Metro Areas

$y = -3.9943x + 4.2443$
$R^2 = 0.0187$

Source: U.S. Bureau of the Census (1980a, 1990, 2000a).

local ratios into account when making settlement decisions, and thus began to avoid metropolitan areas in which the ratio was unfavorable.

The history of the rent-to-wage ratio in Los Angeles reflects the same process. In 1980, the ratio of average Mexican immigrant rents to average Mexican wages was 26 percent in Los Angeles, a comfortable burden. By 1990, a decade later, Mexican immigrants were paying 50 percent of their wages for rent on average, a serious economic hardship. Mexicans' dispersion from Los Angeles increased around 1990, and by 2000 Mexican immigrants in Los Angeles were paying only 24 percent of their wages in rent, a comfortable burden again. Even so, Spanish-language newspapers covered the subsequent movement of rents in the Los Angeles region, nervously fearing additional increases and complaining about high rents.[64] The Spanish-language press also attributed Latino settlement in the neighboring San Bernardino metropolitan region, just east of Los Angeles, to high housing costs in Los Angeles.[65]

The experience of the affluent Asian Indian immigrants had some points of similarity with that of impoverished Mexicans and some of difference. At the beginning, Asian Indians had a very favorable rent-to-wage ratio in the forty-seven metropolitan regions in which they had settled above trace numbers. Figure 2.4 shows that in the average metropolitan region, Asian Indian immigrants were paying about a tenth of their wages as rent in 1980,

Figure 2.4   Mean Rent-to-Wage Ratio of Asian Indians, 1980, and Metropolitan Growth Rates, 1980s

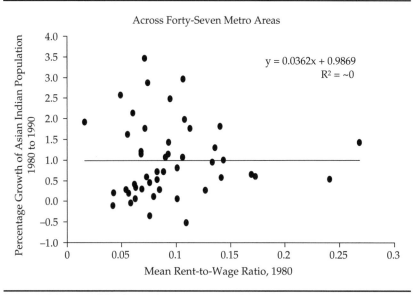

Across Forty-Seven Metro Areas

$y = 0.0362x + 0.9869$
$R^2 = \sim 0$

Source: U.S. Bureau of the Census (1980a, 1990, 2000a).

a very favorable ratio. Unsurprisingly, then, growth of the Asian Indian population of the forty-seven metropolitan regions in the 1980s bore no relationship to the rent-to-wage ratio in 1980. Asian Indians settled where they listed, unconstrained by those ratios.

Doing so, however, had slightly adverse consequences by 1990. The metropolitan areas in which Asian Indians had prevailingly settled in the 1980s tended to have higher ratios in 1990. As was also true among Mexican immigrants, Asian Indian influx in the 1980s apparently drove the rent-to-wage ratio up among Asian Indian migrants, causing a deterioration of the immigrants' economic situation by 1990. In those metropolitan regions in which Asian Indian population had grown most in the 1980s, the rent-to-wage ratio was most unfavorable to Asian Indians in 1990. But figure 2.5 also shows that, despite adverse change in the previous decade, Asian Indian rent-to-wage ratios were still very favorable in 1990. In only about 20 percent of metropolitan regions were Asian Indian migrants overpaying rent in 1990. Their Mexican counterparts, however, were overpaying in 90 percent of metropolitan areas in 1990.

Even so, in the 1990s, the rent-to-wage ratio began modestly to constrain Asian Indian immigrants' settlement decisions. True, in the 1990s, growth of that population was stronger in those metropolitan regions whose rent-to-wage ratio had been most unfavorable in 1990 (figure 2.6). The network continued to dominate the Asian Indians' settlement decisions in the 1990s.

Figure 2.5   Metropolitan Growth Rates in 1980s and Mean Rent-to-Wage Ratio of Asian Indians, 1990

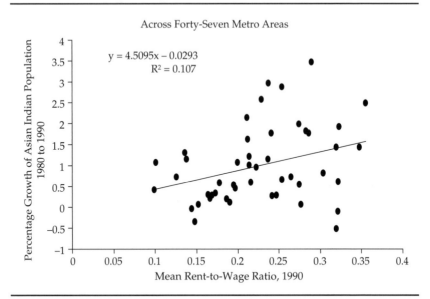

Source: U.S. Bureau of the Census (1980a, 1990, 2000a).

Figure 2.6   Mean Rent-to-Wage Ratio of Asian Indians, 1990, and Metropolitan Growth Rates in 1990s

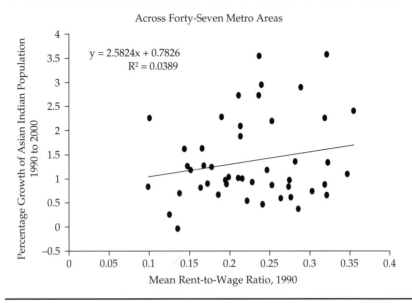

Source: U.S. Bureau of the Census (1980a, 1990, 2000a).

Indians settled where they listed. But, as indicated by the changing slope of the two equations, the rate of adverse change in the 1990s declined by about 45 percent relative to what it had been in the 1980s. Again, as had been the case for Mexicans, the slower growth of unfavorable rent-to-wage localities did not reduce the average rent-to-wage exposure of Asian Indians in 1990 relative to 1980. The 1980 and 1990 distributions remained about the same. But slowing of growth in unfavorable localities prevented the Asian Indian rent-to-wage ratio from deteriorating in the 1990s, despite an influx of new immigrants.

Networks Versus Markets

The ratio of average rents to average wages is a measure of group economic welfare, and ratios above one-third mean economic hardship. Because the ratio exerts little influence on immigrant settlement as long as that ratio is low, migration networks initially offer a free choice of location to users. For both Mexicans and Asian Indians, low ratios did not restrain settlement in the 1980s, the halcyon days. But, in both cases, a decade of network-driven settlement worsened the rent-to-wage ratio in network destinations. For Mexicans this change was adverse and catastrophic; for Asian Indians, adverse but mild. Because of their very low initial wages, rising rents and even lower wages drove Mexican immigrant populations into desperate economic vulnerability in the 1990s. Thanks to their affluence, Asian Indians did not sustain anywhere near equivalent hardship, though their ratio also deteriorated.

After ratios rose in 1990, the next decade's growth of immigrant population began to reflect market-induced restraint. Among both Mexicans and Asian Indians, growth in the 1990s favored localities with lower rent-to-wage ratios. For Asian Indians, this countertrend slowed the tendency of Asian Indian populations to grow most in prime network destinations. For Mexicans, it dramatically reversed directions, causing the most growth to occur in those metropolitan regions that had had the most favorable wage to rent ratio in 1990. Either way, the first decade's immigrant settlement involved migration networks ignoring markets, and the next decade's growth involved a countertrend in which markets constrained networks.

Did Acculturation Cause Dispersion?

It is necessary now to address the possibility that acculturation caused Mexicans' regional dispersal, not rents and wages. Both the Mexican and the Asian Indian immigrant population acculturated between 1980 and 2000. In 1980, virtually all immigrants were newly arrived. As such, the immigrant population had less language and cultural fluency in 1980 than in 1990. Both Indian and Mexican migrants arguably depended more on networks in 1980 than in 1990. Acculturation may reduce that dependence, weakening the network and inviting individualized dispersion.[66] This is a possibility. Arguably, acculturation enhanced migrants' sensitivity to quality of life including, but not limited to, the rent-to-wage ratio. To this extent, the retreat of new settlement from unfavorable to more favorable rent-to-wage destinations, which occurred among both Mexicans and Asian Indians in the 1990s, might have reflected heightened cultural competence as well as the real decline in economic welfare that arose in the decade.[67] In that case, growth of the new settlement states might have resulted from resettlement of immigrants already acculturated in traditional states.

Conversely, to the extent that the new settlement states attracted immigrants directly from Mexico, rather than from traditional settlement states, then acculturation cannot explain the regional dispersion. Table 2.1 already showed that the three traditional states (California, Texas, and Illinois) for Mexican settlement exhibited a lower percentage of foreign Mexicans who entered the United States in the 1990s than the other forty-seven states. Bump, Lowell, and Pettersen examined the provenance of Mexican migrants to new settlement states in comparison with those living in traditional states in 2000. They reported that only 15 percent of settlers in new settlement states came from traditional states. Most came from abroad. "The pattern of immigrant movement into new settlement states appears to be primarily a phenomenon of new arrival and not one of redistribution away from traditional states."[68] This result is compatible with the supposition that rents and wages drove the resettlement; it is not compatible with the supposition that acculturation caused the dispersion.

That conclusion also agrees with the results of Elsa von Scheven, who compared the demographic characteristics of the settlers in eight new settlement states with those in Los Angeles County and the top three reception states. Mexican immigrants in the traditional destinations, she found, were about the same age as those in new settlement states in 1990, but that in 2000 they were about a year older. Also, in 1990 Mexicans in traditional areas had approximately as many children in their households as their counterparts in new settlement areas. By 2000, however, those in the traditional areas had appreciably more children in their households. Finally, in 1990, the ratio of males to females ("the sex ratio") was 4 percent more male in traditional areas than in new settlement areas. By 2000, the difference approached 7 percent (table 2.8). Apparently, Mexican immigrants into the new settlement states during the 1990s were disproportionately young men without children. Young men without children are typical new migrants, straight from Mexico, not long settled in the United States, and still unacculturated.

The magnitude of the demographic contrast is additionally apparent when Los Angeles and New York City are compared. Of all the new settle-

Table 2.8   Demographic Characteristics of Mexican Immigrants
Eighteen or Older

	Los Angeles County	California	Three Traditional States	Eight New Settlement States	Other States
Age					
1990	29.6	27.5	28.1	28.3	28.4
2000	29.6	29.5	29.7	28.5	28.5
Years of education					
1990	8.1	8.0	8.0	7.8	8.3
2000	8.2	8.2	8.3	8.5	8.6
Children in household					
1990	0.7	0.7	0.7	0.6	0.6
2000	2.0	1.9	1.8	1.4	1.4
Persons in household					
1990	6.2	6.3	6.0	4.9	4.8
2000	6.1	6.2	5.7	5.3	5.3
Percentage male					
1990	58	59	58	62	63
2000	55	55	56	63	65
1990, N	12,200	27,373	36,199	3,828	4,093
2000, N	15,600	27,685	49,793	18,201	19,901

Source: U.S. Bureau of the Census (1990); U.S. Census Bureau (2000a), 5 percent PUMS.

ment metropolitan areas, New York City contained the largest population of Mexican immigrants in 2000; and Los Angeles had the largest population of immigrant Mexicans of any of the traditional metropolitan regions. As figure 2.7 shows, only about one-third of Los Angeles's foreign-born Mexicans had entered the Los Angeles metropolitan area during the 1990s, versus two-thirds of those in the New York City region. Because the Mexican population had lived longer in Los Angeles on average than in New York City, the contrast implies that Mexican immigrants in Los Angeles were more settled than those in New York City during the 1990s. Additionally, among immigrant Mexicans who entered Los Angeles during the 1990s, the sex ratio was much closer to balance than among those who entered New York City during the same decade. The surplus of males in New York City reflects an unsettled Mexican population because, once

Figure 2.7   Settlement and Sex Ratio of Foreign-Born Mexicans

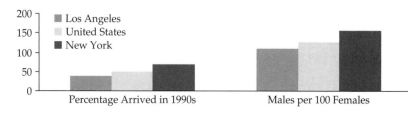

Source: U.S. Census Bureau (2000b).

settled, Mexican men marry or send for their wives in Mexico. Still unsettled and predominantly male, the Mexican population of New York City was also less acculturated than that of Los Angeles in 2000.

Additional evidence bearing upon the acculturation hypothesis derives from the research of Rubén Hernández-León and Victor Zúñiga. Using ethnographic methods, these authors studied the processes that brought Mexicans to new settlement destinations during the 1990s. They report that the Mexican migration network transported foreign-born Mexicans directly from Mexico to Dalton, Georgia, or Tar Heel, North Carolina, both new settlement destinations.[69] This evidence signals the survival and redirection of the Mexican migration network, which introduced new destinations and did not shut down. It also shows that the Mexicans' regional dispersal proceeded on the strength of new arrivals straight from Mexico and entirely unacculturated.

A Two-Step Settlement

Although Douglas Massey and his colleagues championed the role of social networks in migration, when seeking to explain the regional dispersion of Mexican immigrants to new settlement destinations in the 1990s, they offered a political explanation instead. They laid the responsibility for dispersion of Mexicans on IRCA and enhanced border enforcement. Their arguments are inconsistent with the census evidence just presented and with David Heer's earlier results. Using data derived from the 1980, 1990, and 2000 public-use census, Michael Johnston and I have shown that Mexican and Asian Indian immigrants settled where they listed in the 1980s. In that decade, metropolitan rent-to-wage ratios were favorable. Immigrants could afford to follow the network. However, a decade later, the rent-to-wage ratio had dramatically worsened among low-wage Mexicans and slightly worsened among high-wage Asian Indians. At that point, the ratio, an overall measure of economic welfare, began to constrain Mexican settlement decisions, diverting new immigrants' settlement from traditional to new settlement areas. A comparable but much milder constraint affected Asian Indians in the 1990s as well.

These results support a two-step model of network settlement that may generalize to other immigrant groups. In the first phase, migrants select destinations without regard for economic conditions and slavish dependence on friends' and relatives' prior settlement decisions. As a result, the immigrants' rent-to-wage ratio gradually deteriorates in prime network destinations. In the second phase, unfavorable ratios induce new migrants to disperse to nontraditional destinations. In the second phase, the network adapts to the users' changed economic realities, and reinvents itself around a new schedule of destinations. The migration network does not disintegrate in the second phase. Non-prime destinations are upgraded; prime destinations are downgraded, but the network continues to introduce unacculturated migrants. This two-step model offers a potentially generalizable approach to immigrant settlement in reception localities when immigration volume is massive and protracted.

= Chapter 3 =

Is Migration Still
Demand-Driven?

I N THE BROADEST sense, globalization refers to all processes that incorporate the peoples of the world into a single society.[1] These processes are economic, cultural, and political. However, in the narrower economic sense used here, globalization means movement toward a globally integrated market for labor and capital, especially capital, but increasingly labor as well. Globally integrated markets for labor imply increasing international migration. Global restructuring is economic globalization in process. Very popular in policy circles, global restructuring theory accounts for a multiplicity of linked changes around the world in terms of the resurgent power of financial capital in a world with ever fewer barriers to trade. At the core, restructuring theory calls attention to local economic changes produced by resource shifts in the newly globalized market. In that global market, capital flows freely across international boundaries in response to profit incentives and labor, more inhibited, flows more freely than before.[2] This scenario depicts the production of the local by the global in that the local exists because of the global.

The Elements of Global Restructuring

Theorists of global restructuring proclaim the supremacy of big capital. The agents of global restructuring are transnational corporations and money-center banks that, spanning continents, reallocate jobs and work among them in response to profit incentives and indifferent to political or cultural loyalties or boundaries.[3] These transnational institutions are the dominant actors in the globalized economy. Global restructuring theory also claims that profit incentives have created an international urban hierarchy centered on three world cities and a number of supporting major cities. "The foreign investment that drives economic globalization is managed from a small number of global cities, whose structural characteristics create a strong demand for immigrant labor."[4] From these supreme

48

organizing nodes—London, Tokyo, and New York, in Saskia Sassen's influential account—transnational business corporations reach out to control the regional economies they penetrate.[5] As a result, local and regional economies operate more than previously as players in an international script written by distant financiers.

Restructuring theory extracts four key propositions from this scenario. First, in the new, globalized world, multinational and transnational corporations strip middle-level production jobs from high-priced workers in developed countries, assigning their tasks to factories in cheap-labor countries. Second, as jobs export proceeds from the developed countries, transnational corporations centralize financial control, producer services, and advanced technology in Japan, western Europe, and the United States.[6] Third, jobs export and financial centralization both polarize the income structure of these developed countries.[7] That is, expanding these highly paid sectors increases the number and share of the most affluent, whereas firing the production workers whose jobs were exported increases the number and share of the poor.[8] The middle class dwindles as the numbers of the wealthy and of the poor increase.[9] Finally, globalization attracts two types of migrants to the developed core countries. A minority are skilled professionals, who earn high incomes.[10] The Asian Indian migrants discussed in chapter 2 belong to this class, as do the Korean and Chinese immigrants discussed in chapter 7. The majority, however, are poor people from the developing world, who flood into big cities in response to demand for informal sector jobs (such as nannies, gardeners, roofers, construction workers) on the part of newly wealthy households. The Mexican and Central American immigrants belong to this category.

Globalization, Migration, and Informalization

Moore and Pinderhughes declare that "the growth of an informal economy is part and parcel of late twentieth-century economic restructuring."[11] This judgment epitomizes restructuring theory, which explains the growth of informal economies in the developed countries as a spontaneous by-product of newly polarized income distributions arising from global restructuring.[12] Restructuring theorists explain immigration and informalization in terms of expanded and persistent demand for cheap, immigrant labor.[13] Informalization means that a growing share of the labor force works in the informal sector.[14] The informal sector consists of "income-generating activities taking place outside a formal regulatory framework within which similar activities are in effect regulated."[15] Informalization has become increasingly obvious in the United States since 1980, and in Europe as well.[16] Receiving wages in cash is a standard indicator of participation in the informal sector. Massey, Durand, and Malone found that in 1980 and 1981 only 16 percent of undocumented workers in California were receiving wages in cash, and next to none of the legal immigrants were doing so.[17] Twelve years later, 45 percent of undocumented immigrants and 25 percent of legal immigrants in California were receiving cash wages.

Globalization theorists explain both immigration and informalization on the basis of demand-pull.[18] In their view, global restructuring changes the income structure of the advanced countries, especially within the biggest cities, increasing the number and share of the wealthy in total income and decreasing the share of the poor but increasing their number. The resulting hourglass income distribution creates demand for cheap goods the poor can afford as well as for luxury goods and personal services the rich consume.[19] The rich buy in fancy boutiques; the poor buy on the street, in swap meets, and in discount warehouses. Responding to the expanding demand of the newly rich for personal and domestic service, immigrants from poor countries swarm into the great cities of the developed world, where they become gardeners, nannies, cooks, roofers, and domestic servants. They also work in the hotel and restaurant industries, whose customers are affluent as well. Additionally, responding to the demand for cheap goods, which emanates also from the newly poor ex–middle class, the poor immigrants find employment in low-wage factories and discount retail stores. Much of their work is informal. Whether they work for wealthy households or for industrial sweatshops, poor immigrants receive substandard pay and benefits, often illegally substandard, and are usually paid in cash. Expanding the low-wage immigrant sector is essential to the supply of high-wage workers. Sassen declares that "expansion of the high-income workforce . . . depends on the availability of a vast supply of low-wage workers."[20] In her view, the demand for cheap immigrant labor arises in the most advanced sectors of the most advanced economies and pulls immigrants into world cities.[21]

In essence, the globalization-derived explanation of informalization adds many immigrant workers at the bottom of the income distribution for every few added at the top. The result is polarization of incomes in reception cities as, thanks to immigration, the numbers of rich and poor grow relative to the number of the middle class. However, globalization theory does not propose that the poor immigrants become poorer as their immigration continues. In its view, the poor Third World immigrants enter a world of expanding demand for their cheap labor. The theory proposes only that the share of poor immigrants in the population increases relative to the share of those who are not poor. Informalization increases in the reception cities because more poor immigrants inhabit them, not because they contain more poor immigrants who are also growing poorer. If the numbers of poor immigrants increase, and the poor immigrants also become poorer, the immigrants' economic situation would be appreciably worse than the gloomiest globalization scenario. That outcome would not fit the demand-driven model of immigration on which globalization theory rests either. Yet, because the immigrants became both poorer and more numerous in Los Angeles, the conceptual distinction has realistic implications. If this situation is true generally, the standard demand-driven explanation does not fit reality. Globalization's demand-driven theory cannot explain declining incomes of immigrants, whereas a supply-driven explanation can.

Existing Critiques of Restructuring Theory

Global restructuring theory links economic processes in industrial and developing countries, thus crafting a coherent and parsimonious vision of a master process of which immigration and informalization in the developed countries are just by-products. No wonder global restructuring theory has enjoyed such popularity. However, as arguments matured, the theory also attracted multiple criticisms. Before adding new ideas to this debate, I review the existing critiques, none of which is superseded by what will later be added. One criticism addresses restructuring theory's overemphasis on globalization at the expense of local agency as well as its economism and linear determinism.[22] Here, economism means overemphasizing market forces to the neglect of cultural, social, and political responses to those forces.[23] Globalization theorists think that the global market gives orders to states and to the cities within them. Determinism means eliminating immigrant agency.[24] If the global market is the czar, then neither cities nor immigrants have choices. Rejecting this determinism, John Logan and Todd Swanstrom observe that the literature of global restructuring represents markets as natural forces independent of and superior to national and local states.[25] In other words, globalization theorists depict markets as all-powerful rather than just powerful. Disagreeing, Logan and Swanstrom insist that "a great deal more [political] discretion exists to shape economic and urban restructuring than is commonly believed."[26] Although they do not specifically mention it, this local discretion could include the choice of how much immigrant poverty cities tolerate. Robert Kloosterman similarly declares that interregional differences prove that restructuring does not determine urban outcomes.[27] If it did, no interregional differences would exist within developed countries, but they do exist. Huge regional disparities in immigrant settlement is compatible with the claim, made in chapter 2, that migrant networks structure immigrant settlement despite the presumably homogenizing effects of globalization. Mark Gottdiener and Nicos Komninos wish to escape "one-dimensional, deterministic explanations" to forge "approaches that consider political and cultural as well as economic dimensions."[28] These neglected dimensions might include the capability of cities to enforce laws governing slums and sweatshops.

Another criticism addresses restructuring theory's neglect of national demographic realities in favor of poorly fitting, aprioristic generalizations. Roger Waldinger and Michael Lichter have shown that demand for low-wage labor in American cities did not really require immigrants as global restructuring theory assumed. After all, unlike their European and Japanese counterparts, American cities already had a labor reserve of underemployed, the native-born blacks. As Mexican President Vicente Fox acknowledged, these native-born blacks were available to take the low-wage service and manufacturing jobs that globalization handed to Mexicans. Why did American employers hire immigrants rather than blacks? The causes of this perplexing outcome, Waldinger and Lichter declare, must be sought first in the folklore that disparages the work ethic of black Americans.[29] Employers consider that working-class black Americans have an entitlement mentality and a weak work ethic. This belief explains why employers preferred Latino immigrants over native-born black Americans. Second, in Waldinger and Lichter's view, the social networks of the immigrants permitted them to out compete native blacks for initial access to the growing informal sector, and thereafter to exclude native blacks from their newly acquired industrial niches if only by using Spanish on the job.[30] To this extent, differential and unequal social networks also contributed to the demand for immigrants.[31] This conclusion is compatible with the claim that immigrant networks structure immigrant settlement even when globalization is in progress.

A third critical direction claims that restructuring theory wrongly attributes Third World immigration to globalization. The key evidence is migration networks, whose independent effects on migration globalization theorists have ignored. As argued in chapter 2, these networks build strength as migrations mature, and cumulatively cause the migrations they track. In so doing, they eclipse the demand-driven causes of the migration, which global restructuring theorists identify as economic globalization.[32] Migration networks are much older than globalization and have existed without it. Migration networks do not depend upon globalization, but the opposite is not true. Even where globalization independently initiates demand-driven migration, migration networks develop, then become cumulative as they mature. Indeed, for this reason globalization cannot sustain long-term immigration except through the medium of migration networks. Thus globalization does not singlehandedly produce migration from the Third World.

In an ingenious aside, Emilio Reyneri observes that migration networks' participants notoriously exaggerate job opportunities in the destination economy, promoting more immigration than the destination economy can actually absorb. A century ago, European immigrants naively thought that American streets were "paved with gold." As a result of such illusions, Reyneri suggests, immigrants anticipate a rosier job supply than actually exists at their destination. If so, even network-driven immigrants think they are responding to job opportunities even when no jobs exist for them. However, even in this case, globalization-induced demand does not really drive the migration. Rather, the illusion of demand drives the migration. If that illusion is a product of the network, as Reyneri maintains, then the network (not the reception economy) is actually driving migration. Phantom demand cannot salvage demand-led immigration.[33]

A fourth criticism addresses the supporting roles of the immigrant economy and of the ethnic economy in the immigrant-reception cities. Immigrant and ethnic economies are the employment sector that arises when immigrant employers hire other immigrants. If they hire coethnics, they create an ethnic economy; if they hire immigrants who are not coethnics, they create an immigrant economy. As immigrants congregate, ethnic economies and immigrant economies expand, thus permitting the migration flow to continue beyond the level that native-born employers could sustain.[34] This expansion may be substantial. Immigrant employers in San Diego hired one-third of all immigrant employees in that city, expanding the immigrant job base by one-third beyond what native-born employers could have provided.[35] Native-born employers thus do not create all the demand for immigrant labor as Fred Krissman maintains.[36] The immigrants themselves create new demand that attracts other immigrants. Chapter 5 addresses the immigrant economy in the Los Angeles garment industry to amplify this argument with evidence.

Finally, global restructuring cannot exclude path-dependent explanations such as cumulative causation. As Massey and his colleagues have observed, "the conditions that initiate international movement" need not "perpetuate it."[37] Although they criticize migration network theory, Douglas Gurak and Fe Caces acknowledge that Massey's is a "reasonable argument."[38] Similarly, Philip Martin and Edward Taylor declare that it is quite common "for demand-pull foreign worker recruitment to set migration for employment in motion, and for supply-push and network factors to become more important as a migration stream matures."[39] In this case, path-dependent etiologies offer more satisfactory explanatory models for long-term migrations than simple demand-pull does. Pursuing this approach, the concept of "spill over migration" denotes migrations whose motor changes from demand-driven to network-driven in midstream.[40] In such cases, as Hamnett has explained, declining incomes at the bottom end result from labor markets saturated by network-driven migration rather than from independent dynamics of the host economy.[41]

Spill-Over Migration:
Two Historical Illustrations

Two historical cases show that important American migrations switched motors in midcourse. During the Great Migration of European whites to the United States, real wages of the native whites declined about 10 percent between 1880 and 1914. Although the wages of the incoming Europeans were as high as those of the native whites, their real wages declined.[42] Nonetheless, European migration continued strong after immigrant real wages had begun to decline. Even the robust economy of the United States could not absorb all the immigrant labor that arrived without wage declines, but the wage decline did not immediately reduce the influx of Europeans. However, precisely that absorption defines demand-driven immigration. Therefore, in a strict sense, the Great Migration of European whites was not demand-driven after 1914 even if it had been earlier.

A second example tells a comparable story. During the interwar migration of five million native blacks from the American South to northern, central, and western cities, a major transformation of American society in the twentieth century, the later black migrants received real wages as high as those paid the earlier.[43] This situation lasted until 1929. In that depression year, demand for urban labor collapsed. The real wages of black migrants dropped, remaining low until 1942, when war production began. Black migration from the South declined at the beginning of the Great Depression in apparent response to declining real wages. The simultaneous decline of real wages and of interstate black migration signaled a true demand-driven migration because, when the wages slackened, migration also slackened. War production abruptly increased the real wages of southern blacks, reinvigorating their migration.[44] When World War II ended in 1945 and war production slowed, demand for black production workers slowed. The real wages of migrant black workers declined through 1970, when the black migration from the South finally ended.[45] Nonetheless, the black migration continued unabated from 1945 until 1970 despite those declining wages.[46]

This second example shows that, judging by its decline after 1929 and recrudescence in 1942, the internal migration of blacks from Dixie was demand-driven only up to World War II. The migration then switched motors and continued until 1970 despite declining real wages. Noting the discrepancy, George Groh attributes the postwar continuation of interstate black migration to technological change in agriculture, a push that compelled them to exit.[47] Of course, there was also the decided preference of southern blacks for northern destinations as reflected in the folklore declaration, then quite popular, that "I'd rather be a lamp post in Chicago than the President of Dixie." This was a cultural preference. In any case, like the migration of the European whites, that of southern blacks passed through a demand-pull phase into a supply-push phase when the motor of migration changed. Neither the European nor the southern migration remained demand-driven: real wages declined, but migration continued anyway. These historical examples suggest that current migrations may also continue for many years after their demand-driven phase has ended.

Does Demand Cause Migration?

An entirely new critique is based upon close analysis of the concept of demand-driven immigration. The claim that immigration results from employer demand is widely quoted and widely believed on Main Street, on Wall Street, in the media, and even in the academy.[48] "As long as demand exists, there will be migrants" is the ubiquitous watchword, and the unspoken implication is, "so nothing can be done." Joining the chorus, global restructuring theory also claims that employer demand drives the immigration process to world cities.

But, exactly what does demand-driven migration require? Global restructuring theorists have not raised this question, much less answered it. The issue is trickier than it initially appears. Peter Fischer and Thomas Straubhaar declare that migrations are demand-driven when "the number of people who would like to migrate is smaller than the number of those who are wanted."[49] Thus construed, demand is a continuous variable, not a binary one that is either present or absent. As the number who migrated approximates the number wanted, demand gradually diminishes. By extension, when the number who immigrated exactly satisfies the number wanted, demand vanishes. Demand is at that point saturated.

Although it conveys the principal idea, Fischer and Straubhaar's definition has several limitations. First, employer demand can persist over time, but migration does not ensue because the wages offered are too low. Demand exists, but migrants refuse to come for such low wages. In this condition, employer demand exists but the employer demand does not cause migration. Therefore, the blanket assertion that employer demand causes migration is not correct.[50]

Of course, protracted immigrant influx cannot proceed in the face of zero employer demand. Zero employer demand means that employers would not hire workers at any wage. This powerful observation, wrongly but widely deemed irrefutable, actually leads to another objection to the demand explanation of immigration. Employer demand cannot vanish. Employer demand always exists in the sense that at some ridiculously low wage employers will hire additional immigrant workers. In neoclassical economic theory it is impossible that employer demand does not exist; all that is possible is that demand attracts no takers. Hence, the moment can never arise when immigrants stop coming because no employer demand exists. Because employer demand always exists, but immigration is historically intermittent, employer demand is not always and not even mostly followed by immigration. But effects always follow their cause.

Third, Fischer and Straubhaar's phrase, immigrants "who are wanted" leaves open the question "wanted by whom and for what at what price?" Are immigrants wanted if they enter a country illegally to take work that pays illegally low wages under illegal working conditions? Are they wanted if they live under illegally crowded conditions in illegally dilapidated structures? Are they wanted if their employers operate illegally? Even if all these questions are answered yes, as neoliberals must answer them, wanted immigrants will not amount to a migration if their illegal entry does not eventuate in employment. When employers import immigrants whom the reception state prevents them from employing, the state has the last laugh. Hence, again we cannot assume that employer demand invariably produces migration.

Fourth, the neoliberal logic of the globalization theorists assumes that immigrant wages can drop to any level, no matter how low, but this assumption is unrealistic. Laws and regulations in reception cities, regions, and national states specify minima beneath which wages, industrial conditions, and housing conditions may not drop. Minimum wage laws are an example. If these laws are enforced, effective demand for immigrant labor ends when wages hit the lawful minimum. In that case, state regulation curtails effective demand well short of its economic limit. Effective demand for illegal labor depends upon the zeal with which local, regional, and national states enforce housing, occupational, and industrial laws.

Finally, a migration could easily start as demand-driven under Fischer and Straubhaar's definition, then become supply-driven. Such a migration would start with legal immigrants, who saturate the mainstream's job offerings, then continue with immigrants who find employment in the informal economy. When immigrants keep coming as demand declines, the spillover pattern, demand plays a decreasing role in their generation. The final decoupling of the business cycle from immigration volume, with immigration rising as employment declines, would signal a point at which immigration grows as employer demand slackens. Camarota maintains that such a point was reached in the United States after 2000: "The market-driven perspective on immigration is passé."[51] From the point of view of migration networks, degeneration into supply-driven immigration is the expected product of demand-driven migrations from poor countries.

What Is Demand-Driven Migration?

A realistic definition of demand-driven immigration requires maintenance of real immigrant welfare over time despite sustained migratory influx. This is basic. The reason is equally basic. The economist Oded

Stark writes that "under normal conditions, an increased supply of labor, unless outpaced by increased demand, will tend to depress wages or slow their rise."[52] From this elementary proposition, it follows that, in real demand-driven migrations, immigrants' economic welfare does not decline as the migration matures. There is a simple reason. For every new immigrant received, demand expands to create another job at the same wage level as the first. Several corollaries derive from this proposition. First, in demand-driven migrations, immigrants' productivity-adjusted wages remain stable over time. While they last, demand-driven migrations are insatiable consumers of migrant labor because, as the receiving economy grows, the demand for additional immigrant labor keeps pace. The more immigrants enter, the more the economy grows; and the more the economy grows, the more immigrants its labor markets demand. The key indicator of stable demand for immigrant labor is constant wage levels. Another indication is a low and stable unemployment rate among immigrants. Another is absence of low-end growth in ethnic economies, especially growth of the informal sector.[53] Another is a low and stable immigrant poverty rate. Additionally, when immigrations are demand-driven, immigrants' housing quality does not decline as the migration progresses.

Demand-driven immigration is in a race with economic growth. As long as economic growth keeps pace with influx, immigration remains demand-driven. Conversely, as soon as immigrant influx outstrips economic growth, the influx becomes supply-driven. This transition has predictable consequences that enable us to distinguish demand-driven immigration from network-driven, which is here treated as synonymous with supply-driven. High-volume network-driven migrations reduce immigrant earned income over time whereas demand-driven migrations do not. Therefore, if immigrant earned income is declining over time, migrations are network-driven, not demand-driven, whatever may have been true in the past.

Admittedly, welfare states have the short-term capability to disguise a decline in immigrants' earnings by extending and expanding immigrants' access to welfare benefits and to transfer payments as employer demand for immigrant labor falters. In effect, the state then soaks up the surplus immigrant labor at taxpayer expense. Such policies artificially bolster immigrants' incomes, concealing the decline in income that would otherwise have occurred. However, realistically speaking, the protracted ability of welfare states to administer immigrants' earnings and to stabilize their standard of living is threatened by long-term network-driven immigrations. States' resources are limited and their burdens heavy. At some point in the course of sustained, network-driven migrations, welfare states reduce immigrants' welfare benefits and transfer payments. When this moment arrives, immigrants' earned income trends downward as excess labor finds the sagging market, thus identifying the migration as network-driven.

Implications for Policy

The globalization argument has already attracted a number of criticisms. Admittedly, these criticisms were quite general. Nonetheless, all are compatible with the key propositions advanced in chapters 1 and 2. That is, migration networks structure migrant settlement under globalization; even if initially demand-driven, Third World migration could very well spill over into supply-driven migration over time; localities retain the capability to constrain and redirect migratory access even when globalization is under way.

A new, and conceptual, critique addresses globalization's vaunted dependence upon demand-driven migration from Third World countries. The underlying assumption holds that employer demand for immigrant labor expands under globalization, and thus pulls immigrants into the most developed cities in the developed countries without immiseration. This argument requires and assumes that demand is either present or not, and when present causes immigration. The trouble here is that demand is variable, not constant. The strength of employer demand varies from high to low, and, when trending lower, demand is losing explanatory power if migration continues unabated. Declining demand cannot explain constant immigration. Additionally, when present, employer demand does not—as globalization theorists assumed—always cause immigration. Employer demand for cheap immigrant labor is always present, but only sometimes causes immigration. Because a cause must be followed by its effect, we cannot conclude that employer demand always causes immigration. Sometimes demand does cause immigration, but sometimes it does not. We have to specify exactly when it does, and globalization theory has not yet offered this specification.

When migrations are demand-driven, immigrants' living standards do not trend downward as the migration matures. They instead remain constant because employer demand expands to accommodate additional migrants as they arrive. When employer demand does not expand, but the influx of migrants does, then a migration has become supply or network-driven. It has, in Massey's phrase, become cumulatively caused. The terms "network-driven" and "supply-driven" are almost synonyms because network-driven migrations are supply-driven.

This argument thus offers a way to distinguish when immigrations are supply-driven and when demand-driven. If the migrants' living conditions trend downward as the migration matures, we can infer that the migration is supply-driven; if they are constant despite continuing influx, then it is demand-driven. It follows that empirically identifying the trend of immigrant living conditions in a world city, such as Los Angeles, enables us to infer what kind of migration globalization is depositing there. Moreover, when we observe supply-driven migration, theories that predict demand-driven migration can be empirically rejected.

But the distinction between supply-driven and demand-driven is not merely academic: it has implications for public policy. Demand-driven migrations have structural supports within the labor-importing country such that politically obstructing migration would obstruct economic growth as well. If employers cannot obtain the workers they require, they cannot expand, and economic development languishes. On the other hand, if immigrations are supply-driven, at least some of the migrants (not all) are adding little value with their labor. Low-value workers contribute little or nothing to economic growth, and possibly divert public resources from productive uses to their support. If, additionally, localities can and do deflect unwanted supply-driven migrants, then localities are not powerless to protect themselves from unwanted immigrants even though globalization is the master process governing the world's economic development.

═ Chapter 4 ═

Hard Times in the Barrios

L os Angeles had undergone thirty-five years of well-documented globalization by 2000. Global restructuring created the Pacific Rim trading area, of which Los Angeles became the second-ranking city behind Tokyo. During this transition, manufacturing industry left southern California for the Pacific Rim, leaving behind high technology, aerospace, defense, and immigrant-staffed sweatshops.[1] The real wages of native-born manufacturing workers stagnated and declined in the protracted egress of jobs.[2] New jobs in service industries employed many of those displaced from manufacturing, but usually at lower wages.[3] On the other hand, growing information services and management occupations increased the proportion of high-wage earners in the labor force. As a result, economic inequality increased in Los Angeles. As elsewhere, newly rich millionaires became more prominent on the high end and desperately poor, unskilled immigrants at the low end of the income distribution.[4]

Declining Immigration

In this southern California region, where the pace of globalization was feverish, was Latino migration really demand-driven throughout the period as, according to globalization theorists, it should have been, or did it become supply-driven? If demand-driven, the immigrants' earned incomes and economic welfare should have kept pace with native incomes; if supply-driven, they should have dropped. The actual trend of immigrants' incomes affects how one explains Los Angeles's diminishing share of the total foreign-born population of the United States. If immigrant incomes were declining, it is plausible to attribute their diminished share of the region's population to local economic hardship.

The two largest categories of immigrants in Los Angeles were Latinos and Asians, but Mexicans alone accounted for two-thirds of the foreign population. When combined, Asians and Latinos accounted for 82 percent of international migrants in 1995.[5] Between 1970 and 2000, the foreign-born

Table 4.1   Foreign-Born Population, City of Los Angeles and United States

Year	United States	Los Angeles	Los Angeles as Percentage
2000	31,100,000	1,512,720	4.9
1990	19,767,316	1,336,665	6.8
1980	14,079,906	804,818	5.7
1970	9,619,302	410,870	4.3
1960	9,738,091	311,677	3.2

Sources: Gibson and Lennon (1999); U.S. Census Bureau, American Fact Finder (2000).

increased from 11 percent to 36 percent of the population of Los Angeles County.[6] Except for non-Hispanic whites, all the immigrant groups in southern California fielded increasing immigration cohorts in every decennial year between 1970 and 2000. As a result, the foreign-born population of the city of Los Angeles quadrupled between 1970 and 2000, reaching an apex of 6.8 percent of the total foreign-born population of the United States in 1990 (table 4.1). However, in the 1990s, even though the national foreign-born population increased by 11,332,684 that of the city of Los Angeles increased by only 176,055. As a result, Los Angeles's share of the national foreign-born population dropped from 6.8 percent in 1990 to 4.9 percent in 2000, a decrease of approximately 28 percent. In hard numbers, the city's foreign-born population in 2000 was 1,512,720 rather than 2,114,800. In other words, thanks to the drop in its relative attractiveness to foreigners, the city had 602,080 fewer immigrants in 2000 than it would otherwise have had.

In the case of Mexicans, the immigration cohorts grew consistently in size between 1980 and 2000, nearly quadrupling the foreign-born Mexican population. But the five-county Los Angeles metropolitan area share of the total U.S. population of foreign-born Mexicans declined in this period, from 31.7 to 16.7 percent. Although the area was still the largest settlement of Mexicans in the United States in 2000, its share of the nation's total Mexican-origin population had fallen 50 percent since 1980. Of course, this decline reflected the dispersion of Mexican population from traditional settlement regions discussed in chapter 2. But the local demographic consequences merit separate attention. If the Los Angeles metropolitan area had retained its 1980 share, metropolitan Los Angeles would have had a Mexican-origin population of 2,491,068 instead of 1,530,280. The difference would have added an additional 960,788 foreign-born Mexicans to the metropolitan population. This additional Mexican population would have represented a 10-percent increase in the total population of the Los Angeles metropolitan area.

Signs of Declining Welfare Among Immigrants

Why did Los Angeles reduce its share of the national population of foreign-born and of foreign-born Mexicans in the 1990s? Possibly, immigrants found Los Angeles less attractive because their living conditions had declined there. However, if Los Angeles were sustaining demand-driven immigration, as Sassen maintains that world cities do, then those conditions should not have deteriorated. Conversely, if the Mexican immigration had become network-driven by 1980, sustained Mexican immigration thereafter should have swamped Los Angeles, exceeding the area's capacity to offer suitable jobs and housing to newer immigrants. In this case, the expected outcomes would include declining wages for Mexicans in Los Angeles, growth of the Mexican share of the metropolitan population in poverty, expansion of the informal economy and of the Mexican share of it, declining stature for the Mexican ownership economy, high rents and overcrowding among Mexicans, the spread of slums, and development of metropolitan social movements reflecting growing intolerance for immigrant poverty. All these are empirical issues whose resolution enables one to decide whether the evidence better supports a demand-driven or a supply-driven scenario for immigration. *All* these telltale signs of network-driven migration materialized in Los Angeles after 1980.

Working Poverty Increases

Unlike northern European welfare states, where labor markets were administered, labor markets in Los Angeles were relatively free. Immigrants' wages could drop below the poverty level—and they did. Poverty rates rose in California between 1970 and 2000, but dropped nationally.[7] The Latino proportion of the population living in very poor neighborhoods—with neighborhood poverty rates of at least 40 percent—increased more than threefold between 1970 and 2000. By 2000, immigrants were 61 percent of the poverty population of southern California.[8] Low employment was not the cause. Latinos had high rates of labor force participation, but fell into poverty because their wages were low. By the 1990s, policy analysts perceived an increase in "working poverty" in Los Angeles importantly as a result of sustained immigration from Mexican and Central America.[9] Mexican scholars reached the same conclusion.[10] Los Angeles's venerable Spanish-language newspaper, *La Opinión,* reported it to readers.[11] By working poverty was meant fully employed workers living in poverty because their wages were low. True, during the affluent 1990s, rates of poverty in California generally declined about 10 percent after having nearly doubled in the preceding two decades. However, the general decline of poverty did not equally benefit California's Latinos among whom the rate of poverty was only stable (at one-third) rather than declining, as was everyone else's rate of poverty.[12] Moreover, despite the general decline in the state's poverty rate, a statistic that included recipients of welfare benefits, Latinos were specifically responsible for working poverty. In 1997, Latinos represented 70 percent of California's working poor but only 40 percent of its employed.[13]

Antipoverty Social Movements

This worsening economic situation among Latinos came to be perceived as a social problem. To remedy it, multiethnic social movements mobilized to combat low wages among immigrants. Raising the minimum wage was a favored approach. In 1987, three Los Angeles affiliates of the Industrial Areas Foundation undertook a successful campaign to raise California's minimum wage to $4.25 an hour, the highest in the nation.[14] They succeeded—putting California's minimum wage at 105 percent of the federal, up from 102 percent in the 1970s. During the 1960s and 1950s, California's minimum wage had coincided with Washington's. However, after this 1987 increase, California continued to set its minimum wage higher than the federal, reaching 112 percent in 2000.[15] The state's high minimum wage discouraged low-wage firms from remaining in California, and thus helped to deflect the low-wage workers who would otherwise have held jobs in those firms.

The social movements typically operated as coalitions that came together to back various antipoverty projects. The Living Wage Coalition, the Labor Community Strategy Center, the Task Force on Low-Wage Immigrant Workers, The Los Angeles Coalition for Economic Survival, The Los Angeles Alliance for a New Economy, and the Coalition for Humane Immigrant Rights of Los Angeles were prominent among the independent movements that coalesced around the protection of vulnerable workers, especially domestic workers, day laborers, and garment workers. The partners undertook advocacy, organizing, and policy reform. As in New York City, the Los Angeles movements educated workers, developed leadership, issued and publicized reports that brought the workers' plight to the attention of police and public officials.[16] They staged noisy demonstrations on behalf of legalization of illegal immigrants,[17] and both conducted and published research reports.

The Los Angeles Alliance for a New Economy presented evidence of extreme overrepresentation of Latinos among the "working poor." This report galvanized the formation of the Los Angeles Living Wage Coalition, which came together with grassroots support of trade unions, religious congregations, and community groups.[18] Overcoming the mayor's veto, the coalition secured the passage by the city council of a municipal living wage ordinance in 1997.[19] Applying only to municipal jobs, this ordinance compelled the City of Los Angeles to pay its lowest-level employees $9.78 per hour, a minimum wage much higher than the California minimum wage, then $5.75 an hour, which was itself already higher than the federal minimum wage.[20] Somewhat earlier, the Service Employees' International Union organized the Justice for Janitors campaign to mobilize public support behind higher wages for immigrant maintenance workers in high-rise office buildings.[21] Highly publicized marches of chanting Latino janitors drew public attention to the low wages these workers earned. The public responded with sympathy.[22] These social movements show that by the 1990s Los Angeles churches, civic agencies, and trade unions had become aware of working poverty among Latino immigrants, were troubled by the conditions, and sought to remedy them by political action. Political protests brought pressure on private employers and on the city government to improve the wages of the working poor, and they were somewhat successful. In the words of Norma Chinchilla and Nora Hamilton, "these efforts have had some success in improving wages and working conditions and reducing exploitation in typical immigrant occupations."[23] Paul More and his associates similarly argue that, when compared with wage declines in California, slight improvement in real average wages in Los Angeles during the 1990s proves that local political pressure improved the wages of the lowest-paid workers in Los Angeles.[24]

Declining Wages

Mexican immigrants' relative wages in Los Angeles were low and dropping in the late twentieth century, and, according to Lisa Catanzarite and Michael Aguilera, they were lowest in workplaces "saturated with coethnics."[25] Much evidence corroborates this conclusion. Kevin McCarthy and Georges Vernez reported that Mexican and Central American immigrants in California earned 40 percent less than native workers in 1970 "and their relative earnings level" declined to 50 percent less in 1990.[26] Shannon McConville and Paul Ong concluded that "a large supply of less-skilled workers has depressed wages and created more competition at the bottom end of the labor market, which is disproportionately composed of minorities, immigrants, and second-generation workers."[27] Hagan found that Latino women competed with one another for domestic service jobs, driving down their wages.[28] Deborah Reed showed that between 1969 and 1997 male immigrants increased from 10 percent to 36 percent of California's labor force in which they were wildly overrepresented in the lowest three deciles.[29] Georges Vernez reported that Mexican men's average wages declined from 67 percent of white men's wages in 1960 to 60 percent in 1980.[30] Comparing four ethno-racial groups in southern California between 1970 and 1990, Ivan Light and Elizabeth Roach found that the wages of whites in the private sector increased fourfold in the twenty-year period; wages of Asians increased as much as those of whites; but the wages of Hispanics increased only 72 percent as much.[31] David Lopez, Eric Popkin, and Edward Telles undertook a cohort analysis of the earnings of Salvadoran, Guatemalan, and Mexican immigrants in Los Angeles, comparing real earnings in three successive periods.[32] Their evidence compared mean earnings of immigrant men aged twenty-five to sixty-four from 1975 to 1979, 1980 to 1984, and 1985 to 1989. All three Latino groups showed continuous decline in 1989-dollar earnings over each successive period. Overall declines were between 30 percent and 40 percent of initial real wages. Paul Ong and Evelyn Blumenberg found that real hourly compensation in the private sector of Los Angeles increased only 14.5 percent between 1969 and 1989 compared to 98 percent between 1948 and 1969. However, among immigrants, real wages declined 13 percent between 1970 and 1980.[33] Studying three cohorts of Mexican immigrants to Los Angeles, Vilma Ortiz also found evidence of declining real wages between 1970 and 1990. Mexican immigrants of the 1960s cohort maintained their earnings, but "subsequent cohorts" saw real and relative earnings continuously decline.[34] Real wages of Mexican women immigrants declined even more than those of Mexican men.[35]

Mark Ellis compared wage trends in Los Angeles and four other immigrant reception cities with national trends.[36] Like previous researchers, he found that wages of Hispanic immigrants in Los Angeles declined between 1980 and 1990. On the other hand, he found that wages of native-born workers rose in the same period. The overall result was a widening gap between the wages of immigrant Hispanics and those of native-born workers. Comparing the period 1970 to 1995, William A. V. Clark reached the same conclusion for the entire state of California: native-born workers' wages increased, whereas those of immigrants in general and Mexicans in particular declined.[37]

James Smith and Barry Edmonston collected comparative wage deciles for foreign-born workers in six high-immigration states, California, and Los Angeles in 1990.[38] They ascertained what percentage of immigrants was in the lowest wage decile for native workers within each reception area. They reported that 29.5 percent of immigrant workers in Los Angeles were concentrated in the metropolitan region's lowest wage decile compared to 22.7 percent in California, and 17.7 percent in the six high-immigration states. This concentration was the highest among the most recent immigrants in each of the three reception areas, an unsurprising result, but Los Angeles always had the highest proportion. In Los Angeles, 44.5 percent of recent immigrants were in the lowest native wage decile in 1990 (figure 4.1). The more concentrated the immigrant workers, the lower were their relative wages.

Using unpublished census data, Michael Francis Johnston (personal communication) tracked the mean wages of foreign-born Asian Indians

Figure 4.1   Foreign-Born in Lowest Wage Decile by Region, 1990

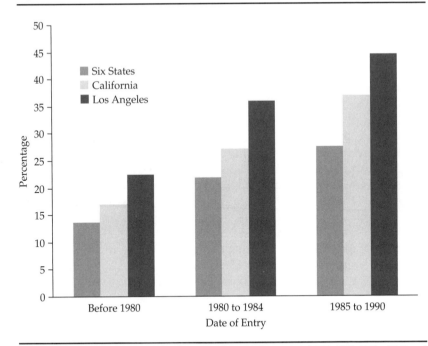

Source: Reprinted with permission from Smith and Edmonston (1997, 180). © the National Academy of Sciences, courtesy of the National Academies Press, Washington, D.C.

and foreign-born Mexicans between 1980 and 2000 reveals a significant finding. The comparison is important because high-education immigrants, such as Asian Indians, entered a labor market in which demand for their technical skills was firm. On the average, Asian Indian immigrants were much better educated than native-born white Americans and as such closely approximated high technology migrants on the cusp of global restructuring. In contrast, foreign-born Mexicans entered a labor force in which the share of jobs for unskilled workers was declining. Although this trend has, as Elaine Levine has observed, an ominous long-term implication in the shipwreck of the American Dream, it has also disadvantageous short-term implications for Mexicans in declining relative wages.[39]

Figure 4.2 uses index numbers only and illustrates the trend of wages from 1980 until 2000 across national-origin groups. Obviously Mexicans were a much larger group than Asian Indians. In 2000, the Los Angeles–Long Beach metropolitan region was home to 837,000 Mexican but only 21,020 Asian Indian wage earners. Figure 4.2 displays only the trend of mean wages for both immigrant groups relative to the rest of the metropolitan area population, the aggregated metropolitan areas of six high-

Figure 4.2   Wage Changes, 1980 to 2000, Percentage Above or
Below Average

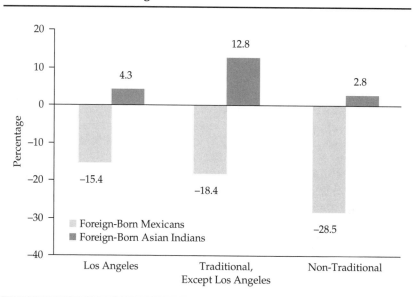

Source: U.S. Census Bureau (2000a, 2000b, 2000c), 5 percent PUMS.

immigration states excluding Los Angeles, and the aggregated metropolitan areas of "nontraditional" reception areas.

Results confirm what Peter Stalker reported about the contrasting
trend of Mexican and Asian Indian wages for the 1970 to 1990 period, but
extend his results to 2000.[40] Between 1980 and 2000, Mexican wages
increased less than the mean wages of "All Other" workers in every setting. In the Los Angeles metropolitan region, Mexican immigrants' wages
decreased 15.4 percent relative to those of All Others in the twenty years.
In other traditional destination areas, they decreased a relative 18.4 percent. Finally, in the nontraditional, high-growth cities, Mexican immigrants' wages fell a relative 28.5 percent behind All Other between 1980
and 2000. That result is initially surprising. One wonders why Mexican
immigrants would rush into nontraditional regions in which their relative wages were falling the most. On the other hand, the nontraditional
reception areas experienced a massive thirteenfold increase in their Mexican population in those twenty years. It is thus plausible that the huge
influx itself depressed the wage growth of Mexican immigrants in the
nontraditional areas.

The wage experience of foreign-born Asian Indians was quite different than that of foreign-born Mexicans. In every setting, Asian Indian

immigrants' mean wages increased more rapidly than those of All Other earners in the twenty-year period. In the Los Angeles–Long Beach metropolitan area, the relative gain was 4.3 percent. In traditional metropolitan settlements, excluding Los Angeles, it was 12.8 percent. Finally, in the nontraditional growth metropolitan areas, it was 2.8 percent.

These results imply two conclusions. First, Mexican immigration was probably not demand-driven from 1980 to 2000, whereas the Asian Indian immigration probably was. The Asian Indian data show that sustained immigrant influx need not reduce wages. No matter what the preceding influx, Asian Indians gained income relative to everyone else. Conversely, where Mexican influx was greatest, in nontraditional areas, their wage increases were smallest. The strong and even growing demand for high-technology workers in this period supported the wages of highly skilled Asian Indian immigrants despite their influx. By contrast, given the diminishing share of unskilled labor in the United States, the declining relative wages among low-skilled Mexican immigrants imply labor demand that, already saturated in 1980, began thereafter to shrink as network-driven immigrants continued to arrive. Second, global restructuring theory fits the Asian Indian influx much better than the Mexican. The skilled Asian Indian immigrants were demand-driven throughout, whereas the unskilled Mexican immigrants became network-driven.

Even assuming that global restructuring once fit the Mexican case, since about 1980 it has not. Therefore, we confront the necessity for modifying the claim, commonly encountered in the popular as well as in the academic literature, that low-wage immigration just responds to employer demand.[41] This claim is simplistic for the reasons explained in chapter 3. Although some demand was still there for low-skilled workers in 2000, demand was appreciably weaker in 2000 than in 1980. Declining wages signal declining demand, and Mexican wages were declining.

Growing Informalization

Informal sectors expand when network-driven immigration oversupplies the mainstream labor market, causing the unemployed and under-employed to undertake marginal self-employment. Mexicans did not create the informal sector of Los Angeles. The informal sector in Los Angeles still consisted largely of blacks in 1972.[42] But the ethnic composition changed thereafter. Enrico Marcelli reported that Latinos increased from 49 percent to 59 percent of workers in California's informal economy between 1990 and 1996, and, in the same period the percentage of informal economy employees earning poverty level wages rose from 27 to 36 percent.[43] Marta López-Garza found that Mexicans and Central Americans made up 80 percent of the workers in the informal economy of Los Angeles in 2000.[44] Their jobs consisted largely of domestic service, street vending, gardening, and landscaping. Of informal sector workers, only 14 percent were not immigrants. In 2001, "approximately 20,000 day laborers" competed every day for casual jobs on street corners in Los Angeles. "Virtually all of them are immigrants—20 percent Central American, the rest Mexican."[45] Abel Valenzuela estimated that between ten and twenty thousand day workers sought jobs every day on Los Angeles street corners. Of these, 99 percent were foreign-born, and 84 percent were illegally in the United States. None had health insurance.[46]

Chinchilla and Hamilton studied Central Americans in street vending. Most street vendors had worked up to self-employment in the informal sector from wage work in the informal sector. Half had opened their informal business six years after their arrival, and one-third did not start in the informal business until eleven years after their arrival in Los Angeles.[47] Two-thirds of their employees were Latinos, mostly coethnics.[48] The Los Angeles Municipal Code prohibits pedestrians from selling food or merchandise on public streets without a license.[49] Operating without licenses, immigrant street vendors operated illegally. They reported frequent "harassment and arrest, and in some cases rough treatment" by the police.[50] In the aftermath of the Los Angeles riot and arson of 1992, Latino street vendors formed a trade association that obtained some favorable legal changes.[51] Street vending was legalized in special districts, but vendors had to be members of the association, and the number of members was limited.[52] Affiliation with the formal sector's ethnic business owners and support from Central American governments additionally stabilized and institutionalized street vending in Los Angeles. This maneuver improved economic welfare of association members, but tended to exclude more recent migrants from street vending.

In a research project fielded by the Economic Roundtable, a quasi-governmental research center, Pascal Joassart-Marcelli and Daniel Flaming estimated informal sector employment in Los Angeles County.[53] Using restricted government data, they compared official estimates of employment, then measured the discrepancies between series. Essentially they found "a significant gap between the number of people claiming to be employed" and "the number reported by employers." Many more people claimed to have jobs than employers acknowledged employing. This gap suggests informal economic activity. The Joassart-Marcelli and Flaming evidence suggests that informalization had increased in the 1990s. In 2001, there were almost 500,000 fewer employer-reported jobs in Los Angeles County than there were employed residents in Los Angeles County. In 1990, there had been only 100,000 fewer jobs than employees. The discrepancy implies a fivefold increase in informal economic activity in the decade 1990 to 2000.[54] Using nine different tests based on incompatibility of data series, Joassart-Marcelli and Flaming reached nine different estimates of the size of the informal sector in Los Angeles

Table 4.2   Industries Employing Illegal Latino Immigrants in
Los Angeles County, 1990

Industry	Total Employment	Percentage Illegal Immigrants
Textile	16,660	49
Apparel	94,634	47
Leather	3,913	45
Furniture	32,325	42
Rubber and plastics	20,307	39
Agriculture, forestry, and fisheries	49,124	37
Lumber and wood	9,487	37
Miscellaneous manufacturing	69,597	33
Private households	45,288	31
Food and tobacco manufacturing	40,623	31
Primary metal	16,994	29
Paper and allied products	14,513	29
Eating and drinking places	177,865	28
Fabricated metal	44,089	28
Stone and concrete	16,811	27

Source: Joassart-Marcelli and Flaming (2002), with permission from the Economic Roundtable.

County. Their estimates of the informal sector ranged from 9 percent to 29 percent of total employment; the median estimate was 15 percent.[55] Illegal Latino immigrants were heavily overrepresented in what Joassart-Marcelli and Flaming identified as heartland industries of the informal sector (table 4.2). For example, in the textile industry nearly half of the workers in these industries were illegal immigrants even though illegal workers represent no more than one-tenth of the Los Angeles County labor force.

Intended for consumption by government agencies, but reported as well in the press, this report raised economic and social criticisms of the informal sector.[56] On the economic side, Joassart-Marcelli and Flaming pointed out that workers in the informal sector paid no taxes. This lost revenue amounted to an estimated $1.2 billion in 2001. Additionally, employers who hire illegal workers "are also likely to break other types of regulations" such as those related to health, safety, and wages. Therefore, Los Angeles's burgeoning informal economy really represented an employers' crime wave. Finally, most employees of informal firms did not earn a living wage. Three-quarters of the Los Angeles population in poverty was Latino in 2000 even though Latinos were only half the population.[57] On the social side, Joassart-Marcelli and Flaming noted, "There are broad and widening differences in the distribution of wealth in the Los Angeles region." The deprivations of the low-wage population are "made tolerable" if low-wage workers can escape initial poverty, but in Los Angeles informal economies offered no escape in 2000.[58]

To combat informalization, Joassart-Marcelli and Flaming offered four recommendations. Of these, the first was to "enforce existing labor regulations in a more systematic way."[59] All who have studied the informal sector in Los Angeles have endorsed this remedy. Marta López-Garza is one example: "I favor vigorous enforcement of laws, ensuring fair and safe working conditions to eradicate sweatshop operations. This requires more vigilant oversight by the state . . . in the enforcement of existing labor laws as well as health and safety codes and regulations."[60]

Deterioration of the Mexican Ownership Economy

Ethnic ownership economies open another employment buffer to network-driven immigration.[61] The ethnic ownership economy of any group consists of the self-employed, their unpaid family workers, and their coethnic employees.[62] Whites are ethnics too, and their businesses belong to the ethnic ownership economy of their groups. Firms in the ethnic ownership economy are not informal. Unlike informal firms, however, they pay taxes, somewhat respect occupational and industrial laws, and have telephones, real premises, regular business hours, and business licenses. Governments collect statistics about them. They report earned income and are subject to some government monitoring. As elsewhere, wages in the ethnic ownership economy of Los Angeles were somewhat lower than in the mainstream, but not 80 percent lower, as they were in the informal economy.

Although the growth of Hispanic self-employment in the 1990s was a national, not just a local phenomenon, growth of immigrant self-employment in Los Angeles was exceptionally strong in that decade.[63] Tarry Hum reported that 54 percent of Mexican immigrants and 54 percent of Central Americans in Los Angeles worked (owners or employees) in ethnic economies in 2000.[64] Among Central Americans who entered the United States in the 1990s, Hum found that fully 88 percent worked in the ethnic ownership economy of their group. Hum's estimates did not include the informal sector, discussed earlier, in which Central Americans and Mexicans predominated. Among the most recent immigrants, ethnic ownership economies provided half the employment in Los Angeles in the late 1990s. According to Hum, virtually none of the Hispanic immigrants found employment in the mainstream labor market in the late 1990s. Along with its informal sector, the ethnic ownership economy had virtually become their only source of jobs.[65] In other words, had the migration of the 1990s depended on the mainstream economy for jobs, migration to Los Angeles would have ended in the 1980s. As it was, by

Table 4.3   Indices of Change in Employment for Southern California, 1970 to 1990

	Employment	Self-Employment
Native-born white men	100	139
Native-born white women	140	259
Foreign-born white men	115	194
Foreign-born white women	134	182
Foreign-born Asian men	911	1,331
Foreign-born Asian women	994	NA
Foreign-born Hispanic men	610	756
Foreign-born Hispanic women	691	1,660

Source: Light and Roach (1996, table 7.4).
Notes: Index = Percent change in category/percent change in native white employment × 100.
NA = data not available.

2000 the employment buffers (informal economy plus ethnic ownership economy) had approximately quadrupled the labor absorption capacity of Los Angeles County's employment mainstream.

Census data expose the uneven impact of globalization on self-employment rates in Los Angeles between 1970 and 1990. Globalization's impact on self-employment in Los Angeles was complex, and affected natives as well as immigrants. Under a regime of global restructuring, native workers' self-employment increases in regions that export jobs, such as southern California. Self-employment of native-born workers increases because the exportation of production jobs in manufacturing, a defining characteristic of globalization, strips native-born workers of their wage jobs, encouraging self-employment. Additionally, the previously non-employed wives of redundant men then become self-employed in order to shore up their family's declining income. For this reason, as shown in table 4.3, self-employment among native-born white women in Los Angeles increased more than it did among their male counterparts between 1970 and 1990, but increased for both more rapidly than their wage employment did.[66]

However, one should distinguish the jobs-export self-employment of the native born from the network-driven self-employment of immigrants. Although both changes originated in globalization, their immediate causes were different. Demand-driven immigrations need no support from self-employment because an attractive wage awaits every immigrant. In the course of network-driven migrations, as wages drop and unemployment increases, immigrants turn in desperation to self-employment. Doing so, they scrape the bottom of the barrel. More immigrant business owners chase a constant volume of consumer dollars, thus driving down the average economic returns of self-employment.[67]

Self-employment increased in southern California between 1970 and 1990 among all ethno-racial groups, native as well as foreign. Combining all four census ethno-racial categories, aggregate self-employment increased 229 percent in the twenty years whereas employment in the general labor market increased only 180 percent.[68] Incorporated and unincorporated self-employment both increased. The increase in the number of incorporated self-employed occurred among the native born of all ethno-racial categories, and promoted the growth of the highest income stratum in each, thus contributing to income polarization. Increases in unincorporated self-employment were less universal. These are legally proprietors. Increases in unincorporated self-employment outstripped those in wage employment among native whites and native Hispanics. Rates of self-employment increased faster among Hispanic women than among any other group. Among the foreign born, increases in self-employment outstripped those in wage employment among whites, Asian men, and Hispanics.

Declining Income of the Self-Employed

Varying money returns to self-employment expose realities masked by self-employment rates. Thanks to globalization, the incorporated self-employed of Los Angeles earned as much in 1990 as they had in 1970 relative to native white wage earners. Globalization, however, did not equally support the unincorporated self-employed, who earned relatively less in 1990 than they had in 1970 relative to native white wage earners. As is clear in table 4.4, among Asians, whites, and Hispanics, the earnings of the unincorporated self-employed failed to keep pace with those of coethnic wage earners in the private sector, much less those of white wage earners.[69] Among Hispanics, the unincorporated self-employed earned 67 percent of the average earnings of white employees in the private sector, whereas Hispanic private sector workers earned only 53 percent as much as whites. The unincorporated Hispanic self-employed lost ground relative to Hispanic wage earners between 1970 and 1990, but in 1990 still earned absolutely more than coethnic wage earners (table 4.4). Relative to white incomes, Asians fared better than Hispanics in all categories but did not equal the whites.

Earning declines among the self-employed Hispanics did not result from declining educational levels. The mean educational levels of Asian immigrants in Los Angeles and in the United States, however, did decrease between 1970 and 2000. Those of Hispanic immigrants were stable or increased slightly.[70] Because Hispanic immigrants' relative self-employment and wage earnings declined the most, but Hispanic educational levels were stable, the deterioration of the Hispanic immigrants'

Table 4.4   Index of Mean Earnings Changes, Los Angeles Region,
1970 to 1990 (Ages 25 to 64)

	Earnings Growth	Earnings, 1990
Whites		
Private sector wage earners	100	100
Incorporated self-employed	101	209
Unincorporated self-employed	59	109
Hispanics		
Private sector wage earners	72	53
Incorporated self-employed	53	102
Unincorporated self-employed	53	67
Asians		
Private sector wage earners	95	78
Incorporated self-employed	89	150
Unincorporated self-employed	65	95

Source: Light and Roach (1996, table 7.2).
Notes: Indices = Percentage growth = Percentage change in earnings of group/
percentage change in earnings of whites, 1970–1990 × 100; Earnings, 1990 = average earnings of group/average earnings of white employees in the private sector × 100.

economic welfare cannot be attributed to declining educational qualifi-
cation of later arrival Hispanic cohorts.

In addition to declining earnings and sharply increased self-employment
rates, telltale signs of self-employment's declining health, new evidence
bears on the percentage of specifically Mexican firms with employees and
their gross receipts between 1969 and 1997 (see table 4.5). The percentage of
Mexican-owned firms with employees plummeted between 1969 and 1997
everywhere in the United States. The decline was worse in California than
nationally, but worst in Los Angeles. In Los Angeles, employer firms
declined from 32.1 percent of all Mexican-owned firms to 13.1 percent in
those twenty-eight years. This severe reduction amounts to a qualitative
decline in the economic level of the entire Mexican ownership economy.
It is plausible to ascribe this qualitative decline to a massive invasion of
under- and unemployed Mexicans, who opened undercapitalized one-
person firms in a desperate attempt to find work. A similar conclusion can
be drawn from the mean gross receipts of Mexican-owned firms. In current dollars, their mean gross receipts increased only 90 percent as much
in Los Angeles as they did nationwide, a relative slackening of earnings
in southern California. The presumptive cause is again heavy influx of
new and marginal business owners in overcrowded Los Angeles markets,
resulting in declining earnings per firm.

Table 4.5   Mexican-Owned Firms in United States, California, and
Los Angeles

	1969	1997
Percentage employer firms		
United States	32.5	19.2
California	33.6	15.9
Los Angeles	32.1	13.1
Mean gross receipts per firm		
United States	$33,728	$156,147
California	$34,230	$155,293
Los Angeles	$31,512	$139,902

Sources: U.S. Bureau of the Census (1971, tables 1,2,6); U.S. Census Bureau (2001, tables 5, 7).

Spread of Slums and Overcrowded Housing

Declining incomes reduce the quality of housing immigrants can afford. Low wages mean that slums, overcrowding, and overpayment all increase. Overpayment means housing costs higher than incomes can normally afford, and is conventionally pegged at housing costs in excess of 30 percent of household income.[71] When network-driven immigration concentrates new immigrants in selected locations, as it did in Los Angeles, the network accentuates the immigration's impact on housing costs in immigrant neighborhoods. Network clustering of immigrants put additional upward pressure on regional housing prices that were trending upward for other reasons as well. The combination trapped Mexican immigrants in Los Angeles between declining wages and rising rents in Los Angeles just as chapter 2 showed it did nationally. The whipsaw represented the spontaneous response of the housing market and labor market to long-term network-driven immigration of the unskilled. Carried far and long enough, this market response significantly reduced Mexican and Central American immigrants' quality of life in Los Angeles and southern California, especially the quality of life of the newest, younger, and less established immigrants.

In 1970, when the immigration began, housing costs in Los Angeles were already 60 percent higher than the U.S. average. During the 1970s and 1980s, however, they increased in Los Angeles faster than elsewhere in the country.[72] By 2000, they were twice those in the average American metropolitan area. Unsurprisingly, as the costs of housing rose, and relative incomes fell, lower income households began to crowd more people into residences. Between 1980 and 2000, the percentage of Los Angeles households overpaying increased from 28.7 to 35.9 percent, and the per-

Table 4.6   Southern California Residents in Overcrowded Housing
(Percentages)

Immigrants Year of Immigration	1980	1990
1980 to 1990	NA	47.9
1970 to 1979	35.2	36.0
1960 to 1969	16.6	16.3
Before 1960	4.0	4.8
Native-born	1.9	3.2

Source: Myers and Lee (1996, 57), with permission.
Note: Overcrowded housing is defined as more than 1.5 persons per room.

centage who were overcrowded increased from 13.0 to 25.6 percent.[73] The burden fell most heavily on the poor and on immigrants.[74] Dowell Myers and Seong Woo Lee showed that 35.2 percent of immigrants who had arrived in southern California during the 1970s lived in overcrowded housing in 1980.[75] A decade later, 47.9 percent of recent immigrants did so (see table 4.6). In contrast, in 1990, only 3.2 percent of the native born did. In many cases, overcrowding represented a violation of law. Aware of the overcrowding, officials of the Los Angeles Building and Safety Department were reluctant to enforce existing density laws for fear of creating mass homelessness. "We don't want to kick people out into the street with no place to stay."[76] There was also political corruption. After slumlords contributed to his political campaign, the Los Angeles City Attorney reduced the penalties his office sought from them.[77]

Los Angeles County's worst housing was in the heavily Latino, suburban city of Santa Ana. Santa Ana also had the second highest percentage of foreign-born residents of any city in the United States in the 1990s. In one of its dilapidated single-family homes lived Gloria Valadez, her twenty-six-year-old daughter, and her six grandchildren. Valadez shared this two-bedroom house with eight other tenants, bringing the total occupation to sixteen. Her detached garage also housed paying tenants. Occupants "put up with mice, cockroaches, broken windows and faulty plumbing." A lodger even paid $150 for the right to sleep eight hours on the couch.[78] This housing situation was unpleasant and unattractive, but it was also illegal because of overcrowding, infestation, dilapidation, unauthorized occupancy, and substandard plumbing and electrical connections.

Along with the overcrowding, occupation of substandard housing also increased in Los Angeles between 1970 and 2000. The main development was the proliferation of dilapidated, tenement housing in the central city, but especially in Pico-Union, the Central American neighborhood west of downtown. Servicing impoverished immigrant tenants, landlords collected rents but ceased to maintain properties. Apartment houses became slum tenements. Occupied garages emerged as colorful, regional solutions to high housing costs. Lacking plumbing, heating, ventilation, and windows, and lit only by one dangling light bulb, unconverted garages could not legally serve as residences. However, facing high housing costs, poor immigrant families sublet the detached garage to even poorer families.[79] Mornings and evenings, garage dwellers emptied their slop bucket into the toilet in the main house and showered.[80]

Los Angeles had endured poor public transportation for decades. A third of its Latinos owned no car, and depended on an inferior public transportation system in 2000. This was a hardship because, as the Mexican American Legal Defense and Education Foundation declared, "costly, unreliable and untimely public transit" made job holding difficult.[81] In the wake of the Los Angeles riot of 1992, a Bus Riders Union was formed by the Labor Community Strategy Center. The Bus Riders Union took the Metropolitan Transit Authority to court and came away with both fare reductions and court-ordered new buses and bus lines to serve minority and immigrant neighborhoods.[82] Bus service improved slightly in consequence, but remained inadequate. To escape the bus, most Latino immigrants purchased cars and trucks. Needing to drive, they needed driver's licenses, which California initially issued to any applicant regardless of immigration status. California first required driver's license applicants to prove legal residence in 1994.[83] Because this requirement prevented illegal immigrants from obtaining driver's licenses, spokesmen for the Hispanic community subsequently sought to eliminate the law, but Republicans successfully defended it.[84] California's requirement reduced the state's attractiveness to illegal immigrants, who were subject to arrest when they drove without a license, but could neither obtain a driver's license nor commute conveniently without driving. The requirement also probably deflected some illegal immigrants to other states.

Because of the low wages, immigrant households required many earners, each wanting a car to get to work. This need led in turn to crowded, immigrant neighborhoods with too many cars. Many households had rented the detached garages as living units and therefore parked on the street. Street parking could not accommodate the overcrowded houses. Immigrant families therefore parked their vehicles on the setback in front of their homes, transforming it to a parking lot. So popular was this image of Hispanics in southern California that it found expression in *Crash*, a 2004 movie about ethnic diversity in Los Angeles. However, there was more to this complaint than discomfort. In many cities of Los Angeles County, municipal ordinances forbade parking on a house's setback because it was an eyesore. Police attempted to enforce the no-parking provisions on overcrowded immigrant houses only to learn that immigrant households could not comply with municipal parking requirements. There was no other parking than the setback, and the cars were needed as transportation to work. Vigorous parking enforcement, a strictly local issue, thus became a tool of immigration control inasmuch as immigrants could not work without parking illegally.

Seeking cheaper housing, low-income families in Los Angeles moved to outlying areas of the region, such as Palmdale. This intraregional movement threatened to reduce the socioeconomic standards in Palmdale, so Palmdale took action. When poor homeowners failed to maintain their front yards to city standards, Palmdale officials threatened prosecution under a municipal ordinance that required an attractive front yard. A city report found that 3,000 homes lacked adequate landscaping under the new law, but half would require financial subsidies from the city to enable them to comply.[85] Because Palmdale's law had been passed after the migratory influx of poor residents had begun rather than before, it appears that the city passed the ordinance to deter and deflect the incipient influx of poorer residents. Such a policy is not the same as the post factum enforcement of existing housing laws, discussed in chapter 7, but it nonetheless illustrates how suburban cities used housing codes to deflect unwanted residents.

Antislum Crusades

As news of deteriorating housing conditions spread and public concern grew, successive mayors of Los Angeles appointed housing commissions to investigate. The first Blue Ribbon Housing Commission did so in 1988, the second in 1996. Both reports documented the growth of slums, the increase in housing costs, and the spread of illegal housing conditions.[86] In their report, the second omission lamented, "the filth, the lack of proper sanitary facilities, rats, the absentee landlords and everything else which is associated with slum housing conditions."[87] It estimated that one-fifth of Los Angeles's rental units were substandard. Substandard meant illegal, not simply deplorable. Both commissions found that existing housing conditions violated municipal fire, safety, health, sanitation, and earthquake regulations. However, they also found that municipal agencies lacked the personnel, the budget, and the political will to enforce the housing code. To create that political will, explicitly conceptualized as a requirement of the moment, a multiethnic reform coalition formed behind housing reform after the 1996 report appeared. It included the Roman Catholic hierarchy, the Los Angeles Coalition for Economic Survival,[88] trade unions, immigrant defense organizations, centrist and center-left politicians, the *Los Angeles Times*, universities, interfaith coalitions, and some prominent civic and business leaders. Although left of center, the reform movement attracted a broad-based spectrum, and did not depend upon either socialists or Hispanic voters. It successfully garnered political support in city hall. Although elected as a neoconservative, Mayor Richard Riordan declared that "slum housing can no longer be tolerated in the City of Los Angeles."[89] Riordan proposed his own antislum campaign to rehabilitate the city's 156,400 substandard apartments, and the 108,000 apartments infested with rats.[90] The next year, the Los Angeles City Council funded a housing inspection program with a tax upon apartment houses. Successfully defended in the courts against landlords' legal challenge, Riordan's "systematic code enforcement program" opened with an annual budget of $8 million, big money for this hitherto ignored municipal responsibility.

Private actors also entered the lists against slums. In cooperation with the Environmental Law Foundation, the Legal Aid Foundation of Los Angeles brought suit on behalf of nineteen Latino tenants of a notorious slum tenement. The building lacked hot water, gas, and electricity. It was infested with roaches and rats. Lead paint was peeling off the walls. The landlord had earlier pleaded nolo contendere to charges of maintaining a slum tenement, but thereafter refused to make required repairs. After a Los Angeles Superior Court judge awarded $3.5 million in damages to the tenants, City Councilman Eric Garcetti declared that "being a slum lord does not pay and will not be tolerated in . . . Los Angeles."[91] There was some truth to this claim. The crusade actually reduced the growth of slums. Reviewing the reform effort, Bill Pitkin concludes that the Blue Ribbon committees successfully revamped Los Angeles's housing code enforcement program, permitting the city to control slum conditions and "prevent further deterioration in the housing stock."[92] Of course, controlling slums did nothing to make decent housing available to Latinos at affordable prices. The housing crusaders reduced access to slums without replacing the cheap housing the slums had provided.[93] The crusade thus actually intensified the rent pressure on Latinos in Los Angeles in the short term. In turn, the augmented rent pressure deflected some Latino immigrants from Los Angeles.

Decade of Action Result: A Mixed "Blessing"

In 2004, two-thirds of New York City's growing Mexican population consisted of Mixtecans. When the *Los Angeles Times* asked those Mixtecans why they had selected New York City for residence rather than Los Angeles, the Mixtecans answered that Los Angeles already contained so many Mexicans from other states in Mexico, it was now impossible for Mixtecans to "get a foothold" there.[94] That answer is compatible with the supposition that Mexican migration had saturated economic opportunities in Los Angeles, and the Mixtecans knew it. Global restructuring explains many features of southern California's economic trajectory between 1970 and 2000, but it does not explain this Mixtecan answer nor why, more generally, Latino immigrants avoided Los Angeles in the 1990s.[95]

In southern California, a globalizing region, the immigration of uneducated, low-skill workers from Mexico and Central America outstripped initial labor demand within a decade. Around 1980, demand-driven migration spilled over into a network-driven migration that, as it propagated itself, undermined the economic well-being of low-wage Latino immigrants already in the region. Immigrant wages began their downward slide, immigrants' self-employment rates increased but their earnings declined. Latino firms grew smaller. The region's informal sector expanded, as did the Latino share of it. Working poverty increased, as did the immigrant share of it. Immigrant housing costs increased, overcrowding and overpayment increased, slums spread, and immigrant welfare declined. Reacting to this squalor, which threatened their self-interest and offended their social conscience, trade unions, churches, immigrant defense organizations, assorted left-wingers, and even metropolitan business elites rejected the increasing economic inequality that immigration had produced in the Los Angeles metropolitan area. They rallied the public behind demands for affordable housing, higher wages for the unskilled, paid medical care for all workers, and slum clearance. They supported immigrant defense organizations, such as Justice for Janitors. Unlike Proposition 187, which California voters passed in 1994, this public reaction was pro-immigrant. No one should live in a slum or earn less than a living wage was the implicit slogan. Unlike Proposition 187, this slogan was humane and generous in inspiration rather than punitive.

Nonetheless, along with Proposition 187, which was manifestly antiimmigrant, the successful defense of immigrant living conditions deflected some Latino immigration away from the Los Angeles metropolitan region. Raising legal minimum wages in California and in Los Angeles reduced the supply of low-wage jobs for new immigrants. Banning slums improved the quality of vested immigrants' housing, but, without an increase in the affordable housing supply, the measure reduced the availability of the most affordable housing, slums. Regional and local no-growth policies contradicted the needs of immigrant households, some still in Mexico, but not of immigrant households already vested in southern California.[96] In all, immigrants in Los Angeles encountered a shortage of affordable housing that a decade's political action only aggravated while their incomes declined. In view of these hardships, and quite apart from the possible effects of IRCA and Operation Gatekeeper that Massey, Durand, and Malone proposed, Mexican immigrants had realistic economic motives for looking outside Los Angeles for jobs and housing in 1990.[97] When unwrapped and examined, the case of Los Angeles corroborates and amplifies the national analysis presented in chapter 2, but it does not fit the globalization theorists' image of demand-driven migration.

= Chapter 5 =

How the Garment
Industry Expanded

G LOBALIZATION HAD many economic effects on Latinos in Los Angeles
between 1970 and 2000. Expansion of employment buffers in the
face of network-driven migration from Mexico and Central America was one of these. Although associated with declining economic welfare
of Latinos, buffer growth permitted Los Angeles to support more immigrants than would have been possible without it. The two buffers were the
ethnic ownership economy and the informal sector, the latter technically a
subsector of the ethnic economy. Based on that recitation, one might fairly
conclude that the expanding ethnic economies provided the requisite
buffer. This chapter shows why that was not quite accurate. True, ethnic
ownership economies did grow. In so doing, they soaked up unemployment among immigrants, permitting more migrants to live in southern California, and thus aggravating the economic burden. However, even when
combined, these two sectors—ethnic ownership economies and informal
economies—cannot explain all the new employment that actually materialized in response to the network-driven migration. The problem is conceptual, not empirical. The concept of an ethnic ownership economy is too
narrow to encompass the reality. To explain what happened, a new economic concept is essential. This is the new concept of an immigrant economy. This goal of this chapter is to introduce and clarify the concept of
immigrant economy, to demonstrate its empirical fit, and to integrate it into
the sociology of immigration.

Critique of Migration Network Theory

Migration network theory has a blind spot. It addresses only the facilitation
of searches, especially those for jobs and housing, but ignores the resource
expansion that migration networks accomplish in destination localities.
That is, networks make it easier for immigrants to find jobs, housing, protection, and companionship. Indeed, as they mature, networks increase

81

search efficiency, their raison d'être.[1] Efficient networks promptly expose every available job, residence, and companion in some destination, thus lowering search costs. Without increasing the supply of jobs or housing, migration networks only facilitate participants' access to the existing supply. As noted, however, mature networks aggravate job and housing shortages in destinations even as they improve search efficiency. The contradiction is a fundamental one: migration networks enhance search efficiency but diminish resource availability.

In that case, how long can network facilitation continue in a single destination? If the migratory influx is massive and protracted, every locality ultimately runs out of jobs and housing. Then the influx ends. As Peter Gregory observes, the supply of jobs exercises a "restraint on the volume of migration."[2] The same judgment would fit housing as well. Economic saturation exists when a locality can offer no work or no housing to new migrants. Under fully saturated conditions, a newcomer can only obtain a job or housing when an incumbent vacates, just as revelers find a parking space in Santa Monica on a Saturday night only when someone else vacates a space. Even hyperefficient social networks cannot find jobs, housing, or parking spaces where none exist. Network or none, immigrants cannot stay where they find no food or shelter. Knowing that such a situation exists, new migrants avoid the destination.

Networks and Immigrant Entrepreneurship

As the migration network delivers additional workers, local economic development must keep pace or a backlog of job-hunting immigrants builds up. Impending saturation diminishes the network's access to the saturated locality, diverting it to new ones. A saturated locality's immigration influx ends abruptly, but this is a theoretical projection. Although immigration has ended in one locality, or possibly just slowed, it continues elsewhere, possibly more rapidly. The deflection of networks from partially saturated regions, however, has already been addressed. Here we address the migration network's unappreciated role in expanding the job supply in targeted destinations. This expansion is the work of buffer formation. To the extent that the migration network itself expands the job supply in the short run, it also provides the essential conditions for self-propagation beyond the maximum that earlier would have limited it. To the extent that migration networks manufacture the conditions for their self-propagation, they are more dynamic than currently realized, and less subject to realistic limitations, whether demographic or economic.

The general topic is how networks increase migrant-accessible resources in destinations. A preliminary distinction is essential. Networks expand migrants' access to local jobs and housing in one of three ways. Either they improve the efficiency of searches or they increase the supply of jobs and housing in the destination, or both. These routes lead to quite different outcomes. Improving efficiency reduces search time, and increases the array of scanned vacancies. If networks direct immigrants to unwanted vacancies, they improve the immigrants' search, reducing their costs, without adverse economic effects upon native workers. These are the famous jobs no one else wanted to do. However, if hyperefficient networks also enable immigrants to get jobs that nonimmigrants were also trying to secure, as Waldinger claims happened sometimes, the immigrants' hyperefficient migration network excluded natives from jobs without increasing the job supply.[3] The migrants' hyperefficient network thus transferred existing jobs from nonimmigrants to immigrants. This is one way immigrants take jobs from nonimmigrants.

Hyperefficient networks are not just very efficient; they are more efficient than networks nonimmigrants mobilize. Where they exist, immigrants' hyperefficient networks are a competitive resource.[4] They increase the access of immigrants to resources in a destination without increasing the total supply of jobs or housing in the destination. They may drive non-immigrants out of local labor markets, garnering short-term advantages for immigrants. Although much social science literature addresses the possible impact of immigration upon nonimmigrant workers, only Waldinger and his associates have stressed the critical role of networks in this process. Social networks mediate the competition of natives and immigrants. In the struggle for economic advantage, victory goes to the most efficient social networks. Showing this outcome represented a distinct contribution to the migration literature, but, that said, even Waldinger overlooked the long-term limitations: in the long run, hyperefficient migration networks collapse because they do not increase the resource supply; they simply permit migrants to outcompete nonmigrants. When the network has found and appropriated the last job and the last apartment in town, then what?

Networks that Create Jobs

The process whereby migrant networks also increase the jobs available in localities merits attention. Yes, migration networks improve the efficiency of searches, but by adding new jobs to the aggregate job supply, the networks also postpone saturation. They create jobs when they support immigrant entrepreneurship. The ethnic entrepreneurship literature acknowledges that networks are a powerful tool in job creation.[5] The same networks that relocate coethnics from one nation to another can strengthen the migrants' entrepreneurship in the destinations. First, migration networks encourage nonimmigrant entrepreneurs to create new jobs in immigrant reception localities in order to take advantage of immigrant labor that, thanks to its network organization, is easily accessed. This shift enhances the supply of jobs available to immigrants at no expense to nonimmigrant workers. Second, immigrant entrepreneurs buy existing firms from nonimmigrant owners, or start new ones, staffing them with family members and immigrant employees.[6] In the former case, immigrant entrepreneurs transfer jobs from the nonimmigrants to immigrants, increasing immigrant-accessible jobs without increasing the aggregate job supply. In the latter case, immigrant-owned firms make jobs available to other immigrants from the expanded job supply rather than from the prior and unexpanded supply.[7] Here, new immigrant-owned firms create employment for their owners and for immigrant employees without displacing nonimmigrants.

The immigrants' ethnic ownership economy consists of self-employed immigrants, their unpaid family members, and their coethnic employees.[8] This is the classic definition. All immigrants build ethnic ownership economies, and, Antoine Pécoud notwithstanding, white immigrants do as well.[9] Ethnic ownership economies augment the job supply available to coethnics, who now have three places (the ethnic ownership economy, its informal sector, and the general labor market) to search for employment rather than only one. Indeed, the main advantage of the ethnic economy for employees is precisely that: it provides an additional job supply to search.[10] Hence, any treatment of immigrant networks that ignores immigrant entrepreneurship, concentrating only upon employment in the general labor market, underestimates the carrying capacity of destination economies.[11] It also exaggerates the extent to which hyperefficient networks deprive non-immigrant workers of jobs, thus exaggerating the conflict of economic interest between native workers and immigrant workers.

Existing migration network theory makes this error. Even in Massey's magisterial synthesis of this literature, one finds no reference to entrepreneurship in the index or any appreciation in the text of its implications for job creation.[12] Although Massey acknowledges that migration networks "put a destination job within easy reach of most community members," he neglects the enhanced access to business ownership that migration networks also afford immigrants, and the additional immigrant-accessible jobs that enhanced business ownership conveys.[13] Immigrants generally have slightly higher self-employment rates than coethnic nonimmigrants so the effect of their entrepreneurship is slightly greater than the effect of entrepreneurship in the mainstream economy.[14] Overlooking this point, Massey acknowledges only the response of the host economy to immigrant employees: The more efficient the immigrant networks, the more efficiently host capital responds. This response augments the job supply in the general labor market, delaying economic saturation, and protracting cumulatively caused migration, just as Massey claims, albeit at the possible expense of nonmigrants, as Waldinger noted.[15] But Massey's recital overlooks ethnic economies because contemporary network theory ignores their economic role.

When immigrant networks support coethnic entrepreneurship, thus creating or expanding an ethnic economy, they expand the existing econ-

omy in the destinations their network reaches. The expanded ethnic economy buffers the influx. This buffer permits the destination economies to
raise their saturation threshold, thus permitting more immigrants to find
work than would otherwise have been possible. Ethnic economies create immigrant-accessible employment. Their buffering effect is serious.
Wayne Cornelius found that of San Diego employers who had hired
immigrant labor, one-third were themselves immigrants. In other words,
approximately one-third of the jobs immigrants secured in San Diego were
provided by other immigrants, who were not living in San Diego when the
immigration began.[16] In this sense, the immigrant employers, themselves
a product of the immigration process, had increased by one-third the number of immigrants who could inhabit San Diego. Naturally, the immigrant-
caused expansion of the destination localities begins after the migration has begun to land workers. The length of lag depends on political
restraints on immigrant enterprise as much as on the economic resources
immigrants bring. These political restraints are much more prominent in
European countries than in the United States.[17] Nonetheless, the network's
favorable modification of the target economy everywhere sustains and
supports the cumulatively caused migration network. Migration networks
are more effective than network theory acknowledges because the networks not only lower the costs of migration, they also create jobs at visited
destinations.

Immigrant and Ethnic Economies

If migration networks facilitate entrepreneurship in destinations, then why
do immigrant groups have unequal self-employment rates?[18] Facilitation
best fits immigrant groups that develop numerous entrepreneurs such as
Israelis, Chinese, Iranians, and Koreans. Entrepreneur-rich immigrant
groups have big ethnic ownership economies that expand the jobs available to coethnic workers. But what of working-class migrations, such as
those from Mexico and Central America? These contain few entrepreneurs.
All by themselves, their small ethnic ownership economies cannot mas-
sively expand the supply of coethnic-accessible jobs. In southern California, Korean, Chinese, Israeli, and Iranian immigrants had self-employment
rates much higher than native whites, whereas Mexican and Central American immigrants had lower.[19] Clearly, the ethnic ownership economies of
the well-endowed groups had great potential to expand the employment
available to coethnics in southern California, but the ethnic economies of
the Central Americans and Mexicans did not.[20]
    The explanation has a short and a long component. First, the short:
informal sectors expand to employ the working class immigrant groups,
whereas ethnic ownership economies expand to employ the higher status
groups.[21] Informal economies require minimal resources of those who

become self-employed, but they nonetheless buffer immigrant influx. With a tin can and some pencils, anyone can become an entrepreneur, and, thanks to this business, may survive, provided the police are not overzealous. On the other hand, ethnic ownership economies buffer immigrants who have more extensive capital resources. These are resources of human, financial, social and even cultural capital. People with these resources can start businesses in the mainstream.

Although true, this concise response overlooks synergies that bring working-class immigrants into middle-class immigrants' employment.[22] A longer explanation is therefore also necessary. What if immigrant entrepreneurs hire immigrants who are not coethnic? The existing concept of ethnic ownership economy, which is based on immigrant entrepreneurs who hire coethnics, cannot encompass such an employment relationship.[23] When immigrant entrepreneurs hire immigrants who are not coethnic, then, a new concept is needed.

An immigrant ownership economy consists of immigrant employers plus their immigrant but not coethnic employees. Because immigrant employers give hiring preference to coethnics, immigrant economies do not arise when equally entrepreneurial immigrant groups cohabit a municipality. In such a case, employers of group A prefer employees of group A, and employers of group B prefer employees of group B. In this case, ethnic economies occupy the entire terrain. Immigrant ownership economies arise when workers from low-entrepreneurship groups take jobs provided by employers from high-entrepreneurship groups. This arrangement is common. Steven Gold found that 77 percent of Israeli immigrants in Los Angeles were self-employed.[24] As a result, only 23 percent of Israelis were available to work for wages in the Israeli ethnic ownership economy. Without non-Israeli labor, two-thirds of Israeli entrepreneurs could not have become employers. Similarly, Dae Young Kim reported that so many Koreans started their own business that few Koreans were available to work in them for wages.[25] Therefore, Korean employers had to hire Latino labor, and to learn Spanish.

"Ethnic crossover" expands the economic opportunities of entrepreneurs and of workers by linking the networks of employers and workers across ethnic boundaries.[26] Sociology has understood this point in a general way. Writing in 1992, Gurak and Caces explained that weak ties "reduce the self encapsulation of networks and expand the opportunities available to the network."[27] Tamar Wilson explained that strong ties could be used to gain weak ones.[28] Somewhat later, David Heer noticed that cumulative causation stalls out unless migrants develop weak ties with non-coethnics in the destination.[29] The concept of immigrant economy concretizes these insights. This weak tie between employers and non-coethnic workers bridges the social networks of two immigrant communities, enhancing the economic opportunities of both.[30] Bridging networks enable employers to access the social network of non-coethnic employees, and vice versa. This capacity is mutually advantageous. Thanks to the bridges, immigrant employers readily obtain non-coethnic immigrant labor by advising their existing employees of a vacancy. This news travels via the migration network, and affects migration decisionmaking at home. "My employer, Mr. Park, has a job for you. Come to Los Angeles." Bridged networks reduce the cost of hiring and being hired, facilitating job growth in the destination.

When Mr. Park hires Mrs. Lopez, an immigrant Korean entrepreneur employs an immigrant Mexican seamstress. This arrangement buffers the local economic opportunities available to both Koreans and Mexicans. On the employer's side, access to Mexican labor permits Mr. Park to operate a factory, employing himself and supporting his family. Without Mexican labor, Mr. Park would confront a Korean ethnic economy lacking enough Korean workers to staff even one more garment factory, his own. Therefore, the immigrant ownership economy here expands by one household (Mr. Park's) the number of Koreans who live in Los Angeles. On the worker's side, access to a Korean employer permits Mrs. Lopez to escape unemployment caused by the limited size of the Mexican ownership economy. The immigrant economy thereby expands by one household (that of Mrs. Lopez) the number of Mexican immigrants who can find work in Los Angeles. Without Mrs. Lopez and others in her immigrant network, Mr. Park could not live in Los Angeles; but without Mr. Park, Mrs. Lopez could not live there either. Thanks to bridged networks, the immigrant ownership economy permits Los Angeles to support two additional immigrant households.

Expanding the Garment Industry

We now turn to how the garment industry of Los Angeles expanded between 1970 and 1996, providing the single most important buffer for the network-driven migration. Evidence shows the immigrant economy was more important than all the multiple ethnic economies combined. That is, the immigrant economy contributed more to the growth of the garment industry than did the ethnic ownership economies of the various immigrant communities. Immigrants have always dominated garment manufacturing in Los Angeles. Immigrants were 93 percent of all personnel in that industry in 1990. In 1979, garment-manufacturing employees had been heavily Asian, but Latinos increasingly replaced them thereafter.[31] Among the industries of Los Angeles, the garment industry's reliance on immigrant workers was extreme, showing how immigrants create whole industries, grafting them onto reception economies. The immigrants provided the financial capital, the human capital, the cultural capital, the labor, and the social capital that the massive Los Angeles garment industry required.[32] At its peak, that industry employed 160,000 people. It therefore represents the kind of migration-caused increase in a destination economy's job base that unexpanded network theory cannot explain.

The Los Angeles garment industry was very large in 2000, but estimates of how large were impossible to determine because the industry's informal sector was about 40 percent.[33] Ignoring the informal sector, the California Employment Development Department estimated total apparel employed in Los Angeles at 92,000 as of 2002. Adjusting upward for the underground sector, the Los Angeles Jewish Commission on Sweatshops estimated that "as many as" 162,000 people worked in the garment industry of Los Angeles County.[34] In the 1990s, California for the first time required garment contractors to register their factories.[35] Conducted in 1993, a city of Los Angeles survey identified 3,642 garment factories; the mean employment of each was 27.1 persons. That relationship yields an estimate of 98,700 workers in the city's known industry. In terms of total employment, garment manufacturing ranked fourth in Los Angeles County in 1996, behind engineering and management services, but ahead of the Hollywood film industry.[36] The garment industry's workers represented 5.5 percent of Los Angeles's immigrant labor force in 1990.

These statistics do not indicate how much of the garment industry was a product of ethnic ownership economies (including their informal component), how much of an immigrant ownership economy, and how much of the mainstream economy. That information is what this chapter seeks to estimate. Existing literature does indicate that the immigrant economy hired the lion's share of garment industry employees in Los Angeles. Edna Bonacich reported that Asians owned 51 percent of garment factories, and that most of their employees were Latinas.[37] Dong Ok Lee's study of Korean garment factory owners found that 85 percent of their employees were Hispanic.[38] Lee's estimate corresponds closely with that of Hess, who reported that Hispanics represented 87 percent of the employees of the Korean-owned garment factories.[39] Clearly, Asian employers were hiring more Latino than Asian workers. Therefore, the garment industry of Los Angeles mainly consisted of a large immigrant economy in which, Richard Appelbaum avers, immigrant Asian, European, and Latin American entrepreneurs hired Mexican and Central American seamstresses.[40] Some Mexican and Central Americans employed coethnics, but these apparently accounted for a third or less of Hispanic employment in garment manufacturing.

Estimating the Immigrant and Ethnic Economy

Using census data, figure 5.1 cross-tabulates race and class of the garment industry personnel. For this and subsequent tables from the 1990 census, Richard Bernard defined garment industry workers as "sewing machine operators," by far the largest category of worker in this industry.[41] He also defined employers as self-employed persons in the garment manufacturing industry whose occupation was managerial and administrative.[42]

Figure 5.1   Los Angeles Garment Industry by Ethno-Racial Category, 1990

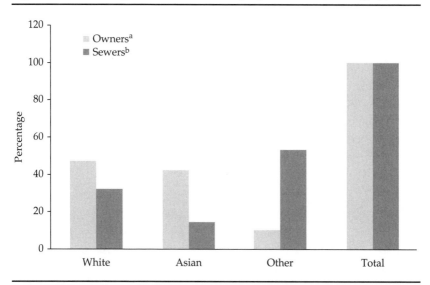

Source: U.S. Census Bureau (1990), 5 percent PUMS (of Hispanics 48 percent identified themselves as white).
[a] Owners are persons self-employed in garment manufacturing whose census occupation was "managers and administrators." Owners were excluded if their occupation did not suggest supervisory responsibility for sewers.
[b] Sewers are wage earners in garment manufacturing whose census occupation was "sewing machine operators." This category was the biggest in garment manufacturing. Other industry employees were ignored if their job title, such as accountant, did not imply production work with a sewing machine.

When these definitions were used, whites were 47.3 percent of employers, but only 32.2 percent of workers. Asians were 42.4 percent of employers, but only 14.5 percent of workers. White employers, in principle, could have employed 68 percent of white workers. But Asian employers could not have employed so high a proportion of Asian workers. Obviously, Asian-owned garment factories had to employ mostly non-Asian workers. Without non-Asian workers, Asian employers would have been unable to recruit all the labor they needed.

The objective now is to estimate the share of the immigrant ownership economy, the ethnic ownership economies, and the mainstream economy in constituting the Los Angeles garment industry in 1990. Census data do not permit matching employers and employees by ethno-racial origin. The best researchers can obtain from the U.S. Census is juxtaposed lists that show the nativity of garment industry factory owners on one side and of sewing machine operators on the other. Nonetheless, from these lists, if permitted some assumptions, we can estimate the share of the labor force that was employed by each of the three sectors—mainstream, ethnic economy, and immigrant economy.

Table 5.1 lists the percentage of garment factory owners and garment factory employees by place of birth. Two lists are juxtaposed. Census data indicate that, contrary to folk wisdom, some native-born persons did work in the Los Angeles garment industry. In fact, the native born made up 28.5 percent of factory owners and 6 percent of sewing machine operators. Looking over the other forty-four nations listed, which the table clusters into eight regions, table 5.1 shows that six of the eight furnished more owners than employees. These were Europe, Asia, the Middle East, the Caribbean, South America, and Africa. Only North and Central America furnished more employees than owners. Mexico and Central America furnished 9.3 percent of factory owners and 72.2 percent of employees. The rest of the world furnished 90.7 percent of employers and 27.8 percent of workers. From this array, it is apparent that Mexican and Central American factory owners could have employed only 9.3 percent of the garment industry's actual workforce if we assume that Central American and Mexican firms employed as many workers as did the others.

Apparently, much employment in the Los Angeles garment industry crossed ethno-national boundaries with employers from one immigrant group hiring workers from others. The problem is to estimate the share of the mainstream economy, the ethnic ownership economies, and the immigrant economy in the garment industry's total employment from the array in table 5.1. Making this estimate requires simplifying assumptions. Assuming that all employers hired twenty-one employees—the industry mean—and that employers preferred coethnics to others, one can extract estimates from the census data. Accepting these assumptions, an immigrant group's total ethnic ownership economy is the lesser of its percentage share of total ownership or its percentage share of total employment—provided only that the group has some representation in both. Thus, from table 5.1, the ethnic ownership economy of Mexicans in the garment industry is 6.1 percent, the share of Mexicans among the factory owners. Although Mexicans were 53.6 percent of sewers, they were only 6.1 percent of employers. Even if Mexican employers hired only Mexican sewers, they could hire only 11.4 percent of the Mexican sewers in the labor market, leaving 88.6 percent of the Mexican workers to find non-Mexican employers. Thus the Mexican ethnic ownership economy amounted to no more than 6.1 percent of the garment industry. Similarly, mainland Chinese comprised 6.8 percent of owners and 5.5 percent of workers. Therefore, even if mainland Chinese owners hired all the mainland Chinese workers, they would absorb only 90 percent of the Chinese labor, leaving the other 10 percent of Chinese workers to find non-Chinese employers.[43]

Summing the separate estimates of ethnic ownership economies in table 5.1, we obtain 30.3 percent for all forty-five countries shown. This

Table 5.1   Place of Birth of Personnel in Garment Industry of Los Angeles, 1990

Place of Birth	Owners	Sewers
North America	35.3	59.7
United States	28.5	6.0
Canada	0.7	0.1
Mexico	6.1	53.6
Caribbean	4.7	0.8
Puerto Rico	0.0	0.1
Cuba	4.0	0.5
Dominican Republic	0.7	0.1
Haiti	0.0	0.1
Europe	5.6	0.7
France	0.0	0.1
West Germany	0.6	0.0
Italy	0.4	0.2
Poland	0.7	0.1
Romania	0.0	0.1
Spain	0.0	0.1
Sweden	0.7	0.0
United Kingdom	1.6	0.0
Soviet Union	1.6	0.2
Asia	40.1	13.2
Cambodia	3.1	0.4
China	6.8	5.5
Hong Kong	0.8	0.6
Japan	0.4	0.2
Korea	19.3	3.1
Laos	0.0	0.2
Philippines	0.0	0.5
Taiwan	3.7	0.3
Thailand	2.1	0.5
Vietnam	3.9	1.9
Middle East	6.5	0.5
Iran	3.7	0.2
Iraq	2.1	0.0
Lebanon	0.7	0.2
Turkey	0.0	0.1
Central America	3.2	18.6
Belize	0.0	0.1
Costa Rica	0.0	0.1
El Salvador	1.4	11.0
Guatemala	0.0	5.4
Honduras	0.0	0.8
Nicaragua	1.8	1.2

(Table continues on p. 92.)

**Table 5.1   Place of Birth of Personnel in Garment Industry of
Los Angeles, 1990** *(Continued)*

Place of Birth	Owners	Sewers
South America	3.9	1.9
Argentina	0.0	0.1
Brazil	0.0	0.1
Chile	0.8	0.1
Colombia	0.9	0.3
Ecuador	0.5	0.7
Peru	1.1	0.5
Uruguay	0.6	0.1
Africa	0.7	0.1
Egypt	0.0	0.1
South Africa	0.7	0.0
Total	100	95.7[a]
N	(3,181)	(67,883)

Source: U.S. Bureau of the Census (1990), 5 percent PUMS.
[a] missing data.

Table 5.2   Economic Location of Garment Industry Personnel, 1990

Mainstream	22.5%	
Native hires immigrant		22.5%
Immigrant economy	47.2	
Immigrant hires non-coethnic immigrant		47.2
Ethnic economy	30.3	
Immigrant hires coethnic immigrant		24.3
Native hires native		6.0
Total	100%	100%

Source: U.S. Bureau of the Census (1990), 5 percent PUMS.

number is listed in table 5.2, which estimates the three employment sectors' contributions to total employment in the garment industry. This estimate (30.3 percent) represents the share of total garment industry employment that took the form of immigrant employers hiring coethnic immigrant workers.[44] Similarly, the mainstream economy's contribution to garment industry employment was 22.5 percent. This employment was strictly native-born employers who hired immigrant workers. From a technical standpoint, and given the limitation of this evidence, one must call this the mainstream economy because native-born employers hired immigrants. The last sector, the immigrant ownership economy, arises when immigrant employers hire non-coethnic immigrants. When Mr. Park hires Mrs. Lopez, this employment relationship falls into the immigrant economy.

Our estimate of the immigrant economy's size, obtained by subtraction, is 47.2 percent of total employment in the garment industry. The immigrant sector is the sum of the immigrant economy plus all the ethnic ownership economies, excluding native-born Americans hiring other native-born Americans, which occurred in 6 percent of the cases. In the Los Angeles garment industry, the immigrant employers created 71.5 percent of the jobs.

Ethnic Classification

Ethnic classification is problematic here. The ethnic ownership economy encompassed those 6 percent of cases in which native-born employers hired native-born workers. In terms of the accounting scheme, these two groups are coethnics. The sector must thus be called the ethnic ownership economy of the native born. However, some native-born employers were ethnic Jews, Chinese, Pakistanis, or something else altogether, and their native-born employees were coethnics in some variable sense. For example, some native-born employers of Mexican origin hired native-born coethnics with whom they spoke Spanish. However, of the native-born employers, 89 percent were white, and 66 percent had European origins. Many of these white garment employers were the rear guard of the previous generation's garment industry, and probably were Jewish. Obviously, native-born Jewish garment employers could not hire Jewish sewing machine operators in 1990 as they did in 1900. There were few Jewish sewers in 1990, but there had been plenty in 1900. When Jewish owners hired native-born sewing machine operators they probably hired Asians or Latinas. Therefore, the relationship of native-born, European-origin employer to native-born sewing machine operators was more complex than simply the relationship of one white American to another white American selected at random from the melting pot. Unfortunately, our accounting scheme conceals this complexity.

Second, these estimates required the assumption that all employers hired the same number of workers. This assumption is of course flawed. Some ethnic groups' firms were bigger than others'. Hess reported that Korean-owned garment factories employed an average of 47.7 workers, nearly twice the industry average.[45] In that case, the estimates used in table 5.1 and 5.2 would deflate the immigrant economy's share of total employment and inflate the ethnic ownership economy's share. Because the chapter introduces the concept of immigrant ownership economy, explaining its utility, the estimation procedure is conservative.

Third, the computation assumed that coethnic employers exhausted coethnic labor before they turned to others. This assumption is compatible with the literature's outlook and with what informants reported, but it is too extreme.[46] It is realistic to suppose that employers prefer coethnic labor, but they rarely hire all of it. Even if most employees are coethnics, some are not. The effect of this bias is to increase the estimate of the ethnic ownership economies' share of the garment industry at the expense of the immigrant economy. Again, because the chapter introduces the concept of immigration economy, it was conservative to introduce this bias.

Finally, coethnicity is more complex than these procedures suggest. It was measured by matching immigrants from the same nation, the usual procedure. However, as is well known, sometimes immigrants from the same country do not regard themselves as coethnics. A published case in point addresses the Iranians of Los Angeles, who are divided into four ethno-religious subcommunities (Armenian, Bahai, Jewish, Muslim). In this case, "Iranian" coethnicity mattered little in the construction of the four ethnic ownership economies, the Iranian Armenian ethnic ownership economy, the Iranian Bahai, the Iranian Jewish, and the Iranian Moslem.[47] To clarify the ancestry of the garment industry's native-born population, Richard Bernard obtained detailed lists (not shown) of native-born owners and native-born sewing machine operators by ethno-racial origins the respondents volunteered. Owners of European origin comprised 66 percent of all native-born factory owners, but sewers of European origin comprised only 15 percent of native-born sewers. Among the European-origin, native-born owners, we counted thirty-seven single and multiple ethnic origins, of which the two largest sources were Germany and Russia. In view of the history of this industry, the Germans and Russians were very likely Jewish. If to German and Russian ancestry claimants we add German-Polish multiple identifiers, all of whom might well be Jewish also, we obtain 292 owners, about one-third of the native-born owners of European ancestry. If Jewish is the master identity, say, then a Jewish Pole who hires a German Jewish or German-Irish Jew would represent an ethnic economy connection. If nationality is the master identity, then a Pole hiring a German coreligionist or, indeed, a German-English multiple identifier hiring a German need not represent an ethnic connection. Finally, if current nationality (U.S. citizenship) is the master identity, then any native-born American hiring any other native-born American would represent an ethnic employment relationship. Working out the ethnic character of the relationships thus sketched must be the work of subsequent research.

Ethnic and Immigrant Economies in Tandem

Although a big improvement over individualistic theories of migration, migration network theory can be expanded by recognition of the migration network's capacity to increase migrant-accessible jobs in destination economies rather than simply to facilitate job searches. Migration networks thus increase the number of immigrants who can live and work in a destination well beyond the immigrant-support capability that existed there when the migration began. Taking account of the job-creation function of networks, we distinguish simple ethnic ownership economies and the immigrant economy. Simple ethnic ownership economies contain coethnics; immigrant ownership economies connect non-coethnic immigrants as employer and employee. Immigrant economies allow non-coethnics advantageous access to otherwise inaccessible networks. Immigrant economies arise when entrepreneur-heavy immigrant groups run out of workers and turn to entrepreneur-poor immigrant groups for labor. In the bimodal migration stream characteristic of Los Angeles's globalization, wealthy Asians and poor Latinos, this arrangement recurred often. The exchange is mutually beneficial: some immigrants can become entrepreneurs who otherwise could not, and some find jobs who otherwise could not. As a result of the immigrant economies that buffer the mainstream, Los Angeles supported many more immigrants than would have been possible had the garment industry depended upon ethnic ownership economies.

Turning to Los Angeles's garment industry for illustration, we found that three-quarters of this large and expanded industry arose from current immigrants' capital and labor power. Most of the residual one-quarter arose from the ethnic rear guard of earlier immigration. The rear-guard consisted of native-born but still residually ethnic European Americans and Asian Americans, who now participate in the garment industry predominantly as employers of non-coethnic labor. The Los Angeles garment industry depended more heavily on its immigrant economy than on its forty-seven ethnic ownership economies. Typically, foreign-born Asian employers hired Latino women to compensate for the shortage of Asian employees. In all, these estimates indicate that about 30.3 percent of garment industry personnel were in ethnic ownership economies, 47.2 percent in the immigrant economy, and the remaining 22.5 percent in the mainstream economy. As a conservative estimate, this immigrant-created garment industry supported about 3.5 percent of the labor force of Los Angeles County.

Although these quantitative results ignore the informal sector and pyramid assumptions, they generate estimates that illustrate how important ethnic and immigrant entrepreneurship is to the creation of migration-caused job opportunities for immigrants. The immigrant economy's jobs permitted immigrant populations to expand beyond the number they would otherwise reach if they had depended exclusively on ethnic ownership economies and the general labor market for employment. These results also illustrate the significance of the immigrant economy in supplementing what ethnic ownership economies do to buffer network migration. Previous network literature had considered only how ethnic ownership economies expand employment. This evidence, however, shows that ethnic ownership economies do not exhaust the means whereby immigrant networks expand the job supply in destinations. By itself, the concept of ethnic ownership economy cannot encompass the reality, but in tandem with the concept of immigrant economy, it can.

= Chapter 6 =

Why the Garment
Industry Contracted

IN 1924 LOS ANGELES was only the fourth largest garment-manufacturing center in the United States.[1] New York City was still the nation's capital in the industry, and remained so until the 1980s, when Los Angeles finally passed it.[2] Of course, the inter-city balance had begun to tip before 1980. After 1970, extensive immigration from Asia and Latin America began. In its wake, the number of garment factories in Los Angeles County nearly tripled and the number of employees doubled (table 6.1). Immigration's new provenance gave Los Angeles superior access to foreign-born workers from Asia, Mexico, and Central America. As a result of this supply of cheap labor, so it was universally argued, the garment industry of Los Angeles passed New York's.

This explanation, however, no longer seems entirely creditable. In 1996, the Los Angeles garment industry went into a serious and abrupt decline in respect to both number of employees and number of firms, dropping one-third over the next four years (table 6.1). As a result, 56,823 employees lost their jobs and some left Los Angeles for new settlement states. But why did this abrupt industrial decline occur? After all, in 1996 Los Angeles still boasted the cheap immigrant labor that had supposedly accounted for the rapid growth of the city's garment industry over the prior quarter century. The cause still in place, why did the effect cease to follow? Here we ask why the Los Angeles garment industry, having grown for a quarter century, went into a steep decline after 1996.

Garment Industry Expansion

Garment manufacture became a major industry in Los Angeles between 1970 and 1996. In 1996, garment and textile manufacturing and whole-saling were the largest manufacturing sectors in Los Angeles, which was the top manufacturing region of the United States overall, not just in apparel.[3] Garment and textile manufacturing together represented almost 10 percent

96

Table 6.1   Apparel Manufacturing[a] in Los Angeles County, 1970 to 2003

	1970	1977	1987	1997	2003
Establishments[b]	2,332	2,559	3,349	4,329	3,710
Employees	73,926	78,418	98,541	113,548	68,362
Mean employees per establishment	31.7	30.6	29.4	26.2	18.4

Sources: Geospatial and Statistical Data Center (n.d.); U.S. Bureau of the Census (1972, table 2, p. 64), U.S. Bureau of the Census (2005, table 6, p. 127).
[a] Apparel and other textile products.
[b] In 1970, data were collected for "reporting units." The reporting category was later changed to establishments. "Each manufacturing location of a company is counted as a separate reporting unit. In manufacturing industries, reporting units are, therefore, conceptually the same as establishment in Census Bureau terminology."

of Los Angeles County's economy.[4] Its vast garment and textile manufacturing industry employed 150,000 workers in 1996. This estimate is conservative because the official figures do not include the garment industry's huge informal sector.[5]

Approximately 93 percent of all the workers in the industry were foreign-born in 1990. Of them, an estimated 80 percent were illegally in the United States by 1999. Only 65 percent had been illegal in 1976.[6] About 80 percent were women. The Los Angeles Times acknowledged that immigrants provided virtually all the financial capital, human capital, social capital, cultural capital, and labor power that the city's garment contracting required.[7] Indeed, as Min Zhou observed of New York City, without the immigrant-created garment industry, Los Angeles would not have been able to absorb 150,000 immigrants who, thanks to the industry, were working there in 1996.[8] In this sense, Los Angeles's expanded absorption capacity was a derivative product of immigrant entrepreneurs, immigrant workers, and the immigration process itself. The garment industry thus represented the kind of buffering increase in carrying capacity that chapter 5 proposed.[9]

Before 1982, garment manufacturers were not required to register with the state of California, and employers simply ignored the state's labor code. Enforcement was nonexistent. Contractors paid their employees less than the statutory minimum wage, gave out illegal industrial homework, maintained filthy and unsafe workplaces, and evaded taxation.[10] To improve the enforcement of the labor code, California passed the Montoya Act in 1982, requiring garment contractors to register their factories with state authorities.[11] Registered firms were subject to unannounced inspections by state enforcement authorities, whose agents could seize books and impound bundles. This legislation changed the garment industry a little, but nonregistration was still widespread in the 1990s. The California Safety Compliance Corporation estimated that 40 percent of the garment contractors were still unregistered in 1996.[12] It is not clear how much the

Montoya Act reduced the violations of the labor law, but the effect was not large.[13] A decade after its passage, in 1992, registered and unregistered firms alike continued to pay less than the minimum wage, to give out illegal homework, to maintain unsafe and unhealthy working conditions, and to evade taxation.[14] (Lee 1994). Sarmiento reported in 1996 that 87 percent of garment workers reported earnings below the statutory minimum wage.[15]

These labor conditions were illegal, not just deplorable. That illegal conditions existed was well understood everywhere in California. Newspapers, chambers of commerce, police, unionists, and judges knew that garment industry employers flouted the state's occupational safety, health, and wages laws every day. So, why were illegal conditions tolerated for decades? The answer is complex and has only partly to do with corruption. First, as explained further in chapter 10, enforcement jurisdictions were jumbled. State and federal authorities shared responsibility for law enforcement. The federal government's Immigration and Naturalization Service (INS) had the responsibility for enforcing employer sanctions under the 1986 Immigration Control and Reform Act. This provision of the law prohibited employers from knowingly hiring illegal immigrants. Los Angeles police might have reported illegal immigrants to the INS, but did not.[16] Not reporting was police policy, not just police practice. The INS itself had too few officers to reduce the illegal labor supply of the garment factory employers who were, moreover, immune to prosecution as long as illegal employees had presented bogus immigration documents prior to employment. The federal government also shared with California the authority to prosecute violations of federal wages, hours and safety standards, but failed to do so. Under then current federal law, the U.S. government did not prosecute until the fourth time industrial violations came to its attention. Earlier violations were overlooked in the interest of industrial self-regulation, and out of inspector shortage in the enforcement divisions.[17] In effect, the federal government also failed to prosecute garment factory owners for illegally hiring undocumented immigrants or for operating factories under illegal conditions.

Federal abnegation left regulation of the garment industry to the State of California, which did provide such meager industrial regulation as the garment industry received until the second Clinton administration. California could not prosecute employers for hiring illegal immigrants, but it could prosecute them for violations of state health, safety, wages and hours, and overtime laws. California's Division of Labor Standards Enforcement and California's Occupational Safety and Health Administration (Cal-OSHA) had the legal authority to fine and even shut down industrial violators. Created in 1973, California's Bureau of Field Enforcement authorized agents to enter factories unannounced to oversee child labor law compliance, worksite inspection, audit payroll records, collect unpaid wages, enforce prevailing wage provisions, and confiscate illegally manufactured garments.[18] Because garment industry employers rampantly violated labor laws, the state of California always had the legal authority to simply shut down the entire industry, which effectively lived under a juridical sword of Damocles. However, this authority was hardly wielded until the mid 1990s, and then only lightly. Therefore, the garment industry enjoyed tacit juridical toleration for a quarter century in Los Angeles, thrived in the shadow of this toleration, and, as we shall see, declined when toleration weakened.

Why California Tolerated the Garment Industry

Why did California tolerate illegal conditions in the Los Angeles garment industry for a quarter century? This simple question requires a complex answer. Thanks to the contracting system, law enforcement was difficult and expensive. Shut down on Monday, violator shops reopened under a new name a week later. Law enforcement had a hard time defeating this tactic. Beyond its sheer cost and difficulty, law enforcement also encountered economic, political, and ideological resistance. The history of the garment industry in the United States includes organized crime infiltration.[19] In the literature of organized crime, protracted and systemic evasion of law always signals political and juridical corruption.[20] If law is ignored over the long term, then corruption exists.[21] This conclusion is axiomatic, and needs no documentation of corrupt officials by name. In this sense, the long-term and systemic evasion of labor law in the garment industry implies political and juridical corruption even without corroborating particulars.

Second, resistance to law enforcement also derived from the garment industry's political influence as well as, it must be acknowledged, the political influence of the Latino community. Latinos disliked and opposed law enforcement that put coethnics out of work. The garment industry's paid lobby donated campaign funds to California politicians, including the governor and attorney general.[22] This practice was completely legal. However, the industrialists' donations helped to elect Republican governors who, as Limor Bar-Cohen and Deana Carrillo showed, reduced labor law enforcement staffs below the minimum needed to effectively enforce California's occupational and industrial laws.[23] As a result, the agencies had no realistic choice but to negotiate toothless compliance agreements with garment industry scofflaws rather than to prosecute them.[24]

Third, ideological resistance to law enforcement also contributed to California's legal paralysis. It derived from the nearly ubiquitous belief, a product of the growth ideology, that population growth was always desirable. Because growth of the garment industry promoted growth of population, so the thinking went, the garment industry should be tolerated.[25]

Fatuous though it was, this belief was widely and sincerely held in policy-making, journalistic, and academic circles. Attached to it was the unassailable truth that many immigrant families depended on the garment industry for their livelihood. Were California's labor, occupational, and industrial laws suddenly and strictly enforced, Los Angeles's garment factories would close, and needy immigrant families would lose their livelihoods. Authorities did not want to strip the paycheck from poor immigrant families so they tolerated violations of law by garment employers. Even police have a heart.

Factory Management

It is helpful to understand how garment factories operated. Garment contractors used the progressive bundle system of production. Garments were tied into bundles, which were then routed through a sequence of workstations. At each station, a seamstress performed a repetitious operation such as sewing on a pocket. After completing her operation on all the garments that reached her station, she rebundled them and passed the bundle to the next worker, who accomplished another task. Garment workers were paid piece rates. At best, these piece rates were low but legal. Edna Bonacich and Richard Appelbaum estimated that the average garment worker in Los Angeles earned $7,200 in 1990,[26] when the legal minimum wage would have yielded $8,840, and the official poverty level for a family of four was $13,359 (2000, 181).[27]

Garment contractors often worked in shirtsleeves at a sewing machine along with their workers for at least part of the working day. Many allowed seamstresses to bring their children to the factory, an amenity mainstream employers did not emulate. Because they earned piece rates, the seamstresses did not cost their employers any money when they tended their children instead of their sewing machine. Although this practice was not universal in the garment industry, it was more common there than in other manufacturing industries in Los Angeles, which simply banned children from the workplace. The advantages to the seamstresses are obvious. Employment in the garment industry allowed the mothers of small children to earn. In view of this advantage, many immigrant mothers viewed low-wage garment employment as their best realistic alternative.

The Garment Industry's Three Tiers

The Los Angeles garment manufacturing industry consisted of three hierarchical tiers: retailers, manufacturers, and contractors. At the summit were retailers. Retailers were big department stores such as Macy's, the Gap, Nordstrom, and Kmart. With the exception of the Gap, which peddled its own brand, retailers ordered clothing from independent manufacturers.

In turn, manufacturers designed their own lines, to which they gave fanciful labels like Bugle Boy or Suzie Q. Since about 1970, manufacturers no longer produced the clothing they designed and sold. When they received a contract from a retailer, manufacturers subcontracted production to independent contractors. The numerous contractors actually produced the ready-to-wear clothing in small, owner-directed factories. Thus, when Macy's ordered 10,000 Bugle Boy slacks, Bugle Boy hired contractors to make the pants from patterns Bugle Boy provided. In short, retailers gave contracts to manufacturers, who gave contracts to contractors, who hired seamstresses. There were about three contractors for every manufacturer in the Los Angeles industry in 1990.

Retailers occupied the most advantageous tier and held the real industrial power by initiating the order chains. As the orders descended the hierarchy from retailers to manufacturers, from manufacturers to contractors, and from contractors to workers, they moved into ever more competitive economic environments that finally approximated the price-taking markets of economic theory. The huge influx of contractors into the garment business, a product of demand-driven immigration, tended to weaken the market power of the bottom segment. As a result, the higher tiers appropriated the bulk of the garment industry's revenue. Bonacich and Appelbaum showed that at the top of the food chain, retailers took half the gross revenue from the clothing they sold; manufacturers, 35 percent; and contractors, 15 percent.[28] Production workers were left with only 6 percent. In view of the poverty-level wages garment workers earned, this unequal division of the industrial revenues provoked episodic public outrage in Los Angeles.[29]

Despite the outcry, a recurrent feature of its industrial environment, and despite relentlessly adverse trends in the national garment manufacturing industry, the Los Angeles garment industry thrived until 1996.[30] True, early signs of malady surfaced before 1993, but they were hard to spot. From 1993 to 1996, the number of garment manufacturers and contractors in Los Angeles County increased by 15 percent. In approximately the same period, 1993 to 1997, industry employment expanded by 40 percent, even though it declined nationwide 17 percent in the same time frame.[31] The national drop resulted from the job exports to Mexico. American garment manufacturers began to shift production to Mexico following the approval of the North American Free Trade Agreement (NAFTA) in 1993.[32] The surprise was the continuing viability of garment production in Los Angeles amid the collapse of the American garment industry elsewhere.

Los Angeles was less vulnerable to job exports to Mexico than other garment manufacturing centers, but not invulnerable. In fact, the Los Angeles garment industry experienced an egress of production jobs to Mexico even before but especially after NAFTA passage.[33] Of the largest class, two-thirds of the Los Angeles garment manufacturers with annual net sales of $10 million had some production in Latin America, mostly Mexico, by 1998. In 1993, just before NAFTA, only 12 percent of the garment manufacturers in Los Angeles had kept any production staff in Mexico. In a 1998 survey of all manufacturers, 43 percent indicated that some of their production was now done outside of California.[34] At the 1999 Sewn Products Expo in Los Angeles, trade representatives of seven Mexican states were on hand to promote the relocation of Los Angeles garment factories to their states.[35] Were it not for the outflow of production to Mexico, observers claimed, the Los Angeles garment industry would have added even more employment in the five years from 1993 to 1997 than the 40-percent growth it actually experienced.[36]

Why the Garment Industry Contracted

Mexico's external competition was the industry's most touted problem, but not its only problem. Three local threats indirectly contributed to Mexico's growing popularity with local garment manufacturers. First, in the political aftermath of the Thai slavery case, when public indignation was fierce, President Clinton appointed a White House Apparel Industry Partnership in 1996 to pursue "nonregulatory solutions" to the industry's problems.[37] This voluntary partnership announced that the federal government was watching the garment industry, but did not impose penalties.[38] On the other hand, in the same year, signaling that it meant business this time, the U.S. Department of Labor formed its "no sweat garment enforcement" initiative, whose purpose was to "eradicate garment sweatshops and bring them into compliance with U.S. labor laws."[39] To this end, Labor's Wage and Hour Division joined the Targeted Industries Partnership Program (TIPP), a joint enforcement effort with the California Division of Labor Standards Enforcement and Cal-OSHA.[40] Also participating were the Los Angeles County Department of Health and the California Department of Community Development.

The TIPP created "no new laws" nor novel "procedures with which to contend."[41] The agencies involved simply pooled information and enforcement data, then independently prosecuted cases under their respective existing procedures and laws. Nonetheless, even this limited federal-state collaboration revitalized labor law enforcement in California. By 1999, California had become the state "with the most investigations uncovering violations, the most back wages recovered, and the highest monetary level of penalties assessed."[42] Ruth Milkman and Eileen Appelbaum write that in the late 1990s, organized labor was at the peak of its political power in the state.[43]

Relative to the rest of the country, California had a tough labor-law environment. Business owners denounced California as "a police state," but labor spokesmen complained that enforcement was still grossly inadequate.

The absolute standard is not important. Enforcement of labor law in California was indeed tougher than elsewhere in the United States.[44] In 2001, California's Bureau of Field Enforcement (BOFE) conducted 4,051 investigations of which 29 percent were in the garment industry. It issued 688 citations to "employers of garment workers" and collected $525,999 in penalties as well as millions of dollars of unpaid wages that garment factory employers had unlawfully pocketed.[45] Forty-four percent of BOFE citations were issued for noncompliance with California's Workers' Compensation Insurance requirement, a failure that imposed an employer's injured workers on California's tax-supported hospitals. As a partial result of this augmented enforcement, mandatory workers' compensation insurance premiums rose throughout the state, leading to charges of a hostile business climate.[46] These charges contributed to the recall of Democratic Governor Gray Davis and his replacement in 2003 by Arnold ("the Terminator") Schwarzenegger, his celebrity challenger.

Second, increases to the California and federal minimum wage contributed to the economic hardship in the garment industry. Congress increased the national minimum wage in 1996. This legislation raised the minimum hourly wage from $4.25 to $5.15, and California's Democratic-controlled State Assembly promptly increased California's minimum wage from $5.15 to $5.75. The minimum hourly wage in California was 60 cents higher than the national minimum in 1998, and $1.50 higher than it had been in 1995. Because most garment workers earned the minimum wage, increases in the statutory minimum wage rendered California less competitive as a garment production site. California's minimum wage was now so high, garment industry studies concluded, that garment manufacturing in Los Angeles could no longer rely on cheap immigrant labor to maintain its international position—if employers really had to pay the legal minimum.[47] Thanks to the strengthened enforcement effort, which coincided roughly with the initiation of NAFTA, employers did increasingly have to pay the legal minimum wage. Augmented enforcement increased employer compliance with the minimum wage law in California as, David Weil has shown, it did elsewhere too.[48] Yet, as the state-federal enforcement effort increased in California, wages in the garment industry were dropping ever lower. Wages in the garment industry, already low, fell by 25 percent after 1996 because of international competition. Garment industry employment, which peaked in 1996, fell further after NAFTA than was initially realized.[49] As California's enforcement pressure increased, international competitive pressure also increased. Caught between intensified labor law enforcement at home and intensified competition abroad, the garment industry began to leave Los Angeles.

The garment industry's third, enormous problem revolved around the cost of employee health care. The problem was political as well as economic. Garment industry employers paid for no employee care. Therefore, when sick, fully employed immigrant seamstresses had no health insurance. Diseased seamstresses and their uninsured families turned to publicly supported emergency rooms for free medical care. California taxpayers footed the bill. Externalized to the public, the garment industry's health care bill gradually became a political issue in California on both sides of the aisle.[50] Garment work was unusually unhealthy for various reasons. Sewing all day is hard, grueling work. Studies found that seamstresses experienced neck and upper limb aches, fatigue, sleeping disorders, anxiety, depression, and digestive problems. Their repetitive motions contributed to carpal tunnel syndrome. In addition, workplace formaldehyde, flame retardants, lint, and dust created respiratory and skin problems.[51] Many if not most garment factories were unsafe and dirty.[52] They offered no drinking water, clean toilets, first aid kits, adequate lighting and ventilation, or safety guards on machinery.[53] Garment factories ignored Cal-OSHA requirements to maintain an injury and illness prevention program in the workplace.[54] Garment factory managers routinely insulted, belittled, groped, and even hit the seamstresses, thus creating emotional as well as physical tension and hazards in the workplace.[55] As a result, uninsured seamstresses sustained a high volume of job-related tension, injury, and emotional and physical disease. If the garment industry had maintained ordinary working conditions, its health impact would have been externalized to the public; but, as it was, its below average working conditions were externalized and the public was burdened with an inflated medical bill.[56]

Small California firms were not required to provide health insurance for their employees, and 97 percent of garment industry employers did not provide any. To survive, garment contractors needed to remain internationally competitive. At the low-profit end, they worked on margins too thin to permit health insurance premiums for their workers. At the high-profit end, manufacturers and retailers acknowledged no responsibility to pay health insurance premiums for someone else's (their own subcontractors') employees.[57] Admittedly, the garment industry had plenty of mainstream company: a third of all the workers in Los Angeles County did not have any employer-paid medical insurance in 1999.[58] Even the largest American corporation, Wal-Mart, paid no health care benefits to 40 percent of its employees.[59] Like garment employees, who were immigrants, native-born uninsured workers had to use tax-supported emergency rooms for their medical care so most indigent users were native, not immigrant. But as regards employer-paid health insurance, garment manufacturing was among the worst offenders in Los Angeles, and Los Angeles was the worst offender in California.[60] Aggravating the situation, the Los Angeles garment industry generated more than its share of injured but medically indigent workers. The garment industry thus added its component to the mighty tide of indigents besieging public emergency rooms in California.[61] Large and growing members of medically indigent and injured immigrant workers then turned to public emergency hospitals for free care, imposing uncompensated financial burdens upon them.[62] Los Angeles County spent $80 million on emergency care for the uninsured in 1997, compared with only $62 million in 1992. As the *Los Angeles Times* pointed out, tax-supported hospitals subsidized the health care of the garment industry's immigrant workers.[63] Also true of Wal-Mart, of course, this objection was politically easier to launch against illegal immigrants than against the biggest domestic corporation.[64]

This hidden employer subsidy became a public scandal in 1994. That year, among the largest thirty metropolitan areas in the United States, Los Angeles had the highest percentage of workers lacking medical insurance.[65] Appealing to taxpayers, California's Republican governor, Pete Wilson, induced voters to pass plebiscitary legislation (Proposition 187) that restricted the access of illegal immigrants to public schools and public hospitals in California. Governor Wilson argued that illegal families imposed more costs on the state health care and educational system than they paid in taxes.[66] He argued that immigrants used the state's emergency rooms for free health care, omitting to note that their employers were not providing medical insurance. Nearly two million children in California had no medical insurance in 1998, and nearly all were children of immigrants.[67] Indeed, uninsured children and medically indigent children comprised 7 percent of California's population. Governor Wilson persuaded white voters, then 80 percent of the electorate, that the state could not afford to subsidize the health care of illegal immigrants.[68] Proposition 187 passed, but subsequent legal challenges prevented its enforcement.[69] As a result, illegal immigrants continued to receive free health care in California in subsequent years,[70] and their employers continued to receive subsidies from state taxpayers.

Regulation Happens

California and federal authorities began to subject the garment industry to more effective regulation in 1996. Before 1996, understaffed law enforcement agencies had largely ignored it, maintaining just enough visibility to give an impression of vigilance without actually accomplishing anything. This feeble policy suited the business lobby as well as the Hispanic community. However, in response to Governor Wilson's support of Proposition 187, law enforcement authorities began to police the garment industry in 1996. Since garment factories routinely ignored industrial laws, law enforcement authorities discovered much amiss. The basic enforcement mechanism was the "sweep." Unannounced agents descended upon a plant, seized its books, and questioned employees about their immigration status, arresting any in violation of immigration law. As police barged in the front door, employees ran out the back. In one successful sweep, investigators turned up time-card violations in factories that produced Hollywood celebrity Kathie Lee Gifford's line of women's clothing.[71] Her company's violations of the labor code stirred much criticism in the press, capturing the public's attention, and calling attention to widespread employment of illegal immigrants in the garment industry.[72]

The most spectacular sweep raided the factory where Suni Manasurangkun and her five sons, two daughters-in-law, and two armed men held seventy-two Thai immigrants, mostly women, as industrial slaves in a guarded compound.[73] Manasurangkun ran her factory in a seven-unit apartment complex at 2614 Santa Anita Avenue in El Monte, a western suburb of Los Angeles. Manasurangkun's factory recruited seamstresses in Thailand, where they signed indenture agreements. These agreements obligated each woman to pay $5,000 over three years. The Thai workers in the slavery compound earned only 69 cents an hour, one-tenth the minimum wage. Manasurangkun's sons then smuggled the indentured women into the United States and transported them to the factory compound, a two-story building surrounded by a high wall topped with razor wire. In this guarded factory, gunmen compelled the women to work sixteen-hour days seven days a week.[74] The seamstresses lived on mattresses in crowded dormitories and were not permitted to exit the building. The factory's canteen charged exorbitant prices for their food and supplies. Paid a piece rate, the slaves earned one-sixth the legal minimum wage. At this price, they would have had to work fifteen years to pay off their indenture.

Police raided Manasurangkun's factory and arrested its operators on August 2, 1995. The factory's operators subsequently pleaded guilty in federal court to conspiracy, slave holding, smuggling, and harboring illegal immigrants. They received prison sentences ranging from two to seven years plus a fine of $250,000. Manasurangkun's products had been marketed under various names, including SK Fashion, S & P Fashion, and D & R Fashion. The publicity about the case embarrassed several important retailers, who had sold the products. In 1999 eleven companies agreed to pay more than $3.7 million in damages to a hundred fifty ex-slaves who had labored in the El Monte factory and two affiliated front organizations also run by Manasurangkun. The retailers included Millers Outpost, Mervyn's, and Montgomery Ward, all major retail chains. These of course denied any knowledge of the illegal conditions in their contractor's factories.

Some observers proposed that expanded enforcement explained the apparent growth in employment in the Los Angeles garment industry between 1993 and 1997. From this perspective, the sweeps were seen to have compelled some previously clandestine factories to reopen in the formal sector, thus increasing the legally registered working population without necessarily increasing the real working population. In principle, the enforcement sweeps might account for the entire apparent increase in employment in the period. The actual share of the increase that enforcement efforts explain will never be known. However, the issue is relevant to any interpretation of the garment industry's health between 1993 and 1997. If the industry grew rapidly without any help from the enforcement sweeps, this growth might be attributable to the industry's economic viability. This was the view held by most authorities in 1997. If, on the other hand, as seems equally likely, the apparent growth resulted wholly or largely from enhanced law enforcement, then the industry's apparent growth between 1993 and 1997 really reflected only a deterioration of its political protection. The deterioration of protection flushed illegal firms into the open, giving the impression that new firms had been created.

Serious political heat came down on the garment industry and its protectors after the Thai slavery case broke in 1996. Because of the political heat, federal, state, and local government began finally to examine and regulate working conditions in the Los Angeles garment industry. Signs were cumulative. In 1998, a voter initiative, promoted by labor unions, raised annual funding for California's labor law enforcement agencies from $10 million to $35 million, a level that was thereafter maintained.[75] The U.S. Department of Labor conducted a survey of garment manufacturers in 2000. They found that 98 percent violated health and safety laws. A survey by the California Department of Industrial Relations found an average of seven health and safety violations in every garment firm they examined. In 2001, the Cal-OSHA inspected 312 garment factories. Ninety-five percent had had safety violations, of which 10 percent were serious, willful, or repeat.[76] In 2001, the California Assembly's Committee on Labor and Employment held oversight hearings in Los Angeles. It examined labor law enforcement in the garment and janitorial industries, and found piece rates too low to permit workers to earn the legal minimum wage, workers not paid overtime, unsafe and dangerous factories, and industrial homework.[77] All these conditions were illegal. Prosecutions increased. By 2003 California "stood alone" among American states with respect to its willingness to prosecute employers out of compliance with industrial safety standards whose workers had been either killed on injured on the job.[78] These prosecutions forced greater compliance upon the state's employers, and drove down the injury rate, but spelled diminished political protection for garment industry employers, some of whom could no longer continue in business. Also in 2003, the Democratic-controlled California legislature required "small businesses to provide coverage to one million of the state's working poor, who now rely on tax-supported programs for medical care."[79] This law was a poison pill for the garment industry in particular, but high insurance premiums for workers' compensation insurance, reflecting California's aggressive enforcement, tended as well to undermine low-wage garment firms more than other industries.[80]

Facing diminishing political protection, garment contractors had increasingly to meet rather than evade California's labor laws. Meeting these laws increased production costs, rendering the Los Angeles garment manufacturing industry internationally less competitive. As international competitiveness declined, retailers shifted production to Mexico, and contractor firms shut down. Hugely unsatisfied with even the augmented level of labor law enforcement in Los Angeles, Jill Esbenshade nonetheless agrees that, garment firms "have in fact gone elsewhere" because of enhanced labor law enforcement in Los Angeles.[81] Similarly, in the opinion of Judy Kessler, garment manufacturers moved factories to Mexico to "establish an edge on the competition by escaping the higher California wages and compliance regulations."[82] Because garment production and employment in Los Angeles visibly began to decline after 1997, we conclude that intensified public scrutiny and law enforcement hastened the decline after 1997, but possibly even as early as 1993. In turn, this industrial decline deflected the immigrant population from Los Angeles toward new settlements.

Industrial Decline, Not Elimination

In 2003, aggregate employment in the Los Angeles garment industry was just 60 percent of what it had been at its zenith in 1997. Nonetheless, this large decline did not destroy the industry, which still employed 68,362 workers. The unique survival of the Los Angeles's garment industry requires additional explanation since it occurred despite increased government regulation, which decimated the industry without destroying it. At this point, specific features of the Los Angeles economic environment need to be addressed to explain why the Los Angeles industry flourished until 1997 and then survived the enforcement drive albeit in a diminished state of health. Observers usually attribute the hardihood of the Los Angeles garment industry to two environmental factors. The first is the rapid start-up rates of new, immigrant-owned firms, a supply-side push. California has very high self-employment rates compared with other American states, and the Los Angeles self-employment rates are higher than California's.[83] Thanks to the low start-up costs, many immigrants already had or could easily acquire the capability to start a garment factory. Thanks to the huge immigrant population and continuing influx of new immigrants, many immigrants wished to start small factories. This need partly explains the decreasing average employment size of garment factories between 1970 and 2003. Moreover, contractors earned good incomes in the industry. Even Edna Bonacich and Richard Appelbaum, both harsh critics, acknowledge that many garment contractors earned middle-class incomes; 70 percent of the Korean immigrant contractors owned their own homes and 61 percent had moved out of the inner city to a suburb.[84]

The second factor is the Los Angeles industry's unique market niche. Los Angeles specialized in contemporary clothing and sportswear for the women's and junior markets.[85] Los Angeles apparel makers sold the

"California Look," not just cheap clothing. This was produced quickly and sold at moderate prices to a trend-following international market of young women.[86] Sixty-one percent of the Los Angeles industry's sales were in women's outerwear, a sector in which rapid style changes discouraged production in less fashion-conscious cities.[87] Hollywood had international fashion cachet. Much criticized for its labor policies, Guess? Incorporated was an immigrant-owned Los Angeles manufacturer that specialized in exactly these styles. Its website (www.guess.com) listed its January "hot-picks" for sale: drawstring cropped cargo pants, white peasant top, Velcro wrap-around utility bag, and day-glo pink tee shirt. California Look clothing often bore the logo Hollywood and, thanks to the film industry, this place name commanded prestige recognition from young women all over the world.

Intoleration, Poverty, Decline, and Deflection

The Los Angeles garment industry expanded enormously between 1970 and 1997, a period when garment production in the rest of the United States was decreasing. Although Los Angeles was abundantly endowed with cheap immigrant labor, cheap labor alone does not explain why Los Angeles garment production expanded during this generally unfavorable economic period.[88] Usually overlooked in economistic recitals, the political willingness to tolerate labor exploitation was an essential condition for the prosperity of the Los Angeles garment industry. Without it, cheap labor is not a resource. Here, exploiting cheap labor means tolerating production under illegal conditions, including illegally low wages and illegally inferior working conditions. Although the discovery of cheap labor's contingent dependence on political corruption (broadly understood) is certainly the main theoretical lesson, the topic does not fully explain why the garment industry survived the crackdown. It is probably true, although impossible to prove, that if the crackdown had been more severe, the entire garment industry of Los Angeles would have shut down completely, as it did in Amsterdam. However, given the modest crackdown that materialized, only a partial shut-down resulted. Moreover, in justice to the world of fashion, the California Look must receive appropriate recognition. The garment industry of Los Angeles had this resource too. In the fashion-driven global marketplace, when sewn on labels, the word Hollywood sold clothing. Poor immigrant women were thus able to find jobs in a dynamic and expanding clothing industry located in Los Angeles.

By 1997, approximately 5 percent of employed immigrants in the city of Los Angeles worked in the garment manufacturing industry. The industry expanded, and with it the immigrant absorption capacity of Los Angeles. Approximately 5 percent more immigrants were able to find employment in Los Angeles in 1997 than could have had labor laws been strictly enforced from the beginning. Because the builders of the garment industry were themselves immigrants, the garment industry's expansion amounted to an immigration-driven expansion of Los Angeles's capacity to absorb immigrants. In effect, immigration built the economic condition for its own expansion. However, a quarter century's expansion of the Los Angeles garment industry had implicitly relied on political toleration of illegal labor conditions. Los Angeles garment factories were in blatant and overt violation of wage, health, and industrial standards for twenty-five years, but politicians, judges, and police ignored their violations, enabling scofflaw employers to carry on as if the laws did not exist. Given political protection, reliable until 1996, garment contractors could cut costs by evading the labor code.

The end of reliable protection initiated the decline of the Los Angeles garment industry. The Thai slavery case grabbed the headlines, but health care costs carried the issue forward long after the public had forgotten the cause célèbre of 1996. Their substandard wages and lack of employer-paid medical insurance rendered the garment industry's immigrant huge labor force medically indigent. In effect, garment industry employers had assigned the health care of their employees to the state's hospital emergency rooms. The garment industry's employers had thus obtained a taxpayer subsidy. Because medical care is an essential component of a living wage, garment employees earned wages below the physiological subsistence minimum, that leitmotif of the nineteenth century's dismal science, political economy. Other low-wage immigrant industries in Los Angeles, such as the restaurant industry, obtained the same benefit, but political protection was not as essential to any of them as to the garment industry because of the external competition from Mexico and China that affected the garment industry. When its political cover was exploded, the garment industry could less easily impose its workers' health care on the California treasury. The decline of political toleration of immigrant poverty thus coincided with an abrupt decline in garment industry employment, and the deflection of immigrant Latinos from California.

A Historical Reflection

Taxpayer subsidies of wages are not new. California's hidden medical care subsidy was eerily reminiscent of Britain's Speenhamland Poor Law of 1795, long considered a shining example of unsound industrial legislation.[89] As Britain's Speenhamland Poor Law openly introduced sliding, taxpayer-supported bread for indigent workers, subsidizing their employers, so California introduced an employer's subsidy in the form of tax-supported health care. However, what Karl Polanyi called, "the right to live" was alive in California as it had been alive in nineteenth-century

Britain. For humanitarian reasons, Californians would not permit injured or diseased garment workers to die without medical care, and then be replaced by healthy new immigrants fresh from Mexico or Central America. This solution would have ensured the international competitiveness of the garment industry. But neither were Californians prepared to subsidize the health care of illegal immigrants from the state's treasury. As the Speenhamland Law once encouraged British employers to lower wages in anticipation that taxpayers would increase their subsidies, so California's health care subsidy encouraged not only garment industry employers, but also mainstream employers such as Wal-Mart, Target, Vons, Pavillions, and Ralph's to evade responsibility for employees' medical care in the expectation that tax-supported emergency rooms would foot their bill. As it had Britain two hundred years earlier, the taxpayer subsidy of wages led California down a ruinous path to labor unrest and state insolvency. California's bankruptcy recall election and the protracted grocery clerks' strike in 2003, signaled the fruition of a quarter century's unwise public policy. California's $15 billion bond issue (Proposition 56) in 2004 handed taxpayers the bill for a state government too long tolerant of scofflaw employers.

The immediate causes for the end of the garment industry's political toleration were grandstand political theater. Playing into a growing anti-immigrant backlash, Governor Wilson argued that illegal immigrants were imposing costs on California's treasury.[90] Attacked at the time as anti-immigrant, which in a restricted sense it was, Proposition 187 was also anti-employer in that it threatened to discontinue their health care subsidy. Proposition 187 reduced (but did not eliminate) the previously reliable political tolerance of illegal working and health conditions in restaurants, garment manufacturing, retail trade, and other immigrant-dominated industries in Los Angeles. Decreased political tolerance shrank the vast informal sector of the garment industry, and pressured employers to pay the minimum wage rather than evade it. By political intolerance is meant that, at last, California had begun to monitor the working conditions of immigrants.

Admittedly, the movement toward state regulation collided with an adventitious and unique industrial condition, the California Look. For this reason, the fate of the Los Angeles garment industry is impossible to reduce to political economy. It owed some success to Hollywood's worldwide visibility, without which the garment industry of Los Angeles would have failed to develop as rapidly or extensively as it actually did, and would have declined more rapidly after passage of the North America Free Trade Agreement. Additionally, the increase in the federal minimum wage and the state's subsequent increase and the signing of NAFTA all harmed the Los Angeles garment industry but, thanks to the California Look, they did not kill it.

Political Limits

Important as they were to the abrupt decline of the garment industry, the topic of this inquiry, these environmental changes do not obscure the underlying issue. This issue is not, as Kristine Zentgraf proposes, the mere presence of a large pool of cheap immigrant labor.[91] The mere presence of cheap labor is not sufficient to explain its exploitation. Given the presence of cheap labor, political toleration of its exploitation is essential too. Those who attributed the decline of the Los Angeles garment industry to competition from Mexico have partially misunderstood this lesson. Mexican competition only posed a problem because authorities did not permit wages and working conditions to fall to Mexican levels right in Los Angeles. Precisely because political conditions finally prevented wages and working conditions from falling further, NAFTA damaged the Los Angeles garment industry. To the end, immigrant garment workers were ready to work at lower, internationally competitive wages, but political authorities would not permit it. Even in Los Angeles, once the homeland of the open shop, the political system finally reached a limit beyond which it restrained the further degradation of immigrant labor. That point reached, ready and willing seamstresses were turned away, factories closed, the garment industry declined, and immigrant seamstresses left Los Angeles—or did not come.

= Chapter 7 =

Asian Place Entrepreneurs

A^{LL IMMIGRANTS} are not the same. In the late twentieth century era of globalization, the United States attracted two divergent streams of immigration. One was a demand-driven stream of highly skilled Asians, Europeans, Middle Easterners, and Latin Americans. These immigrants started business firms or took well-paid jobs in growth sectors of the service economy. They received high pay, and brought abundant money and higher educational credentials with them. The second stream—discussed in chapter 8—consisted of working-class Mexicans and Central Americans.[1] Although this stream began in response to increased demand for low-paid and unskilled labor, the low-wage migration switched motors, becoming supply-driven around 1980. As such, the working-class migrations from Central America and Mexico tended to saturate the housing markets they entered, driving up prices and reducing supply.

This chapter addresses the manner in which Korean immigrants and Chinese immigrants found suitable housing in Los Angeles. Representative of the high-wage stream of migration, a distinctive feature of globalization, the Koreans and Chinese had the means to effectuate a successful housing insertion even in Los Angeles's ultra-expensive market. Their means, however, involved more than merely individual wealth, essential though that was. Their insertion required and obtained helpers. First, coethnic place entrepreneurs already in southern California identified cities they deemed both suitable and available for immigrant residential insertion, and then obtained approval from homeland banks and investors to acquire properties. That done, the coethnic place entrepreneurs acquired the housing that coethnic immigrants would need in the future, advertised its availability in their Asian homelands, and sold it to coethnic immigrants once they arrived. Therefore, the story of the Asian immigrants' housing insertion is not of interest because of the hardships they endured, the slums they inhabited, or the overcrowded conditions in which they lived. That is what the Mexican and Central Americans endured. By contrast, the story of these Asian immigrants shows how easy it could be for immigrants to obtain the housing they needed provided they had the support of an ethnic economy. Their red carpet story is of interest because of the alternative template it offers. In the era of globalization, one model does not fit the housing insertion of all immigrants.[2]

However, before globalization became an active force, one model did fit housing insertion. Housing insertion is the process whereby immigrants acquire housing and upgrade it. During the nineteenth and early twentieth centuries, working-class European immigrants entered American society at the bottom, moving up socially and economically over three or four generations. The process was called ethnic succession.[3] The insertion process for European immigrants was largely the same across groups were because—except for the Jews, whose social origins were mixed—European immigrants were basically working-class. To this extent, the housing insertion of southern and eastern Europeans of the late nineteenth century more closely resembles that of Mexicans and Central Americans than it does that of the Koreans, Chinese, Indians, or other highly skilled immigrants of the late twentieth century. In this significant regard, globalization has imposed a new model of housing insertion that requires new approaches to understand it.

From Chicago School to Growth Machines

Early in the twentieth century, sociologists at the University of Chicago pioneered the scientific study of immigrant settlement, and created much of the vocabulary and most of the concepts that we use today.[4] These influential scholars are called the Chicago School. Chicago's leading sociologist, Robert Ezra Park, airily assigned responsibility for immigrant housing to "private enterprise" without paying attention to how private enterprise produced it.[5] Consumption of housing was Park's interest, not its production. Park assumed that housing producers unerringly followed consumer demand. Whatever consumers wanted, housing markets slavishly produced, including ethnically segregated residential neighborhoods. Therefore, the housing market's offerings showed what people wanted, not just what they inhabited. Admittedly, Park's assumption was common, and the Chicago School followed suit. Indeed, the tradition prevails even today in mainstream studies of residential choice and location, which routinely assume that whatever exists is what consumers want.[6] Demand is king, and determines supply.[7]

Reviewing that massive literature, Massey adds that immigrants are "guided to the neighborhood by social networks anchored among friends and relatives who live there."[8] True as far as it goes, and a fair encapsulation of the mainstream view, Massey's generalization ignores institutions that plan, produce, and distribute housing in contact with consumers' social networks. In a state socialist economy, this oversight would be glaring, but, even in a market economy like that of the United States, in which the private sector produces 98 percent of housing, Massey's generalization ignores the production of housing. Specifically, his review ignores firms in real estate, real property development, and building construction.[9] However, in market economies, networks of firms plan, produce, and distribute residential housing to networks of consumers. In international real estate transactions, "local property consultants" link foreign capital to real estate investments in the targeted destination.[10] Social networks refer customers to business networks, and vice versa. Consumer networks cannot guide anyone to housing that does not exist. Therefore, a complete picture of housing access and neighborhood formation requires attention to the supply side as well as the demand side. The existing residential segregation literature pays next to no attention to the supply side.

Happily, outside the residential segregation literature are two influential research approaches that do offer theoretical access to the supply side. Of these, the elder is Harvey Molotch[11] and John Logan and Harvey Molotch's[12] theory of the urban growth machine. This influential theory still offers the best explanation of how urbanization proceeded and still proceeds in the United States.[13] Logan and Molotch locate the motor of urbanization in local interest coalitions (called growth machines) whose prosperity depends on population growth in their locality. The most prominent members of growth machines are the place entrepreneurs. Place entrepreneurs acquire metropolitan land cheaply in the expectation its price will rise later with population increase. To make sure that the prices do rise, place entrepreneurs promote population growth. In the history of the United States, place entrepreneurs brought the railroad or the canal or the federal highway to the towns in which they owned real estate. Following the lead of Logan and Molotch, chapter 6 identified growth machines as the main sources of the pro-growth ideology that uncritically endorsed low-wage Mexican immigration into Los Angeles as it uncritically endorses population growth everywhere. Although place entrepreneurs are their most prominent members, growth machines include more constituents than only place entrepreneurs. They also enroll labor unions, insurance companies, newspapers, churches, the entire retail sector, universities, and transport services around a common, heavily promoted program of local population growth. The participants' common and essential motive is economic self-interest. When the place grows, they prosper. Urban growth creates additional jobs for union members, additional insurance policies for insurance companies, additional customers for retail businesses, additional readers for newspapers, additional congregants for churches, additional listeners for radio stations, additional students for universities, and additional travelers for airports and taxi services. Construction and real estate entrepreneurs are charter members of urban growth machines because the prosperity of both needs a continuous influx of new population, mainly acquired through internal or international migration.[14] Local growth increases demand for housing and road construction and also raises the price of real estate, permitting those to sell dear who earlier bought cheap.

Every city has a growth machine, but some growth machines are more effective than others.[15] The effective ones accelerate city growth above and beyond what macro-economic trends would have otherwise produced. The leaders of growth machines are usually honored, respected, and prominent civic personalities. Streets and public works are named after deceased leaders of the municipal growth machine. Harvey Molotch long ago noticed that the research literature assumed that growth machine leadership comes "rightfully from the higher social circles" without more closely identifying the leadership's class or ethnic origins.[16] Following that tradition, with the exception of Roger Keil, the existing literature pays no attention to the nativity of place entrepreneurs, tacitly assuming that place entrepreneurs are always native whites, which has until recently always been true. In the history of the United States, historians have also tacitly accepted this assumption by dint of not challenging it. Thus, John Higham described nineteenth-century real estate interests in the West that, in conjunction with railroads, actively promoted migration to the West in eastern states as well as in Europe.[17] Higham did not indicate whether any of the immigration promoters were themselves immigrants or nonwhite.[18] In principle, however, immigrants could have joined the urban growth machine in the past and could join it in the present. For example, nineteenth-century immigrants sometimes did become real estate developers or real estate agents, both entrepreneurial roles.[19] In those days, immigrants were Europeans.

Although historical research on the role of immigrants in real estate promotion and investment is scarce, Richard Platkin has documented the role of Jews in America.[20] In principle, immigrant place entrepreneurs could even promote immigration from their homeland to their real property developments in North America. Doing so, immigrant place entrepreneurs would promote international migration out of economic self-interest as immigrant labor contractors have long done. At that point, the immigrant place entrepreneurs would participate in institutionalized promotion of cumulatively caused immigration, giving the migration network a helping hand.[21] Now scholars talk about a "migration industry" that comes into existence to promote the migration on which the industry feeds. A previous generation of scholars used the term "induced immigration" to identify exactly this role.[22]

Evidence that immigrants join urban growth machines as realtors, not just housing consumers, appears in a second urban literature whose connection to the growth machine theory remains insufficiently explored. In a path-breaking study, Risa Palm examined the racial segregation of

Denver in 1982. She found that home sellers selected real estate brokers partially on the basis of race and that real estate brokers tended to work for "brokers of the same race or ethnicity."[23] Moreover, regardless of race, real estate agents steered customers to racially segregated neighborhoods. Black agents steered black customers to black neighborhoods, and white agents steered white customers to white neighborhoods.[24] Because agents followed the same practice, the black agents helped create racial housing segregation in Denver. Reviewing the now substantial literature bearing on racial steering, Eric Fong and Rima Wilkes declare that "real estate agents show fewer housing units to minority groups and steer minority members to predominantly minority neighborhoods."[25] The implication is this: residential segregation is not just a passive reflection of consumer preferences. Acting out of economic self-interest, real estate brokers, not all of whom are white, co-create segregation.

In two recent studies of Portuguese real estate brokers in Toronto, Carlos Teixeira has confirmed this generalization while pushing forward its theoretical implications. Like the other researchers, Teixeira found that Portuguese real estate agents served a predominantly Portuguese clientele of home seekers.[26] In fact, 52 percent of Portuguese homebuyers used a Portuguese agent in their search. Portuguese brokers had "cultural expertise" in dealing with coethnics whose "behaviour and needs" differed from those of non-Portugese.[27] Nonetheless, Teixeira also reported that this coethnic pairing resulted from "successful marketing campaigns" and was not just a spontaneous and unsolicited result of consumers' networks or cultural preference.[28] At this point, Teixeira suggested, Portuguese real estate brokers were actually restructuring the ethnic map of Toronto, and not simply responding passively to buyers' preferences.

The case of Edison, New Jersey, additionally shows how immigrant real estate interests can reenergize a stagnant city. In 1970 no South Asians lived in Edison, New Jersey, a stagnating middle-class suburb of New York City. By 1999 Edison was home to some fifteen thousand Indian immigrants, mostly Gujaratis.[29] An Indian real estate developer started the transition. In 1983 Pradip Kothari started a real estate business and travel agency in Edison. Kothari advertised Edison in Gujerat, advising his coethnics to purchase a home in Edison as their "piece of the American Dream." He promoted Edison so effectively that Gujerati migrants knew "all about Edison and Oak Tree Road" long before they left India. In consequence, Oak Tree Road became the shopping capital for all of Indian New Jersey.[30] Indeed, Kothari's efforts turned Edison into a virtual South Asian enclave. Unsurprisingly, while these changes were in process, Kothari was president of Edison's Indian Business Association and of Edison's Indo-American Cultural Association, both of which he ran from his home on Oak Tree Road.[31] Kothari was a place entrepreneur, and promoting Edison was Kothari's livelihood. Obviously Kothari did not give

Gujaratis the motive to emigrate or the money to buy suburban homes, but his promotional efforts, joined later by other Indian real estate, attracted Gujaratis to Edison who might otherwise have gone elsewhere in New Jersey or even have failed to come to New Jersey at all.[32]

Place Entrepreneurs in Los Angeles, 1970 to 2000

The history of Los Angeles in the late nineteenth and twentieth centuries exemplifies the growth machine's production of urbanization.[33] Echoing Cary McWilliams, venerated father of Los Angeles studies, Greg Hise calls southern California, "a gamble that boosters made on the future."[34] The boosters were place entrepreneurs. They bought Los Angeles real estate cheap, intending to sell it dear to those who might later come. Their gamble paid off when a growing population paid high prices for Los Angeles real property the boosters had purchased cheaply earlier. Similarly, William Fulton declares that during the past century, Los Angeles produced "one of the most effective growth machines ever created,"[35] a conclusion Purcell echoes.[36] Los Angeles's growth machine began with a cluster of visionary entrepreneurs, who lured native-born whites from the Southwest and Midwest with the promise of a balmy climate, a moral society, and a single-family home. This was the intellectual side of the growth machine's appeal. However, the entrepreneurs also promised a handsome capital gain on that bungalow, which most twentieth-century migrants did obtain.[37]

Fulton maintains, however, that Los Angeles's century-old growth machine foundered in the 1980s when sheer size rendered the metropolitan region ungovernable.[38] In Fulton's opinion, the growth machine collapsed because suburbanites "turned angry about traffic jams and high taxes, reducing their tolerance for more suburbs," the growth machine's raison d'etre.[39] Out of their frustration, a slow-growth coalition of homeowners and environmentalists coalesced in the 1980s, the very period, it should be noted, that Latino egress from southern California began. This slow-growth coalition "succeeded in hobbling the growth machine" in the mountains and at the beach, two essential targets already slated by the growth machine for development.[40] In this situation, Fulton concludes, political support for the growth machine collapsed, the leadership of the growth machine bailed out, and "no new paradigm has emerged to take its place." As a result, Los Angeles growth machine lacked leadership, and growth slowed.[41]

To embellish this thesis, the death of the growth machine, Fulton examines the past and present of the Los Angeles metropolitan area. He has no trouble mobilizing historical evidence for his thesis; Purcell[42] offers additional supporting evidence, as does Pincetl.[43] Indeed, three developments, all subsequent to his publication, corroborate Fulton's conclusion. One was the sale of the *Los Angeles Times* to a Wall Street conglomerate in

1999. This sale removed the Chandler family, the newspaper's founder-owner family and key members of the growth machine, from the city's ruling directorate.[44] This removal spelled abdication of charter members of the growth machine. A second was the Environmental Defense Fund's disclosure that between 1981 and 1991, County Supervisor Michael Antonovich took money from property developers to ignore their overbuilding in the Santa Monica Mountains.[45] The third was Michael Dear's influential 2001 report, which concludes that the perimeters of Los Angeles had reached the natural limits of horizontal growth.[46] The sale of the *Los Angeles Times* showed that charter families were bailing out of Los Angeles's growth machine.[47] The Antonovich scandal showed that developers faced slow-growth resistance that limited their ability to build without pay-offs.[48] Dear's report signaled lack of space for new growth.

Nonetheless, Fulton's death-of-the-growth-machine thesis faces two objections. Although Los Angeles does not want growth, the growth machine lives. First, Purcell rightly declares that the Los Angeles growth machine did not really die; it only lost the political consensus in support of growth.[49] However, even Purcell does not observe that the growth machine only lost this control in the native-born population because Purcell ignores the immigrant component of the growth machine. That is unsurprising, because no one has ever addressed immigrant members of the growth machine. As entrepreneurs, immigrants have been consistently underestimated and ignored in countless urban studies, which prefer to treat them as downtrodden rabble lacking resources or agency, still the "wretched refuse" of some "teeming shore." Second, during the period in which the growth machine was supposedly dying, the population of greater Los Angeles increased from 9.9 million in 1970 to 14.5 million in 1990.[50] Components of this increase were 1.7 million additional native-born persons and 2.8 million immigrants. This increase occurred despite the net loss of 83,128 non-Hispanic whites, and thanks to a net influx of 803,532 Asian immigrants and two million Mexican and Central American immigrants. Unfortunately, Fulton's book ignores immigration and immigrant financial elites. Had he examined immigration, he would have learned that many Asian immigrants came to Los Angeles because coethnic entrepreneurs in real estate and property development had encouraged them to come, the classic growth machine process.[51] This is the same myopia that we find in the residential segregation literature.[52]

Chinese Immigrants in Property Development

In fact, immigrant Chinese and Korean immigrant entrepreneurs played a serious role in promoting coethnic immigration to Los Angeles, creating and preparing residential neighborhoods for the new immigrants, and supporting Los Angeles property values, which had never been higher.[53] The Chinese case follows the modus operandi that Michael Goldberg identified long ago: small Chinese investors in real estate operate through social networks; big Chinese investors abroad use coethnic real estate spotters abroad to invest their capital.[54] In 1970, Los Angeles's historic Chinatown was the only Chinese neighborhood in which Chinese predominated, and the only one in which Chinese immigrants could comfortably settle. Los Angeles's historic Chinatown was central, dense, cramped, and working class. However, new Chinese immigrants were middle and upper middle class, not the unskilled working class of yore.[55] The new Chinese immigrants were well educated and arrived with significant capital. In this situation, Charles Wong observes, "Chinese realtors, contractors, and businessmen" moved in on Monterey Park, an inner ring suburb of mixed white and Latino population.[56] The names of this leadership are public knowledge. Born in China, Frederic Hsieh (1945 to 1999) came to Los Angeles to work as a city engineer, but he entered real estate instead.[57] In 1972 at the age of twenty-seven, he moved to Monterey Park, and opened a real estate business.[58] "Hsieh and other [Chinese] entrepreneurs made Monterey Park a desirable alternative to the Los Angeles, San Francisco, and New York Chinatowns."[59] Hsieh's was the first Chinese real estate business in Monterey Park, and Hsieh is credited with planning the suburban city's transition to Chinese control.[60]

Hsieh's modus operandi was vintage growth machine. Hsieh's Mandarin Realty Company promoted Monterey Park in Hong Kong and Taiwan as "the Chinese Beverly Hills."[61] a distinct exaggeration that nonetheless evoked buyer interest abroad.[62] From the beginning, Hsieh intended to make Monterey Park an upscale Chinese residential and business enclave, pointing out, among other advantages, that the city's telephone area code (818) consisted of lucky numbers. In 1977, Hsieh told an astonished and disconcerted gathering of the Monterey Park Chamber of Commerce that Monterey Park would become a "Mecca for Chinese business."[63] This was Hsieh's entrepreneurial vision. Sharing Hsieh's vision, Chinese business firms in Monterey Park initially refused to join the Monterey Park Chamber of Commerce, which had solicited their membership. Instead, they formed their own organization, the Monterey Park Chinese Chamber of Commerce.[64] Later, it is true, experiencing political rebuffs, they joined the Monterey Park Chamber of Commerce as its Chinese committee. Of the forty Chinese firms that took membership in this Chinese committee, fully half were real estate promoters, and the real estate promoters, Wong noted, were the Chinese committee's core activists. When later the Monterey Park Chamber of Commerce declined to endorse a Chinese theme for the suburb, its Chinese committee threatened to secede. By 1979, only seven years after Hsieh opened his real estate business, Chinese were "virtually the only ones investing in the city" of Monterey Park, and the investors tended to be "recent immigrant Chinese."[65] Hsieh profited personally from the development of Monterey Park as a suburban Chinatown. Basically, Hsieh bought land cheaply early in his career, then, having promoted Monterey Park in the interim, resold that land later at inflated prices to Chinese immigrants. Only three years after starting his real estate business, Hsieh assembled several land parcels together from empty and underused commercial lots near Atlantic Boulevard, now a thriving and bustling commercial zone. He called these empty lots Dearfield Plaza. Of course, Hsieh saved a land parcel for his own Omni Bank. Two decades later, Hsieh owned many businesses in Monterey Park—real estate holdings, the Hong Kong Restaurant, a music store, a theater, and insurance and trading firms, and Hsieh had even expanded his operations to Asia.[66] The land on which the businesses sat had appreciated in value in the interim.

Hsieh was not alone. Other Chinese entrepreneurs also profited from the development of Monterey Park. These were members of the Chinese branch of Los Angeles's growth machine. Winston Ko, president of Kowin Development, became a millionaire before he turned thirty as a result of land promotion in Monterey Park. Gregory Tse of Hong Kong's Wing On Realty Group, realized that land was cheap in Monterey Park compared to Hong Kong. Tse bought Monterey Park lots cheaply, then resold them at a profit to wealthy Hong Kong immigrants.[67] By 1994 Monterey Park housed sixty-six Chinese restaurants, fourteen Chinese minimalls, two Chinese newspapers, twenty Chinese banks, six Chinese supermarkets of which Diho Market was the first American-style Chinese supermarket in the United States (Horton 1995, 30).[68] Roger Chen founded the Tawa Supermarket in 1984.[69] The supermarket set up Tawa Commercial Property Development Corporation in 1988. This property developer division built numerous Chinese shopping malls throughout southern California.[70] Currently, nine-centimeters thick, Chinese telephone yellow pages list hundreds of professionals in every imaginable service.[71] All profited from growth of Monterey Park's Chinese population.

Beyond Monterey Park, two adjacent suburban cities, Alhambra and Rosemead, subsequently developed Chinese business and residential centers as a result of the same land promotion and development methodology. Neighboring them, also in the San Gabriel Valley, Arcadia and San Marino became the highest prestige locations for Chinese settlement. In all these cities, Chinese property developers and realtors moved in, promoted the suburban towns in Hong Kong and Taiwan, and then sold lots to immigrant Chinese, who arrived in the United States already informed of the upscale Chinese-speaking communities that awaited their settlement. Indeed, the whole San Gabriel Valley, from Monterey Park to Diamond Bar, had become heavily Chinese by 1999. Horton's analysis of

Chinese telephone books showed that in 1983 Chinese agglomeration in the San Gabriel Valley was already catching up with Chinatown as the largest regional center of Chinese business. In 1983 about one-half of all the Chinese businesses listed in the Chinese telephone books covering greater Los Angeles were located in Chinatown and one-third in the San Gabriel Valley. By 1992, the San Gabriel Valley had 55 percent of all Chinese businesses in Los Angeles, and Chinatown only 6 percent.[72]

The Chinese property developers had access to capital from Taiwan and Hong Kong. Many Chinese banks sprang into existence to support the émigrés as well as to "take advantage of the property boom in California."[73] In 1992, Los Angeles had twenty-four Chinese banks with assets of $5.6 billion. Two-thirds of these banks had been established before 1985. Three of the Chinese banks were among the largest thirty in California. In general, thanks to the Chinese banks, the Chinese had better access to banking than did non-Chinese residents of Los Angeles. Chinese prefer to do business in the Chinese language with bankers who belong to their personal network, and because of this Chinese banks enjoyed a built-in coethnic clientele.

Korean Immigrants in Property Development

"Unlike other minorities," wrote Kyung Lee, "Koreans did not settle in clusters."[74] Los Angeles Koreans had no geographical enclave comparable to Chinatown or Little Tokyo in 1968. Indeed, precisely because it offers a residential and commercial core, Los Angeles Koreatown was long unique among American Korean settlements, which lacked a named ethnic enclave.[75] What is today called Los Angeles Koreatown was known in 1970 as the mid-Wilshire district. Located about five kilometers west of downtown Los Angeles, squarely in the central city, mid-Wilshire was a dreary residential and retail zone that had catered to poor white, black, and Hispanic renters. A decade later, in 1980, the City of Los Angeles officially renamed the mid-Wilshire district Koreatown. The naming ceremony was heavily attended by Korean business leaders and municipal dignitaries. At the time of the naming ceremony, Koreatown housed three hundred Korean businesses, major Korean cultural and civic associations, and thirteen thousand Korean immigrants, who represented 21 percent of Los Angeles's total Korean population.[76] Seeking to explain this remarkable transformation, as fast as any in the urban literature, Nancy Abelmann and John Lie advance a formulaic explanation based on follow-the-leader group process.[77] In their account, Hi-Duk Lee opened the first Korean restaurant in 1971. Other Koreans noticed it, and then settled in the vicinity. Still other Korean business owners settled near them, thus setting in motion what Abelmann and Lie declare an unplanned, spontaneous, and spiraling process of Korean settlement whose unplanned upshot was Koreatown, an inner-city Korean community. This version conforms to the leaderless process version of neighborhood formation that Robert Park endorsed in 1916, and that still rules the urban literature, but the old formula fails to deliver the correct story when upscale immigrants come to town.[78]

Los Angeles Koreatown did not really emerge from a leaderless process.[79] First, Koreatowns are uncommon. Los Angeles was the only American city that developed a residential inner city Koreatown. Other major Korean centers—New York City, Washington, D.C., and Chicago—still did not have Koreatowns in 2000. Second, as Roger Keil has already noted, Korean banks, using Korean money, financed Korean business in Los Angeles, including Korean real estate investment.[80] Koreans built Koreatown without American banks or American capital and without American entrepreneurs.[81] Third, from the beginning, Korean developers and realtors in Los Angeles hoped to transform the mid-Wilshire district into a staging ground for the incipient Korean immigration they intended to promote and ride to riches.[82] This immigration had only just begun in 1970. With access to Korean capital, Korean American immigrant place entrepreneurs assumed the leadership for effectuating that visionary transformation. To this end, they promptly formed the Koreatown Development Association.[83] The development association was a group of Korean immigrant real estate promoters. It is important to understand the role of Hi-Duk Lee in this leadership group, other prominent members of which were Byung Min and Sonia Suk. Hi-Duk Lee was director of the Koreatown Development Association, not just a random restaurateur, who happened to start a business on Olympic Boulevard.[84]

The methods of the Koreatown developers were vintage growth machine. They bought up cheap land in the mid-Wilshire district, and promoted Koreatown in Seoul, the provenance of most Korean immigrants.[85] Korean-born property developers became the major property owners in Koreatown during the 1970s.[86] When Koreans emigrated in the 1980s and 1990s, they already knew that Los Angeles's Koreatown was the right neighborhood in which to settle. Korean immigrants then bought or rented residences from the Koreatown developers. The more immigrant Koreans who settled in Koreatown, the higher the land values in Koreatown, and the greater the profit of the Koreatown developers. This methodology is just basic growth machine.

Everything depended upon promoting Koreatown awareness in Korea as well as in Los Angeles itself. To accomplish this goal, the Koreatown developers coordinated a program of public relations, marketing, government relationships, and publicity.[87] In 1973 the Koreatown Development Association offered free business signs in Korean for firms in the targeted area.[88] They intended thereby to call public attention to Korean concentration, furthering their public relations agenda.[89] The Koreatown developers organized the first Koreatown parade in 1975. This parade drew interracial local crowds and made copy for newspapers in Seoul as well as Los Angeles. The Koreatown developers petitioned the city of Los Angeles officially to designate the mid-Wilshire district "Koreatown." The city of Los Angeles did so in 1980 despite the fact that Koreans were then only seven percent of the residents of Koreatown.[90] Shortly thereafter, the Koreatown Development Association also induced the California Department of Transportation to erect a freeway sign that advertised the exit for Koreatown to passing motorists. This sign identified the neighborhood by its new name, attracted custom, and encouraged Korean settlement. Korean property developers sought to improve their political access, and one of their number, Sang Lee, ran for public office as early as 1988.[91] When crime posed an obstacle to Koreatown's development, the Koreatown Development Association hired a private police force to ensure security for shoppers while demanding more police protection from metropolitan police. To this end, the Koreatown Development Association also raised private funds to finance a sheriff's substation in Koreatown.[92]

Koreatown's initial success probably disappointed its founders. Successful as a central city business center, Koreatown was less successful as a center of Korean residence, especially in the aftermath of the Los Angeles arson and riot of April 1992. However, even by 1985 it was already clear that Koreatown was a first-settlement stopping place for recently arrived Koreans, who relocated to suburbs as soon as they could afford to do so.[93] The Los Angeles riot and arson of 1992, which targeted Koreatown for mob violence, dimmed the luster of Koreatown real estate in the Korean media. The riot of 1992 was a place entrepreneur's worst nightmare. Wealthier Koreans moved to Palos Verdes Estates, Rolling Hills Estates, Rancho Palos Verdes, and Orange County.[94] Undaunted, Korean immigrant property developers orchestrated the suburbanization of the Korean population from Koreatown. Among these was multimillionaire Edward Cho, who immigrated to Los Angeles in 1971, and undertook property development in Garden Grove. Before his suicide in 1994, Cho had been president of the Korean Association of Orange County.[95] The development of suburban Korean areas created a socioeconomic ladder for Korean immigrants to climb upon arrival in Los Angeles. Some Koreans moved directly into the higher class suburbs without enduring a residence in Koreatown.[96] However, most Korean immigrants spent at least several months in Koreatown before moving out to more affluent and desirable suburbs.[97] In this sense, Koreatown was a staging area for Korean immigration and settlement.

After the Los Angeles riot and arson of 1992, during which 700 Korean businesses were burned and looted, Koreatown and mid-Wilshire properties lost value in the short run.[98] Resident Koreans fled to the suburbs to escape future riots. Nonetheless, with heavy backing from Korean banks, Korean American property developers expanded their holdings, thus registering a serious vote of confidence in the battered city's commercial future.[99] By 1999, Koreans owned an additional 3.5 million square feet of commercial property in nearby mid-Wilshire, of which the Korean and Korean-American businesses occupied only 40 percent.[100] The leading Korean American investor was Dr. David Lee, who purchased fifteen office towers on behalf of various consortia of Korean and Korean-American investors.[101] To attract non-Korean tenants, and out of deference to the sensitivities of Latino and Armenian tenants, the Korean Chamber of Commerce finally agreed to stop identifying the office towers as Koreatown properties, and to restrict the use of Korean language signs on the office towers.[102] The real estate pages of the Los Angeles Times pay frequent testimony to the influence on southern California of Korean, Chinese, Japanese, and other Asian developers.[103]

Networks, Agents, and Housing

Accessing a foreign country's housing market is much easier when coethnic real estate developers and real estate salespeople have already settled there. In this case, the coethnic entrepreneurs acquire desirable tracts in advance, holding them speculatively for the anticipated influx of immigrant customers that will finally permit profitable sale. This step requires large capital investment up front as well as the business experience to make the long-term project work. From a consumer's viewpoint, however, the acquisition of these tracts greatly simplifies the process of immigration, settlement decisionmaking, and housing insertion. When they are still in their homeland, prospective migrants can evaluate housing options in reception cities located in different parts of the same country or even in different countries. The consumers know in advance the price and quality of housing they can command as well as the social characteristics of the housing. True, ethnic networks provide comparable housing information, but ethnic networks do not invest large capital up front in expectation of later price appreciation attendant upon the operation of the network. Network-supplied information accurately conveys what exists; it does not expand what exists. Information networks take no political action to bring about desired outcomes either. In contrast, transnational real estate investment projects improved the quality of housing available to coethnics, and also promoted migration, thus securing the long-term profitability of their property investment. Operating as they did with the assistance of migration networks as well as international real estate companies, the Asian immigrants had an easy time finding suitable housing in Los Angeles.

Figure 7.1   Asian Immigrant Place Entrepreneurs in Los Angeles

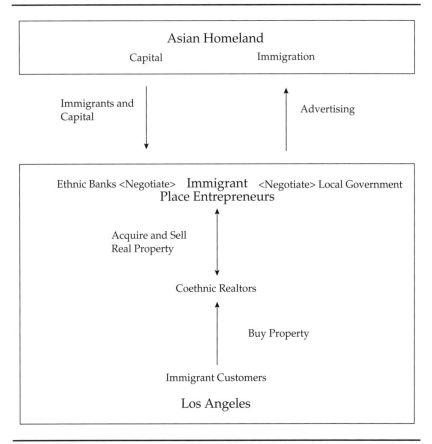

Source: Author's compilations.

The Immigrant Growth Machine

In multiethnic California, growth machines need no longer be all white. Indeed, following Keil,[104] one concludes that in Los Angeles "local space entrepreneurs" could not be white and still attract Asian capital.[105] When immigrants turn to real property acquisition and development, they join the locality's growth machine. As such, immigrant property developers acquire a financial interest in promoting growth in the destination locality. To accomplish this end, Asian immigrant place entrepreneurs attracted coethnic immigrants from Asian homelands, not whites from the Midwest as the nineteenth- and early twentieth-century founders of Los Angeles had done (figure 7.1). Immigrant place entrepreneurs direct urban development down paths of development that nonimmigrant place entrepreneurs could not or would not follow. Therefore, immigrant place entrepreneurs can wax and native-born place entrepreneurs wane. In the 1970 to 2000 period, Chinese and Korean immigrant entrepreneurs reorganized Los Angeles's urban morphology, acquiring entire new communities to house new immigrants. Borrowing from coethnic banks, funded with homeland capital, they advertised Los Angeles properties in China and in Korea, making immigration to Los Angeles easier for prospective immigrants from these countries (figure 7.1). Coethnic realtors promoted their properties to immigrant customers. They produced and marketed upscale coethnic suburbs that attracted to Los Angeles more and higher status immigrants than would otherwise have selected the region for settlement. To the extent that the Chinese and Korean immigrant entrepreneurs promoted emigration from Asia, successfully attracting thousands who would not otherwise have come to Los Angeles, they counteracted the incapacity of the Los Angeles growth machine to attract white people, and the egress of white population during the 1990s. To the extent that they encouraged the emigration of wealthier coethnics, the Asian place entrepreneurs increased the average status and income level of the Los Angeles metropolitan area, strengthening real estate prices in the metropolis. As Fulton and Purcell observed, Los Angeles's historic white growth machine faltered in these thirty years; but they failed to notice that an Asian growth machine had gathered strength at the same time. The contrary trends point to an emergent Los Angeles growth machine, with immigrant leadership, that can continue the region's historic growth trajectory well into the twenty-first century despite the collapse of growth ideology among native whites.

Ethnic Entrepreneurs in Real Estate

Admittedly, this Los Angeles case does not prove that immigrant place entrepreneurs always join municipal growth machines, only that they sometimes do. The role of ethnic minority real estate developers and brokers has become more important in the age of globalization than it used to be, but it was probably more important in the past than is now realized. Historical studies of African American migration and settlement did not stress growth machine dynamics, it is true, but they did mention them.[106] Northern black newspapers, themselves members of the African American growth machine, were voluble and early promoters of black migration from Dixie.[107] Additionally, a black real estate developer, Philip Payton, invented and deployed the technique of block busting, which permitted black people to capture Harlem for residence in the 1920s.[108] Exploiting white owners' fears, Payton panicked them with leaflets that indicated blacks would soon invade Harlem, lowering the whites' property values.

He then bought the panicked whites' houses from them at bargain prices and resold them for a profit to upper-class blacks. The long-term upshot was the transfer of Harlem, a desirable Manhattan location, from white into black hands.[109] Getting Harlem was a major economic victory for black capitalism. Harlem's acquisition represented ethnic minority entrepreneurship in real property acquisition, not a leaderless social process.[110] Possibly the African American growth machine in Harlem was not so powerful in 1920 as was the Chinese growth machine in Los Angeles in 1970, but a black growth machine existed in 1920, and should be recognized in historical studies.

In the case of contemporary working-class Mexican and Central American immigrants to Los Angeles, ethnic property development lags what the more affluent Chinese and Korean immigrants achieved. Although Latino "place entrepreneurs" were appearing in Los Angeles in 2001, the Latino entrepreneurs were then just starting the conscious redesign of the region's morphology that Chinese and Koreans had initiated thirty years earlier.[111] To this extent, then, the residential succession literature legitimately ignores Latino property developers because there were few.[112] The same excuse does not apply to Chinese and Korean residential choice because, in these cases, immigrant place entrepreneurs created the choice context in which coethnic homebuyers and renters made decisions about where they would live. The problem is this: the residential settlement literature never considers the possibility that immigrant place entrepreneurs create choice contexts by conscious entrepreneurial initiative. The default interpretation of residential neighborhood formation is a leaderless social process in which an unorganized free market responds to the initiatives of independent buyers with preferences that just happen to be the same. This default reading is inaccurate when applied to high-status, high-income immigrants in an age of globalization.

= Chapter 8 =

Deflecting Latinos from Suburbs

U NLIKE ASIAN immigrants, working-class Latinos did not have homeland banks, coethnic entrepreneurs, and Mexico-based international real estate developers to prearrange the housing they would
need in Los Angeles.[1] Instead, Latinos crashed into the housing status quo
with no resources except their willingness to overpay and overcrowd.
When the status quo resisted, housing access was curtailed in both the city
and the suburbs of Los Angeles, and some Latinos were deflected from the
metropolitan region.

Institutional resistance of the housing supply to immigrant influx is easier to understand in Europe than in the United States. In European welfare
states, when immigrants occupy public housing, which is a very large share
of what is available, they often trigger resentments among nonimmigrants,
who claim to believe that their own housing chances were thereby diminished. They then politically resist the immigrant influx to preserve their
own housing options. But, how could political conflicts between immigrants and natives over housing erupt in a free housing market such as Los
Angeles?[2] In free housing markets, immigrants and nonimmigrants compete economically for housing, but do not come into political conflict over
it. The Chicago School's theory of succession models intergroup housing
competition in which the central city poor gradually overwhelm their
wealthier neighbors by dint of overcrowding and overpaying.[3] Because
they overcrowd and overpay, low-income households can outbid high-
income households in the housing market, thus obtaining their vacated
housing, and freeing new neighborhoods for low-income occupation.
However, this is economic, not political, competition.

The Chicago School wrote about a bygone world in which metropolitan suburbs did not regulate housing access as they routinely do now.
Long after the Chicago School was defunct, suburbanization stripped the
immigrant poor of the economic tools they had previously used to obtain
housing—overpayment and overcrowding. When the poor overpay, they
can offer more for housing than wealthier households in that housing's
share of their disposable income is higher. When they overcrowd, they can

129

outbid wealthier households because a million paupers each with a dollar have the same effective demand as a millionaire. However, when suburbs and cities legally denied the poor the right to overpay and overcrowd, intergroup housing competition became political, not economic.

Political conflict over housing policy and supply had become serious in Los Angeles by 1990, and, by extension, in other first-reception cities of the United States as well.[4] Admittedly, the conflict was not usually open and conscious. In Los Angeles, metropolitan political fragmentation concealed immigrant-native housing issues rather than exposing them. As a result, parties did not even realize that they were in political conflict over housing. Because the political conflict centered on the disadvantages to nonimmigrants of immigrants' need to amend housing codes, and the nonimmigrants' attempts to preserve those codes unchanged, the conflict offered another context for public debate over law enforcement in the wake of network-driven immigration. Strict enforcement of existing suburban housing codes tended to exclude Latino immigrants, who, thanks to their poverty, required legal laxity or outright law change to gain access. The conceptual similarity with law enforcement against garment sweatshops is obvious.

Recreating the Fragmented Metropolis

Although the nation's second ranked city, the Los Angeles metropolitan area has been the center of immigrant reception since about 1970.[5] This cosmopolitan role is a new one. The city was a center of anti-Chinese sentiment during the agitation that led ultimately to the Chinese Exclusion Act of 1882. Thereafter, with Asians legally excluded, only small foreign communities existed in Los Angeles for nearly a century. Seeking population in the early twentieth century, Los Angeles's growth machine solicited the internal migration of native-born whites from the Midwest and Southwest, who still formed the majority of Los Angeles's white population in 1970.[6] Los Angeles attracted few European immigrants.[7] As a result, the county historically contained a higher proportion of interstate migrants than other major cities in the United States, but a lower proportion of international immigrants.

The founders of Los Angeles had a distinctive vision of the region's urbanism, which they successfully marketed to the native-white Protestants they recruited from Iowa, Oklahoma, and Texas.[8] This vision stressed a low-density, suburban morphology thought to harmonize with the region's mild climate as well as promising full exploitation of the passenger automobile.[9] Unlike the crowded, tenement-ridden cities of the Northeast, the negative pole against which her civic boosters reacted in horror, Los Angeles offered low-density, decentralized urbanism in which residents occupied single-family bungalows on quarter-acre tracts. In the ini-

Table 8.1   Population of Los Angeles by Ethno-Racial Category

	1980	1990	2000	Index
City				
Non-Hispanic white	1,419,402	1,299,604	1,099,188	77
Non-Hispanic black	495,722	454,289	422,819	85
Hispanic	816,075	1,391,411	1,719,073	211
Asian	196,017	341,807	398,888	203
Total	2,966,836	3,485,398	3,694,820	125
Suburbs				
Non-Hispanic white	2,182,518	1,972,758	1,592,890	73
Non-Hispanic black	364,141	391,210	417,155	115
Hispanic	1,173,335	1,801,318	2,284,670	195
Asian	211,922	539,826	746,250	352
Total	3,979,965	4,709,502	5,110,342	128
Metropolitan total	6,946,801	8,194,900	8,805,162	127

Source: Lewis Mumford Center (various years).
Note: Index = 2000/1980 × 100.

tial phase, 1880–1920, the suburbanization of Los Angeles depended upon the world's most extensive streetcar system, the Pacific Electric Railroad.[10] After 1920, as automotive transportation became an alternative, the Los Angeles's growth machine switched its transportation allegiance, encouraging and promoting highway construction and private passenger automobiles rather than streetcars.[11] In the 1950s and 1960s, suburbanization and highway construction proceeded at a frantic pace, and public transportation disintegrated just as fast. The well-documented upshot was a metropolitan region whose urban core was suburban in character, and whose suburbs were numerous, independent, and bucolic. Detractors ridiculed Los Angeles as suburbs in search of a city. However, the Los Angeles region's experiment in decentralized and low-density urbanization became the model around which American civilization organized twentieth-century suburbanization.[12]

By 1970, when the mass immigration of Latinos began, the urban morphology of Los Angeles already was firmly in place. Los Angeles County lies within a five-county southern California megalopolis with multiple central cities, the largest and by far the most prominent of which is the city of Los Angeles.[13] The city of Los Angeles then occupied about half of the county of Los Angeles. The metropolitan suburbs lay within the county of Los Angeles, but by definition outside the city. Table 8.1 shows the population of the city of Los Angeles and its metropolitan region in 1980, 1990, and 2000. In city and suburbs, the population of non-Hispanic whites declined between 1980 and 2000, largely as a result of egress to other states.[14] The population of blacks remained stable, shifting slightly to the suburbs. As a result of immigration, the population of Asians in the region increased threefold, more than that of any other group, and shifted strongly toward the suburbs. The massive suburban shift of Asian population reflects the high socioeconomic origins of Asian immigrants, and the facilitation of their coethnic growth machines, which prepared suburbs for their occupation. Thanks to immigration, the population of Hispanics doubled in both city and suburbs. In both the city of Los Angeles and its suburbs, Hispanics had become the largest single group in 2000. In 1980 and in 2000, more Hispanics lived in the suburbs of Los Angeles than in the city.

The city of Los Angeles represented the urban core of Los Angeles County. About 30 percent of the county's population still lived in the city in 2000. Surrounding the city were eighty-eight incorporated governments of various sizes. The largest was Long Beach, population 461,552. The smallest was Vernon, population 91. These satellite cities were suburbs. Of the 3,684,000 Hispanics who lived in Los Angeles County in 2000, 47 percent were in the suburbs. By contrast, of the 1,013,073 Asians who lived in the county in 2000, 64 percent were in the suburbs. The difference was a matter of 626,000 Hispanics.

Laws that Deflected Latinos

The city of Los Angeles and each of its satellite cities had a housing code that defined what kind of housing was legally permissible. The framers intended to protect the low-density, automobile-dependent style of life their citizens had come to Los Angeles in order to enjoy. City councils framed these housing restrictions with the knowledge and approval of voters in the 1950s and 1960s. Municipal housing codes discouraged multi-family, high-rise housing and public transportation in favor of the preferred housing form, a one- or two-story single-family home with a two-car garage, seated on a large lot, and set well back from the curb.[15] Detached homes were required to have garages to house the automobiles that homeowners were assumed to possess, and without which transportation was highly inefficient and inconvenient. Gasoline was cheap, and air pollution, a problem since 1944, was thought worth enduring in order to enjoy the rest of the lifestyle.[16] Residential density restrictions were a favorite legal device for guaranteeing that a city's built environment would conform to the suburban lifestyle.[17] Suburban cities declared that they could not exceed maxima that had been set too low to accommodate multifamily, high-rise housing. Requiring new houses to have wide setbacks from the street, large lots, and attached garages, city councils built a dependency on automobiles into the code. If a household owned no car, it could not comfortably occupy a suburban house. Municipal regulations even constrained the vegetation home owners could grow. Grass lawns were standard, and required an installed irrigation system because of the region's dry climate. Homeowners who planted drought-tolerant native ground covers (weeds) were subject to citation and fine.[18]

As this legal structure was firmly in place in 1970, when serious Latino immigration began, its designers had no anti-Latino motives.[19] Indeed, this legal structure is common to most American suburbs whose city councils only intended to safeguard the suburban way of life, and to protect the property investment this way of life required.[20] However, after thirty years of low-income Mexican and Central American migration to Los Angeles, what Robert Fogelson had called the "fragmented metropolis" in 1964 now protected a life style incompatible with the emergent housing needs of most Angelinos.[21] When Latinos became the largest group of Los Angeles County's population, Los Angeles's urban past came into conflict with its urban present. Low-wage Latino immigrants needed affordable rental housing, not home ownership on big lots.[22] They needed an integrated public transit system, not automobile dependency. Figure 8.1 shows that Hispanics in Los Angeles County lived in cities that offered abundant rental housing. Asians, on the other hand, a much more affluent category, lived in cities that stressed home ownership. Hispanics also tended to settle in metropolitan cities, where overcrowding and to some extent overpayment were more common.[23] Because single-family homes were expensive, Hispanics tended to live in cities that offered the most and the most affordable rental housing. Residential clustering of low-wage immigrants increased overcrowding and overpayment in heavily Hispanic cities.[24] Those circumstances provided the incentive to seek housing in less immigrant-friendly cities.

Undershirts and Junk Cars

In the Los Angeles suburbs, middle-class residents relied on passenger automobiles for transportation, and parked their cars in the garage with which every site-built house came equipped. When they moved to the suburbs, many immigrant households could not follow suit. First, they could not afford new cars. They bought instead junk cars, and, wearing "wife-beater" undershirts, repaired and restored them on the setback in front of their houses. This practice only became illegal when the cars under repair were left in front for long periods, as they often and unavoidably were. Second, Mexican and Central American immigrants renting suburban single-family homes commonly sublet the garages illegally to other poor families. In 1987, the *Los Angeles Times* reported that two hundred thousand people were living illegally in forty-two thousand metropolitan garages, an average of five inhabitants per garage.[25] Subletting garages for residence permitted homeowners or home renters to reduce their monthly housing bill. According to the *Los Angeles Times*, Latinos "turn to garages because the

Figure 8.1   Asian and Hispanic Housing in Southern California Cities, 2000

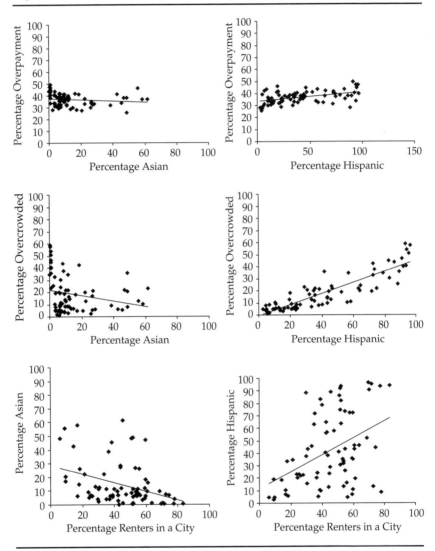

Source: Southern California Association of Governments (2000).

region's supply of cheap housing has failed to keep up with the demand created by this army of immigrants."[26] Unfortunately, renting the garages caused new problems. Illegal dwellings posed fire hazards.[27] Neighbors complained that garage dwellers cut down street trees to plant vegetables (which they ate), hung clothing on fences to dry (having no clothes dryers), loitered on the street (having no adequate living space inside), and urinated into backyard ditches (because their garages contained no toilets). All these practices were illegal. Even after these facts became public, the Los Angeles City Council was reluctant to prosecute landlords for fear of "forcing thousands of tenants into the streets."[28]

Because Los Angeles lacked effective and comprehensive public transportation, most immigrants required a car for convenient transportation to work. Some public officials blamed Latino immigrants for exacerbating the region's freeway gridlock, already the worst in the United States.[29] Because detached houses contained many households, and households many earners, Latino neighborhoods were crowded with old cars.[30] Lacking garages, which had been let to tenants, immigrants parked on residential streets. Parking spaces became scarce. Unable to find parking on the street, residents parked on what had once been the front lawns. Parking on the housing setback, however, was illegal in suburban cities whose housing codes protected middle class residents against this eyesore. At that point, the existing housing code, a political legacy of the previous generation, constricted the ability of Latinos to live in suburban single-family homes. In effect, the housing code stipulated what kind of house one must occupy, but implicitly as well how one must occupy it, and many Latinos could not meet the implicit conditions.

The Growth that Slow-Growth Resisted

Los Angeles County had already experienced a shortage of affordable housing for a generation, but the shortage worsened after 1994, when California's recession ended.[31] In 1999, 40 percent of the metropolitan region's households spent 30 percent or more of their household income on housing.[32] Experts consider housing expenses in excess of 30 percent of household income overpayment; and expenses in excess of 50 percent severe overpayment.[33] True, San Francisco suffered a similar shortage, but the causes were not the same. In San Francisco, new economy wealth had led to gentrification of inner-city neighborhoods, to the disadvantage of the city's middle and working classes. However, in the cities of Los Angeles County, despite a net loss of approximately one-quarter of the non-Hispanic white population, thirty years' influx of low-income Latino immigrants drove up rents in Latino areas and increased overcrowding.[34] Of course, rents were higher for everyone, not just immigrants; and poor and elderly whites as well as Latinos were also forced out of their homes.[35] Latinos alone did not create the high rents. Los Angeles confronted a general crisis of housing affordability in the 1980s and 1990s. The entire United States, in fact, experienced a surge of housing costs in the 1990s. Nonetheless, immigration additionally raised rents in impacted localities. Explaining the national shortage of rental housing in the 1990s, Barbara Alexander and her colleagues observe that immigration "added substantially to the demand" for housing because foreign-born households were one-fifth of all renters in the United States.[36] In Los Angeles, Latinos comprised half the households, and the Latino impact on housing costs was therefore more substantial in Los Angeles and its immigrant neighborhoods than elsewhere.

Urban planners and historians have largely ignored the role of immigrant demand in increasing housing costs in southern California. Explaining the affordability crisis, Fulton[37] and Purcell[38] stressed the slow-growth political ideology that had taken control of city councils everywhere in the Los Angeles metropolitan region.[39] Taking account of this massive shift in public opinion, Fulton even proclaimed the "death of the growth machine," in Los Angeles—a somewhat premature obituary, as chapter 6 disclosed.[40] There is, nonetheless, little doubt that slow-growth political movements in the Los Angeles metropolitan region had captured most city halls in the Los Angeles region by 1990.[41] Los Angeles voters often opposed growth in the interest of environmental protection, but lifestyle and property values were constant concerns as well. Approximately 60 percent of Los Angeles County voters were white in 2000. Mike Davis declared that, "angry homeowners" engaged in a "significant struggle over the politics of growth."[42] The voters' slow-growth ideology discouraged area city councils from opening their low-density suburban cities to high-density housing intended to benefit the poor. In a survey of region city councils, conducted amid loud, public lamentations over the region's lack of affordable housing, Fernando Guerra, Mara Marks, and Harold Brackman reported that "almost all city council members . . . characterize their city's housing policy as aimed at maintaining or reducing current density levels."[43] Although open and frank anti-immigrant appeals played a negligible role in slow-growth ideology, slow growth's political success reduced the housing access of immigrants, who represented the growth that slow-growth resisted.[44]

What Caused the Housing Shortage?

Michael Dear blamed Los Angeles's shortage of affordable housing on the depletion of land available for settlement as decades of sprawl finally collided with natural limits to habitation given by ocean, mountains, water supply, and deserts.[45] In his words, "sprawl hit the wall." He concluded that by 2000 natural limits had foreclosed the possibility of sprawl as usual in response to Los Angeles's unmet housing needs. True, the natural obstacles did exist, and did obstruct urban sprawl. On the other hand, the fact that Los Angeles had reached a natural limit in 1995 rather than 2020 owed much to the unrelenting pressure of immigration continued over the prior twenty-five years. Were Latino immigrants abruptly withdrawn from Los

Angeles in a counterfactual thought experiment, Los Angeles would not so soon have confronted either the need for affordable housing, nor the shortage of affordable housing, nor the natural barriers that aggravated the housing shortage. In that sense, even if natural barriers constrained the access of current Latino immigrants to housing in the region, they had been reached earlier than otherwise would have occurred because of twenty-five years of sustained, high-volume immigration.

Given high-volume, sustained immigration, natural obstacles to horizontal expansion, housing codes that favor single-family dwellings, and no-growth or slow-growth city councils, a housing market raises prices. Housing prices in Los Angeles were still at the national average in 1973. In 2001, the median price of a single-family home in the county was twice the national average. Rents were correspondingly high. High rents particularly impacted low-income, Latino immigrant households. First, low-income housing was generally less profitable than high-income housing and thus little low-income housing was built.[46] Second, low-income Latino households had to compete with higher-income households in the housing market. Just as the Chicago School taught would be the outcome, Latinos competed by overpaying and overcrowding.[47] Unfortunately for them, the old strategy no longer worked very well. What the Chicago School did not teach was that no-growth city councils can politically defeat immigrants' raw economic power. When they do, housing ceases to trickle down, rent-to-wage ratios rise in the working class, and the housing market signals low-income immigrants to "go elsewhere." To the ingenue, this is the spontaneous response of the unorganized housing market, but political choices created the context within which it occurred.

Los Angeles housing prices were faithful messengers of the housing shortage, not its cause. Immediate producers were the municipal housing codes that legally constrained and restricted the ability of the county's eighty-eight cities to convert existing single-family, low-density housing into multiple-family, high-density housing suitable for working-class immigrants. Except for these, the housing market might have converted Los Angeles County from what it used to be, a low-density, suburban region that depended on the automobile, to what it needed to become, a medium-high-density region of apartment houses and public transit resembling the Borough of Queens in New York City.[48]

The Regional Housing Needs Assessment

Metropolitan governments were under conflicting pressures in regard to housing. On the one hand, operating through the Department of Housing and Urban Development, the federal government employed legal and financial incentives to cajole local governments to open their jurisdictions to affordable housing.[49] California also sought to induce suburban governments to comply with open housing laws intended to improve housing affordability by making more low-cost housing available.[50] The state and federal government legal and financial pressure was intense, but it came from outside the suburban cities. Suburban voters rejected and opposed the federal and state housing goals—when applied to their locality. The intended beneficiaries of affordable housing, Latinos could not vote in these local elections because they were not U.S. citizens or, if citizens, not residents of the cities into which they might have moved were affordable housing available in them.[51] Voter opposition prevented suburban cities from complying with federal and state mandates intended to open them to affordable housing.

Evidence for these conclusions comes from the Regional Housing Needs Assessment, which was compiled by the Southern California Association of Governments (SCAG).[52] An umbrella association of independent local governments, as the name implies, SCAG made available to member governments its research on housing conditions in the region and its suggestions on how to comply with federal and state affordable housing programs.[53] Its public website permitted candid access to the dilemmas of local governments facing the shortage of affordable housing in 2001 and 2002. The Los Angeles housing shortage, it claimed, already severe, would grow even worse unless remedied because, "the SCAG region will grow by more than six million people between 1997 and 2020." Latino immigrants were expected to cause most of this growth. Advising member governments on how to reduce the housing shortage, SCAG noted that "[local] political support for housing is critical to the adoption and implementation of local housing programs. The voices in favor of housing, especially affordable housing, are frequently quiet and few, and finding support for local efforts to address housing needs can be difficult." In other words, SCAG anticipated the resistance and hostility of local voters to the very reforms it proposed that local governments undertake.

SCAG recommended multiple "procedural reforms" that would permit construction of multifamily housing in cities whose housing codes did not then authorize multifamily housing. All of SCAG's suggested reforms required legal changes before they could be introduced. The entire program was thus illegal when SCAG proposed it. Of these proposals, the heavyweight champion was simplification and facilitation of the rezoning process, itself a procedural precondition of extensive rezoning.[54] "Recognizing that administrative delay adds to developmental costs," SCAG wrote, "jurisdictions have reviewed and streamlined their land use and development procedures. The intent is to simplify and coordinate the means of obtaining rezonings, use permits, subdivisions, approval of design and engineering plans, and building permits." Another SCAG suggestion requested local governments to waive "fees for publicly desired projects" that would augment the housing supply. Here SCAG recognized that existing zoning laws prevented member cities from expanding the housing supply. SCAG's remedy was political: change existing laws to authorize higher density housing.

SCAG also recommended that local governments lower existing development standards to permit more housing construction. Noting that "site planning and building design innovations can cut the costs of housing construction," SCAG recommended that member cities modify "their requirements on setbacks, street widths, and building materials, or use performance based standards in place of restrictive building and planning standards." By lowering development standards, member cities could authorize cheaper construction, permitting "more affordable housing to be built." SCAG also recommended changes in site design that allow for higher densities or fewer parking space requirements because these changes "can significantly reduce construction costs," thus lowering housing costs. Every SCAG proposal required legal change. Moreover, were all the desired legal changes implemented, the resulting urban environment would consist of higher-rise, multifamily apartment houses that abut the sidewalks, front onto narrower and more congested streets, rely more on street parking, and use cheaper building materials. This construction would have reduced the quality of the built environment in member cities.

Legal zoning densities posed a problem to construction of low-income housing everywhere in Los Angeles County. Required to build more low-income housing in the region, SCAG advised member cities to raise "general plan and zoning densities to allow for higher residential development. This is the *most basic technique* [italics added] for increasing the supply of housing." Lest there be any misunderstanding, SCAG added that the goal of higher density zoning was "to increase the amount of housing that can be built on any given site." The benefit of this legal change would be to increase "the overall potential supply of housing" in member cities.[55] This SCAG proposal amounted to packing more people into higher density housing.

If done, the benefit would accrue to those who did not already enjoy affordable housing, mostly immigrant Latinos, rather than to those who already lived in the existing homes, mostly native whites. To sweeten the pie for area governments, who faced this contradiction, SCAG pointed out that local cities that rezoned could obtain a "density bonus" above what was normally permitted on a site when they provided "some below market rate housing units." The bonus was usually a percentage of the density allowable under existing zoning regulations. "California law required local governments to grant 25 percent density bonus . . . to a developer in exchange for an agreement that the extra units be affordable."[56] Moreover, cities can grant bonuses, "in excess of those called for by state law to encourage affordable housing or other residential development to meet a community's special housing needs." These bonuses provided member city councils with incentives for complying with locally uncongenial state directives.

Vacant land could be made available for affordable housing, SCAG advised member cities. Much vacant land already had been "set aside for commercial, office, and industrial use" rather than for residential use. If existing set-asides could be voided, a regrettable legal obstacle, reserved land would become available for affordable housing. Unfortunately, SCAG observed, "neighbors sometimes resist nearby and infill development."[57] Filling vacant land with affordable housing for nonresidents contradicted the perceived self-interest of suburban homeowners.

Mixed-use development was another strategy SCAG recommended. Mixed-use development combines residential uses with one or more non-residential uses such as office, retail, public, entertainment, or even manufacturing. Mixed uses were illegal in most member cities so legal changes would be necessary to permit the remedy. Unfortunately, SCAG acknowledged, it was not easy to obtain political support for mixed-use development in member cities. "Mixing uses often requires changes to the zoning ordinance or planned unit development regulations."

Infill development occurs on sites that have been bypassed by previous development. SCAG suggested that member governments make such land available for low-income housing developments. Unfortunately, it acknowledged, infill proposals were politically unpopular. "Proposed infill development can cause controversy in the neighborhood due to the threatened loss of local open space, change in community appearance, and increased traffic that may result." Under the circumstances, SCAG concluded, local governments could not expect successful outcomes for infill proposals unless they "anticipate, plan for, and resolve conflicts between builders and local interest groups."

Self-help housing means structures that people construct for themselves. In Mexico, cities are ringed by squalid shantytowns whose inhabitants constructed their own shelter from cast-off materials. The shanty dwellers squat illegally on vacant land, but Mexican cities tolerate their slums. Although shantytowns were illegal in Los Angeles County, SCAG did recommend that member cities permit potential home owners to contribute their own labor "to the construction or renovation" of their home, thus lowering the cost of housing expansion. Like the other SCAG plans, this one required legal changes in member cities where electricians, plumbers, carpenters, and the like must be certified and paid area-standard wages. SCAG asked member cities to relax "city design standards" in the interest of promoting self-help housing in order to make affordable housing available to nonresidents.

Many suburban cities in Los Angeles County had excluded factory-built homes by law for social as well as aesthetic reasons. In the public vernacular, the inhabitants of mobile home parks are called "trailer trash."

Also in the public vernacular, trailer trash are crude, violent, ignorant, noisy, and promiscuous. Mobile home parks are thought to lower the public tone and aesthetic charm of neighborhoods that permit them. Avoiding this inflammatory issue, SCAG declared that factory-built housing was "the least expensive to construct." Cheapness was its sovereign virtue. A more favorable public attitude toward factory-built housing would reduce the average cost of housing in member cities. Therefore, to facilitate factory-home production within members' jurisdictions, SCAG advised member governments to meet, combat, and challenge "citizen resistance due to negative, often inaccurate perceptions of manufactured housing's appearance." Additionally, manufactured housing can be rendered more attractive if local government revised their "design review process to encourage compatible design" with existing site-built homes. Cities like Santa Ana, with large Latino populations, already permitted multiple, large trailer parks.

Shared living provided SCAG another illegal way to lower housing costs. "Shared living has various names: communal living, home sharing, and group living. It occurs when people reside together for social contract, mutual support, and assistance, [or] to reduce housing expenses." For instance, four families can occupy a four-bedroom house, one family to a bedroom, thus permitting each to pay only one-quarter of the astronomical rent. Alternatively, one immigrant family can rent rooms to lodgers, providing them with food and laundry service as well as with shelter. Both cost-reduction practices are, in fact, quite common among Latinos in Los Angeles.[58] The idea is not new. Boarding houses and furnished rooms were essential institutions of the European migration to the United States a century ago.[59] At that time, both were legal even though "the lodger evil" was sanctimoniously condemned. Anyone could open a boarding house. Many women did. However, shared living arrangements now violate the housing code in most Los Angeles suburbs, whose founders wished to put boarding houses and furnished-room living forever behind them and their posterity. Accordingly, SCAG advised local governments to promote shared living wherever possible to relieve the housing shortage while addressing "the misconceptions or lack of knowledge" that cause neighbors to reject shared living.

"A second unit is an additional self-contained living unit, either attached to or detached from the primary residential unit on a single lot." Second units have kitchen space, dining areas, sleeping rooms, and toilets. California law permits second units, but it establishes minimum standards for them. For example, a second unit must have a flushing toilet and electric wiring that meets building code requirements. Unable to ban second units, many Los Angeles area cities regulated the number of second units allowable. Additionally, municipalities regulated the location, size, parking requirements, and architectural compatibility of second units. These regulations made second units expensive to build. SCAG conceded that encouraging second units was not a popular policy in member cities. "Opposition to [second] units generally comes from neighborhood concern over parking and traffic impacts." To promote second unit construction, and therewith the production of additional housing, SCAG advised member government to "legalize existing second units and bring them up to construction codes." As matters stood, thousands of immigrant Latinos lived in unconverted garages, illegal second units, because local governments did not wish to evict them, but neither could they declare that unconverted garages were lawful second units.[60]

In the 1920s, when candor was in style, Harvey Zorbaugh referred to single-room occupancy hotels as "flop houses."[61] Harkening back, SCAG acknowledged that single room occupancy hotels (SROs) "are one of the most traditional forms of affordable private housing for single and elderly low-income people and for new arrivals to an area." Rooms in SRO hotels are tiny. They contain a sink, a closet, a shared toilet, and a shared kitchen. With the enthusiastic approval of citizens, cities in Los Angeles County had earlier excluded SRO hotels on the grounds that they attracted vagrants, criminals, and addicts, and lowered residential quality in the vicinity. These exclusionary laws thereafter inhibited the construction of SRO hotels, a venerable housing type for which strong market demand existed in the 1990s. According to SCAG, member cities should amend "zoning and building codes" that excluded SRO hotels to make affordable housing more available for the lowest income people.

The Challenge of Nimbyism

Finally, SCAG declared NIMBYism to be the "major obstacle hindering the provision of affordable housing" in Los Angeles County. Nimbyism (Not In My Back Yard) must be addressed and anticipated everywhere, SCAG advised its members. Nimbies are homeowners agnostic about how or whether Los Angeles should build affordable housing.[62] Affordable housing is not their problem. Their problem is to maintain the undiminished quality of their neighborhood and their customary life style, and to support their property values.[63] Founder of Homeowners of Encino, Gerald A. Silver is regarded as the founder of Los Angeles nimbyism. A contemporary Horatius at the bridge, Silver singlehandedly turned back a freeway extension that threatened his neighborhood, then went on to institutionalize his movement. "Our goal is to preserve the single-family habitability and lifestyle of Encino," Silver says of his organization's ideology.[64]

Nimbyism was a flourishing and spontaneous, right-wing social movement in Los Angeles County throughout the 1990s.[65] Nimbies did not just oppose Latinos in their neighborhoods; they also opposed prisons, drug offender halfway houses, airport and highway expansions, HIV shelters, homeless shelters, registered sex offenders, corner stores, and factories as well as affordable housing for the middle class.[66] When they opposed affordable housing, nimbies unavoidably also opposed Latino housing. Nimbyism was powerful; nimby websites abounded.[67] In a 2004 editorial headlined "Going Past 'No' on Housing," the *Los Angeles Times* blamed the region's housing shortage on "a backlash of NIMBYism."[68] Wherever city councils proposed to waive, modify, or discard legal impediments to low-cost housing, possibly in response to SCAG recommendations, nimby movements challenged them.[69] Nimbyism used residents' voting rights to resist metropolitan, state, and federal housing policies disadvantageous to their neighborhood.[70] As local voters, nimbies had the power to punish offending city council members at the ballot box. This power they exercised to reduce the compliance their city showed to federal and state directives for affordable housing construction. Were it not for nimbies, local ordinances that obstructed affordable housing could have been readily overturned. Nimbyism was the key political weapon that defended the housing status quo in Los Angeles from changes that would benefit low-income immigrants.[71]

Court Cases

For the benefit of member cities' legal departments, SCAG listed fifteen recent decisions in which courts ruled on affordable housing or group housing issues, the latter chiefly involving disabled persons. Ten of these favored and five opposed the expansion of affordable housing or group home facilities in local cities around the United States. The case law was intended to empower member cities' legal departments when they litigated affordable housing battles. In a representative Los Angeles case, San Pedro Hotel Co., Inc. vs. City of Los Angeles, which SCAG cited, the court ruled that city council members enjoyed absolute personal immunity from federal or state prosecution when they voted against opening local housing to the disabled. This decision was a victory for nimbyism. SCAG also provided representative analyses for housing discrimination cases involving small, medium, and large cities, explaining what actions jurisdictions can undertake to "eliminate impediments." Measures suggested included the introduction of local legislation declaring it illegal to refuse to rent based on a household's source of income (welfare checks the target), the enactment of local ordinances requiring that large developers "set aside" a proportion of affordable units in order to obtain approval from the municipality, and holding "neighborhood forums" to convince "local white residents" they had nothing to fear from affordable housing.

Home Owners Versus Immigrants

The archives of SCAG revealed a regional housing conflict that pitted the perceived self-interest of vested homeowners against those of low-wage immigrants as well as their housing sector allies, the disabled, blacks, the elderly, and the poor of all races. Local governments were trapped between antagonistic pressures. On the one hand, they came under pressure from the federal government, the state government, and SCAG to expand affordable housing in their jurisdictions. On the other hand, city council members faced dismissal from office if they complied. Here emerges a concealed conflict of housing interest between low-income immigrants and homeowning natives. True, this conflict did not involve open hostilities, and the conflict brought certain native-born groups (builders, disabled, elderly, blacks, poor whites) into the lists on the side of immigrants so it was not a strictly immigrants vs. nonimmigrants issue. The public discourse about housing shortage in southern California did not contain antiimmigrant much less anti-Latino themes. In fact, a Latino candidate, Antonio Villaraigosa, only by a slight margin failed to win the mayoralty of Los Angeles in the election of 2001, and did win it in 2005.[72] Nonetheless, native-born homeowners perceived their housing and community selfinterest as antagonistic to those of low-income immigrants. Within Los Angeles County, each metropolitan city's reform plans represented a separate jurisdiction in which a nimby movement opposed housing reform. Indeed, by the time Latino renters actually established themselves in a city, their allies had already won the political fight that authorized the low-income housing in which they lived. The cavalry arrived after the battle was won. For this reason, the parties to the political conflict over housing were not even aware that they were in political conflict.

The well-being of Latino immigrants required that existing housing codes be reformed to permit low-cost multifamily housing in mixed-use tracts served by abundant public transit. Viewing the situation, Dowell Myers declared that the housing impasse required "a redefinition of what constitutes the desired middle-class lifestyle" in California to accommodate the immigrants.[73] If so, accommodation required a revolution in housing. Suburban homeowners had no interest in such a revolution. Their political platform reflected their perceived economic and social self-interest, their satisfaction with the housing status quo, and only then their ethno-racial chauvinism. Moreover, contrary to the sanctimonious official rhetoric, homeowners did not misunderstand their self-interest. In all candor, what was the economic or social advantage to existing homeowners of authorizing self-built housing, low-cost apartment houses, SRO hotels, or boarding houses in their neighborhoods? From their point of view, it was always better that these structures be permitted, if they must be permitted, in someone else's city. Within their self-interested frame of reference, homeowners had a stake in maintenance of residential quality and high housing prices in their city, and they knew it. Deflecting immigration to other regions was not their intention, but it was a consequence of their zealous nimbyism. To the extent that the region's activist homeowners blocked or retarded

Photograph 1 Swap Meet

Source: Photograph by Marissa Manalo.
Note: This "swap meet" happens right on a busy downtown street. Heaps of clothing, appliances, tools, shoes, and other consumer goods line the sidewalk. Low-income consumers dig through in search of bargains.

Photograph 2 Street Vendor

Source: Photograph by Rachel Sarabia.
Note: This vendor sells raspados (Mexican snow cones) on a residential sidewalk in the San Fernando Valley. His income is unstable because raspados sell better when the weather is hot. Because he came from Mexico sin papeles, he cannot get a real job. He sells raspados in order to feed his wife and his four children. Unfortunately, he sighs, vending requires standing many hours in the heat.

Photograph 3   Suburban Eyesore

Source: Photograph by Rachel Sarabia.
Note: Overcrowded homes cause overcrowded driveways. This single-family home in the San Fernando Valley sports five automobiles on a driveway intended for two.

Photograph 4   Car on Set-Back

Source: Photograph by Mayra Marentes and Maria Benitez.
Note: This house is in a predominantly Mexican-immigrant city near the Los Angeles International Airport. This sedan is parked on the set-back in front of the home rather than in the garage.

Photograph 5   Day Laborers

Source: Photograph by Mayra Marentes and Maria Benitez.
Note: These journaleros wait for employers on a corner. The journaleros
are paid in cash. When hired, they earn $80 to $100 for an eight-hour
day. However, on some days they find no work. Their duties can
include plumbing, painting, construction, welding, carpentry, and even
personal tasks. Homosexual employers solicit sex acts from them. These
journaleros claim to have learned trades in Mexico, but, since they are
illegally in the United States, they cannot hold regular jobs.

Photograph 6   Silvestre Cristobal

Source: Photograph courtesy of Los Angeles
Alliance for a New Economy (Moore et al.
2000, 5).
Note: "Most sewing machine workers live
together. We either share an apartment or a
house. That is the only way that we can
make ends meet. We have to help each
other out. For instance, I am currently living with another family. It's the only way I
can provide for my family."
—Silvestre Cristobal, Sewing Machine
Operator, Garment District

Photograph 7   Nimby Handbill

DO YOU WANT HIGH-DENSITY AFFORDABLE HOUSING IN NORTH CLAREMONT?

- 60 rental apartments on 1.9 acres to be built on Baseline Road, East of Towne Avenue between the electrical station and the reservoir.
- Within the Condit Elementary School zone
- The City's General Plan calls for professional buildings for this area.
- The City's General Plan calls for affordable high density housing in South Claremont next to the railroad tracks.
- The Baseline parcel is currently zoned for single family homes.
- The rezoning which is required would be "Spot Zoning" which is illegal in California.
- One of the sites also being considered is on the corner of Monte Vista and Baseline.

WHAT CAN WE EXPECT?

- Be prepared for a major influx of students.
- The proposed high-density apartment complex will set the precedent for additional high-density apartments that could exceed 300 units.
- Traditionally, high-density housing taxes police and fire services.
- While Claremont's schools and families are dedicated to maintaining 20-1 ratios in the primary grades, they will not be able to sustain such goals in light of a substantial increase in students.
- Even if you do not live near the proposed housing, it will affect all of our community.

WHAT CAN WE DO?

- Let your City Council members and officials know you oppose "High-Density Housing" in North Claremont and will hold them accountable.
- Attend the City Council meetings on Sept 14th & 28th at 6:30 p.m. in the City Council Chamber Hall located on 2nd Street to voice your concerns.
- Sept 22nd the Southern California Housing Development Corp will hold a community meeting to inform residents of their plans to develop this area at the Sunrise Assisted Living of Claremont, corner of Baseline and Towne Avenue. Parking is extremely limited. If you can not able to attend, please contact Alfredo of SCHDC at (818) 612-4882.

Brian Desatnik, Redevelopment & Housing Project Manager, at 399-5341.
City Council Office at 399-5444
Mayor Sandy Baldonado 399-5441
Council members E-mail: pheld@ci.claremont.ca.us
Jmchenry@ci.claremont.ca.us
lmiller@ci.claremont.ca.us
Pyao@ci.claermont.ca.us
Sbaldonado@ci.claremont.ca.us

For further information please visit our website at cc4claremont.tripod.com, The Concerned Citizens for Claremont.

Source: Leaflet left on doors by The Concerned Citizens for Claremont (2004).
Note: This nimby handbill was publicly distributed door-to-door in 2004. This handbill urges residents to defeat a proposed affordable housing plan in North Claremont. The proposal authorized multi-family housing intended for police, school teachers, and college students. This affordable housing was not for working-class Latinos, but Claremont nimbys rejected it anyway. Moral: Southern California nimbyism was not directed only at Latinos.

La ley dice que...

Su empleador debe capacitarlo en la seguridad:

■ Cuando el *Programa de Prevención de Lesiones y Enfermedades* se establezca.

■ Cuando comience un nuevo trabajo.

■ Cada vez que se le asigne una nueva tarea.

■ Para cada nuevo proceso, procedimiento, substancia o equipo que cree nuevos peligros.

Su empleador también debe:

■ Comunicarse con usted de manera que usted lo entienda.

■ Alentarlo a informar sobre condiciones poco seguras sin temer recibir represalias.

■ Corregir condiciones o prácticas de trabajo inseguras o insalubres lo antes posible.

■ Cerciorarse que usted cumpla con las prácticas de trabajo seguras.

Source: California Occupational Safety and Health Administration, Publication S1001-91S.
Note: Cal-OSHA pamphlet explains their legal rights to Spanish-speaking workers.

¿Le está causando molestias su trabajo?

► **Molestia o dolor, adormecimiento u hormigueo en los hombros, cuello, espalda y manos** afecta a muchas operadoras de máquinas de coser. Estos síntomas pueden estar relacionados con su trabajo.

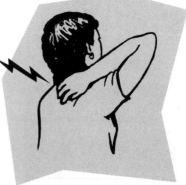

► **Los síntomas pueden empezar gradualmente.** Mucha gente trata de no prestarles atención al principio. Pero si hace esto, los síntomas pueden empeorar y ser más difíciles de tratar. Si tiene síntomas dígaselo a su empleador y obtenga atención médica inmediatamente.

► **Estos síntomas pueden indicar una lesión seria** que puede interferir con su trabajo y sus actividades personales. Hasta pueden conducir a una incapacidad permanente.

Source: California Department of Health Services, Occupational Health Branch, 2001. Available at: www.dhs.ca.gov/ohb.
Note: "Is your work causing pain?" In a pamphlet, the California Department of Health Services, Occupational Health Branch introduced sewing machine workers to possible health injuries from their work, and recommended ways to reduce the risk.

Table 8.2   Housing Conditions and Changes in Los Angeles

				Index		
City	1980	1990	2000	1990/80	2000/90	2000/80
Population (000)	2,966	3,485	3,695	117	106	125
Housing units (000)	1,189	1,300	1,338	109	103	113
Affordability						
Percentage overpaying	28.7	35.0	35.9	122	103	125
Percentage overcrowded	13.0	22.3	25.6	172	115	197
Percentage owner-occupied	40.3	39.4	38.6	98	98	96

Source: O'Hara (2002, figure 1).
Note: Overcrowded is defined as more than 1.0 persons per room (bathrooms, foyers and porches excluded). Includes owners and renters. Overpaying is defined as more than 35 percent of gross household income spent for rent and utilities or homeowner expenses (mortgage, taxes, and utilities). Based on owners and renters.

affordable housing, they derailed the migration networks that had already brought millions of Latinos to southern California and, if able to find affordable housing for them, would have brought another million. With the exception of San Francisco and New York, all other major cities of the United States offered more affordable housing than Los Angeles did in 1990. Lower housing costs elsewhere offered a powerful incentive for immigrants to leave Los Angeles County, and the internal migration of immigrant Latinos from Los Angeles to secondary settlements reflected the pressure of housing costs as well as of low wages.[74]

Deflection Reduced Housing Costs

The joint effects of political nimbyism and house market dynamics are evident in housing statistics gathered by the Southern California Association of Non-Profit Housing. These statistics show that Los Angeles housing costs and overcrowding grew most rapidly and achieved the most dramatic superiority in the 1980s.[75] In the 1990s, housing cost increases in Los Angeles actually abated while they rose elsewhere. Table 8.2 summarizes housing conditions in the city of Los Angeles between 1980 and 2000. Population growth was most rapid in the 1980s, then tapered off in the 1990s as both Latinos and working-class whites quit the region. In the 1990s, Latinos began to explore nontraditional destinations. Corresponding to this sequence, the percentage of overcrowded households doubled in the 1980s, then declined in the 1990s so that Los Angeles Latinos were better housed in 2000 than they had been in 1990. Similarly, the percentage of overpaying households increased 22 percent in the 1980s, then dropped in the 1990s. Housing conditions in Los Angeles improved after people left

Table 8.3   **Median House Value**

	Dollar Cost (000)			Index		
	1980	1990	2000	1990/80	2000/90	2000/80
Los Angeles, city	96	245	223	255	91	232
California	85	196	212	230	108	249
United States	47	79	120	168	152	255
Los Angeles as percentage of United States	204	310	186	152	60	91

Source: O'Hara (2002, figure 3).
Note: Index = later/earlier × 100.

the region. This lagged improvement suggests that emigration from the region expanded affordable housing.

Table 8.3 displays median house values in Los Angeles compared to California and to the rest of the United States for the period 1980 to 2000. In 1970, homes in Los Angeles sold for prices comparable to those elsewhere in the United States. Thirty years later, Los Angeles prices were twice the national average. The biggest difference was in 1990, when the average Los Angeles house was three times more expensive. A decade later, though still very high by national standards, Los Angeles house prices had come down. Indeed, in the 1990s, home prices in Los Angeles grew only 60 percent as fast as those elsewhere in the country and were actually receding toward the national mean. Los Angeles housing was becoming more affordable—thanks to the egress of population from the region.

Los Angeles rents moved in tandem with home prices between 1980 and 2000. This close relationship matters because Latino immigrants were chiefly renters, not homeowners. Table 8.4 shows median national and Los Angeles contract rents for the period 1980 to 2000. In 2000, median monthly rents in Los Angeles were $612 a month, 18 percent higher than the national figure. However, in 1990, a decade earlier, that 18 percent had been 45 percent. In terms of index values, rents were about 10 percent higher at their peak than were home values. Rents actually rose less rapidly in Los Angeles in the 1990s than they did elsewhere in the United States. Like home prices, rents were declining toward national averages in Los Angeles during the 1990s.

These housing statistics suggest that homeowner nimbyism, antislum crusades, slow-growth political power, natural obstacles to sprawl, and sky-high housing prices combined to deflect Latino migration away from Los Angeles in the 1990s. Housing conditions improved in Los Angeles thanks in part to the departure of whites, who had their own reasons for departing, but also because immigrants were deflected. Most deflected

Table 8.4   **Median Contract Rent**

	Monthly Dollar Cost			Index		
	1980	1990	2000	1990/80	2000/90	2000/80
Los Angeles, city	229	544	612	238	113	267
California	252	561	677	223	121	269
United States	198	374	519	189	139	262
Los Angeles as percentage of United States	116	145	118	126	81	102

Source: O'Hara (2002, figure 3).
Note: Index = later/earlier × 100.

immigrants never came to Los Angeles because, while still abroad, they already knew the region was unaffordable.[76] The rough sequence of changes is essential: In the 1980s, housing conditions worsened, and then, in the 1990s, improved. In the 1980s, experiencing network-driven migration, Los Angeles housing prices rose sharply. High and rising housing prices compelled low-wage Latino immigrants to overpay and to live in overcrowded and substandard housing. In the 1990s, confronting sky-high housing costs, homeowner nimbyism, and antislum crusades in Los Angeles, the migration network partially redirected itself away from Los Angeles and toward nontraditional destinations such as North Carolina and Louisiana. As the influx of new migrants slowed, pressure on Los Angeles housing relaxed, prices fell, overcrowding and overpayment declined, and slums ceased to grow.

This argument has overlooked the textbook possibility of augmented housing supply in response to high housing prices. Possibly in the 1980s, high housing costs encouraged new building in the 1990s, thus augmenting the supply of housing, and tending to reduce housing costs. In this case, augmented supply of new housing (not population egress) would account for the relative improvement of Los Angeles housing conditions in the 1990s. However, that textbook scenario did not, in fact, materialize; indeed, the rate of housing construction declined in the 1990s, and the share of multifamily housing construction in total housing construction declined an additional 50 percent as well.[77] For these reasons, Myers and Park called the 1990s, "the great housing collapse in California."[78] That said, there is some tiny merit after all to the textbook's argument because the housing supply did grow a little. Table 8.2 shows that the number of housing units in the city of Los Angeles expanded 13 percent between 1980 and 2000. This was inadequate expansion, but it was expansion. Without the tiny supply enhancement, housing conditions would have been even worse in 2000.

Nonetheless, although the increased housing supply moderated housing costs in the 1990s, augmentation was so meager that it resembled market failure.

Political constrictions caused that market failure. Political constrictions on the supply of affordable housing were both the intent and the predictable consequence of homeowner nimbyism, slow-growth or no-growth movements, and antislum crusades. Suburban homeowners rejected any expansion of housing supply that compromised quality of life in their neighborhoods. Because homeowners were active in most rather than just a few suburban cities, their political impact was almost ubiquitous.[79] Moreover, during the 1990s antislum crusades, discussed in chapter 3, tended also to inhibit the market's ability to provide immigrant Latinos with unconverted garages, self-built shacks, derelict tenements, boarding houses, cheap hotels, and overcrowded slums in which to live inexpensively. Suburban cities rejected any expansion of the affordable housing supply that required these remedies. Both responses prevented the region's housing supply and structure from changing to accommodate the new migrants. Los Angeles deflected more Latinos politically than would have been priced out of a really free housing market complete with the vast, teeming slums that such markets produce. At that point, Los Angeles simultaneously chose a future retentive of its past, and established an immigrant policy for the entire country.

Toward a Zero-Access Housing Supply

Los Angeles was not the only metropolitan region in which municipal regulations raised housing costs. On the contrary, extensive research has shown that comparable regulations raised housing costs in most large American cities—except where regulations were not enforced.[80] As ever, enforcement was the key. Laws meant little without enforcement. Precisely because Los Angeles's regulations occur elsewhere as well, the fanciful opportunity is given to project the deflection process as it worked in Los Angeles onto other reception cites. One then envisions a United States in which all reception cities have housing codes that offer tomorrow's immigrants little or no affordable housing. This hypothetical situation would shut down demand-driven migration from Mexico and Central America for simple lack of housing. Of course, such a scenario extrapolates the Los Angeles case recklessly, oblivious to national and state legislation that could change in the interim. Nonetheless, the extrapolation exposes the anti-immigrant effect of local nimby movements, slow-growth city councils, and antislum crusades all of which, though very different in their political provenance, resulted in pricing many low-income immigrants out of the housing market in Los Angeles, and presumably will do so in other reception cities in the future.

Deflection is not exclusion, but it encourages and promotes exclusion. Los Angeles did not exclude Latinos. It deflected some Latinos, reducing the growth of its immigrant Latino population, but did not stop that growth. Thousands of upwardly mobile Latinos moved into Los Angeles suburbs in the 1990s and paid all the requisite bills when they did so. Nonetheless, by implication, the deflection of some poor Latinos from some suburbs explains how social exclusion resulted from immigrant influx. By social exclusion I mean the involuntary tendency of ethnic minorities to inhabit homogeneous ethnic neighborhoods. American cities explicitly compete to attract the wealthy, and implicitly compete to exclude the poor.[81] The homeless are the most universally rejected.[82] They are tolerated only on skid row, where suburban police surreptitiously dump them.[83] Within metropolitan Los Angeles, poor immigrants clustered in those suburban cities that authorized affordable housing. In immigrant-friendly suburban cities like El Monte, Santa Ana, and Montebello, either housing codes authorized low-cost, multifamily housing (including mobile home parks, which poor immigrants required) or the exclusionary codes were unenforced.[84] Immigration transformed these poverty-tolerant cities into immigrant enclaves. However, suburban cities whose housing and building codes excluded affordable, multifamily housing, and that enforced their existing building and housing code, legally deflected poor immigrants.[85] Social exclusion then characterized residential neighborhoods in the entire metropolitan region because immigrants were deflected from most suburban cities and crowded into only those that ignored housing codes, permitted prefabricated housing, and tolerated overcrowding and slums.

But that is not the end of the local impact on the nation's immigration experience. When first-reception cities restrict immigrant housing insertion, as many of those around Los Angeles did, they deflect migration to second-reception cities. Appendix figure A.1 shows that, despite two decades of deflection, residential overcrowding in 2000 was still most serious in the traditional states of immigrant reception. For this reason, deflection was anti-immigrant in the cities and regions that deflect, but it was not necessarily anti-immigrant in the broader national space. Ultimately, it is true, if deflection continues until every reception city in the country has deflected, a purely hypothetical extrapolation, then the last local deflection would also deflect the entire migration to another country. At that defining moment, the deflecting regions and cities would have managed the demand-driven migration from start to finish without any policy assistance from the national government. Of course, such a hypothetical denouement will never materialize. But the hypothetical is not the point. The point is that to the extent that Los Angeles and other first-reception cities have already deflected immigration, they have already made national immigrant policy. This result is real, and here, now. It is not hypothetical.

═══ Chapter 9 ═══

Racism or Poverty Intolerance?

XPLAINING THE deflection of Latino immigration from Los Angeles, and (by inference) from other traditional destinations, on the basis of intolerance to poverty, these chapters have ignored racism and ethno-racial prejudice. Yet these two factors might plausibly explain why California, Los Angeles, and various suburban municipalities enforced housing, industrial, and occupational laws that discouraged Latino influx and settlement. Los Angeles cities might have strengthened enforcement of existing housing, industrial, and occupational laws on the basis of underlying, if unspoken, racism or cultural antipathy to Mexican and Central American immigrants. After all, Latino authors do complain of racism and anti-Latino bias in California.[1] Additionally, no one can deny the existence of racist attitudes and ethno-chauvinism in Los Angeles or in California. The Golden State rejected Chinese immigrants in the nineteenth century for reasons that included racism and perhaps served Latino immigrants the same way a century later.

Why Racism Cannot Explain Latino Dispersal

However, the plausible does not always survive close examination. When the topic of racism is fully explored, compelling reasons emerge why racism cannot replace poverty intolerance as an explanation of Latino deflection from Los Angeles, from California, and even from other traditional reception states. First, consider southern California's history. Latinos were not the first immigrants deflected. Six decades earlier, southern California had rejected some four hundred thousand English-speaking, native-born white Protestants. During the Great Depression of the 1930s, dust bowl internal migrants fleeing rural poverty ("Okies and Arkies") migrated to southern California. Fearing additional expenses for welfare relief and public education, Los Angeles "declared war" on "the indigent influx."[2] Los Angeles's chief of police dispatched 150 officers to California's southeastern border with orders to form a "bum blockade" against the Okies. Los Angeles police met the Okies' truck caravans at the San Bernardino County border, illegally turning them away.[3] "Don't migrate; just keep on moving," the sheriffs said. "How can I keep on movin' unless I migrate too?" the Okies sang back.[4] Enshrined in John Steinbeck's *Grapes of Wrath*, this reception reminds us that, when they are also poor, native-born, white Protestants have also been unwelcome in southern California. Los Angeles's solution in 1936 was to deflect the unwanted migrants elsewhere. Then as now, of course, deflection was not wholly successful. Some Okies settled in California despite the bum blockade. In 1939, the Federal Writer's Project reported that for these in-migrant Okies, "the workmen's compensation law failed to operate, the State's minimum wage law . . . was ignored, and medical aid was denied."[5]

Second, racism and ethno-religious prejudice were simply not part of the public debate over immigration in southern California during the last three decades of the twentieth century.[6] Squalor was.[7] "Is your community becoming a Third World city?" asked the Save Our State website, home to Los Angeles's most aggressive anti-immigrant movement.[8] This much is a matter of public record. The California public also perceived Latino immigrants as poor, but family loving and hard working.[9] This is a favorable public image, not a hostile one. The public dialogue in southern California did not include racist or xenophobic language. Hence, the claim that racism drove the regional deflection has no visible basis in the public record. Even Victor Hanson's *Mexifornia*, an anti-immigrant diatribe, boasts of the author's numerous Mexican kinsmen.[10] Only an ingenue would suppose that racism and ethno-religious prejudice did not exist in southern California just because certain words were not spoken in public. But anti-immigrant is not the same as anti-Latino, the issue at hand here. Anti-illegal immigrant is not the same as anti-immigrant. Open anti-illegal immigrant opinions surfaced in the 1994 plebiscite on Proposition 187, and in the Arnold Schwarzenegger gubernatorial campaign of 2003. At that time, candidate Schwarzenegger and the California Republican Assembly openly opposed driver's licenses for illegal immigrants. "Stop illegal aliens" was the official CRA slogan.[11] Manifestly anti-illegal immigrant, this political slogan was not manifestly anti-immigrant, much less anti-Latino. If those who opposed illegal immigration in California had also invoked anti-Latino appeals or racist vocabulary, as they did in the nineteenth century, then it would be easier to conclude that their opposition to illegal immigration stemmed from racism.

Third, the geography of racist and neo-Nazi websites offers additional disconfirmatory evidence regarding the putative role of racism in the deflection of Latino population from Los Angeles, California, and other traditional settlements. In 2004, the Southern Poverty Law Center published its *Intelligence Report*, a comprehensive directory of racist and neo-Nazi websites in the United States as of 2001.[12] The number of websites relative to a state's population gives a rough measure of the intensity of organized racism in each state. In descending order, those with the most Klan, skinhead, and neo-Nazi websites were Georgia, South Carolina, North Carolina, and Alabama. When states' hate websites were normed against state population, California had 51 percent, the six traditional immigration states had 69 percent, and the nineteen new settlement states had 148 percent. Unsurprisingly, U.S. racist websites were located disproportionately in the South. The nineteen states of new Latino settlement were wildly overrepresented in racist websites, whereas California and the traditional immigrant settlement states were underrepresented. Latinos who relocated to new settlement states moved from areas of less organized racism to areas of more organized racism. A Latino who migrated to Georgia to escape California's racism jumped from the frying pan into the fire. Moreover, Latinos knew that southern racism was worse than California's. Addressing the membership, the president of the Mexican American Legal Defense and Education Foundation, Antonia Hernandez, called their attention to Ku Klux Klan rallies in Georgia and North Carolina that targeted Latino immigrants.[13] This objection cannot evade the existence of anti-Latino racism in California among the 60 percent who are not themselves Latino, but it does question the likelihood that Latinos would leave the Golden State for Georgia or North Carolina because of it.

Regional Similarities in Anti-Immigrant Sentiment

The decisive question is not whether Los Angeles or California were immigrant friendly. They were not. The question is rather whether they were less so than other regions of the country, especially the new settlement states that attracted Latino settlement in the 1990s. Although the American public's attitude toward immigration changes with the wording of the question pollsters ask, a symptom of volatile public opinion, two decades of polling show that Americans generally have wanted immigration reduced since the 1980s.[14] However, there has been no systematic variation among regions in this attitude. The supreme champion of explanations based on racism, Joe Feagin, acknowledges that the level of anti-immigrant opinion has been equally high in all regions of the United States.[15] Collected by the Pew Hispanic Trust, which is not anti-Latino, polling data show that this equality of the regions prevailed during the 1990s when Latinos in California and other traditional reception states were accelerating their dispersal to new settlement states. Asked in 1992, 1997, and 1999 whether immigration should be restricted, over 70 percent of respondents thought it should be, but, as figure 9.1 shows, there was little interregional variation in opinion. If anti-immigrant opinions were driving the Latino dispersal,

Figure 9.1   "Immigration Should Be Restricted," by Destination

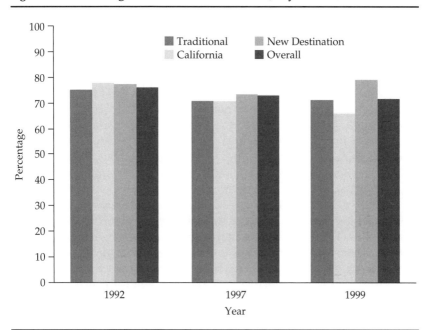

Source: Author's compilations from unpublished data provided by the Pew Hispanic Research Center, with permission.
Note: Data for 1999 do not include Delaware, a new destination state. Also 1999 California estimate is based on a sample size of less than 100, thus highly unreliable.

we would expect higher levels of such opinion in California and other traditional settlement states than in the new settlement states. But the polling data disclose no such variation.

Half the Latinos Are Whites

Only half of Latino immigrants declared themselves non-white in the 2000 Census. If poverty intolerance were a product of disguised racism, then Los Angeles suburbs should have enforced housing codes and antisweatshop laws against non-white Latinos and tolerated the poverty and conditions of white Latinos. Yet none of that happened. Therefore, it does not appear that the color of immigrants influenced the enforcement of industrial and housing codes in Los Angeles. White Latinos and brown Latinos received the same treatment.

As chapter 4 showed, Asian immigrants owned many garment industry sweatshops. In them, Asian employers hired Asian and Latina seamstresses at substandard wages in unsafe working conditions and without medical insurance. To that extent, antisweatshop campaigns threatened

Asian business owners as well as Latino employees. Worse, the creation of low-wage immigrant economies had provided an essential economic buffer for the entire network-driven Latino immigration. Therefore, anti-sweatshop agitation legitimately targeted Asian immigrant employers whose sweatshops enabled more Latinos to live in southern California than would otherwise have been possible. Rich immigrants exploiting poor immigrants make an easy target, but the public dialogue over sweatshops never addressed the ethnicity or nativity of sweatshop employers, who were roundly and repeatedly condemned for their misdeeds, but never for their race or nativity. If racism lay behind the enforcement campaigns, enforcers should have attacked the Asian employers, but none did.

What would it mean to show racial preference to poor white immigrants over poor brown immigrants? Possibly, if confronted with white immigrants as poor as the Latinos, southern California would have tolerated the whites' poverty longer than it did the Latinos'.[16] The longer toleration would then constitute the racial preference the whites received. This is at best a paradoxical advantage. Protracted tolerance for poverty means that poor whites would then have been allowed to work in sweatshops and live in slums longer than poor Latinos, who, because of their color, were not allowed to work or live so long in degraded conditions. Treating co-ethnics worse than others is not what we normally mean by racism, but relying on race to explain dispersal compels this ironic and paradoxical conclusion.

Latino organizations joined interethnic coalitions against slums and sweatshops, taking pride in their success. However, by strengthening enforcement of industrial and housing laws, these campaigns encouraged immigrant deflection. In its 2002 annual report, for example, the Mexican American Legal Defense and Education Foundation (MALDEF) bragged that the organization "successfully co-sponsored legislation to protect undocumented workers from employers that pay less than minimum wage, refuse to pay for overtime, or otherwise fail to comply with other labor laws."[17] If these law enforcement efforts were motivated by anti-Latino racism, then MALDEF was attacking rather than defending the Latino community. The Roman Catholic Church also supported interethnic coalitions that opposed slums and sweatshops. If these coalitions were animated by racism, then the Roman Catholic Church was participating in a racist crusade against Latinos, most of whom were Roman Catholics.

Anti-immigrant political reaction did not reach a ballot in California until 1994, twenty-four years after the mass migration of Latinos had begun. The timing of this reaction raises additional problems for a theory that racism explains Latino dispersal from southern California. Why did California's racists wait so long to begin? If racism began immediately, why did Latinos wait so long to leave? Where racism and ethno-chauvinism are most powerful, they should promote open, visible, and self-conscious anti-immigrant political backlash as soon as immigrants appear—not decades after settlement. Racists need not wait for economic conditions to deteriorate before they move to reject immigrants. Indeed, confronting immigrant Latinos for the first time, some Southern sheriffs sought to dislodge them before they could leave their vehicles.[18] Already in 2003, state police in Alabama had been trained to detect illegal immigrants and to refer them to federal authorities for deportation.[19] State police never did so in California.[20]

Racism and Poverty Intolerance

Even conceding for the sake of the argument that southern Californians' racism played a big role in the political reaction against immigration, what is the likelihood that local poverty intolerance played no supporting role? After cataloging realistic reasons for native white hostility to Latinos, seeking thus to establish an attitudinal basis for anti-Latino hostility, even Patricia Zavella concedes that California's economic problems made it difficult for cities to "house, feed, police or transport" their multiracial populations.[21] Her concession suffices minimally to ground this argument. Strictly speaking, all that need be proven is that regional intolerance for poverty encouraged deflection net of any effects of racism, not necessarily that there was no racism.

It has long been known that racism and ethno-chauvinism are exacerbated by poverty and reduced by wealth. As Booker T. Washington long ago taught African Americans, black millionaires are welcome where black paupers are not. This invitation applies to Latinos as well. Racism and ethno-chauvinism do not extinguish economic self-interest in America, where the almighty dollar atones for many unwelcome personal characteristics. Conversely, as the Reverend Gary Davis sang, accompanying himself on the blues guitar, "Nobody loves you when you're down and out."[22] This song is American folk culture, but translates easily into Spanish. Poverty intolerance need not exclude racism, nor vice versa, for poverty intolerance to deflect migration from one locality to another. The issue is whether independent space exists for local poverty intolerance net of racism in network-driven migrations. The empirical issue is whether economic deterioration and poverty intolerance promoted southern California's egress of Latinos net of the region's racism.

Finally, the exact meaning of racism is now open to debate. Leo Chavez searched for old-fashioned, biological racism in California politics, but found only "neo-racism."[23] The widest definition of neo-racism is that of Roxanne Doty, who defines neo-racism as positing "the insurmountability of cultural differences." That is, having distinguished it from its old-fashioned biological predecessor, such as Hitler espoused, Doty declares neo-racist any doctrine that teaches "the inevitability of conflict" when human beings "of different cultures are mixed in inappropriate numbers."[24] Doty could attack Samuel Huntington's work from this point of view, but the mainstream political discourse on immigration in southern California did not raise the issues of cultural difference or inevitable conflict. Hence, the conflicts arising between nonimmigrants and immigrants in southern California did not qualify as neo-racism either even under Doty's broad definition. If neither racism nor neo-racism can be found in California's political dialogue, then how can either explain the dispersal of Latinos from the state?

Marshaling Evidence

Racism is a privileged variable in social science. Although a cultural variable, racism has been immune to the methodological antipathy that social science has for decades directed to cultural explanations of economic behavior. During the last thirty years, for example, the climate of scholarly opinion has admitted explanations that stress racism without requiring more than circumstantial evidence as supporting documentation. For this reason, racism offers a doughty adversary to any argument that, like this one, does not directly address the topic, but whose results racism might possibly explain. Scholars will not accept a new explanation when a privileged favorite has been neither addressed nor excluded.

The intent of this discussion has not been to reject the claim that racism existed in Los Angeles or in California, or that racism injures those at whom it is directed. Nothing in this chapter supports either inference. However, when racism is introduced as an empirical explanation of immigrants' regional dispersal, then evidence must be marshaled to prove the correctness of the explanation. Seeking that evidence, this chapter found none. Hence, no warrant exists for the claim that racism explains Latino dispersal from Los Angeles, from California, or even from the traditional reception states. The facts do not fit this alternative explanation and the argument of poverty intolerance is thereby strengthened. Even in the worst possible case, hammered together only for the sake of argument, racism cannot exclude poverty tolerance from an ancillary or supporting role in the Latino dispersal.

= Chapter 10 =

Sequential Absorption
and Deflection

WHEN PROTRACTED over decades, the routine operation of migration networks drives immigrants' wages in high traffic destinations down and their housing costs up. For this reason, the
economic welfare of Mexican immigrants gradually declined in Los
Angeles relative to low-traffic destinations. The bad news filtered back to
Mexico, where potential immigrants rethought their settlement choices.
The migration network adjusted, changing the rank order of traffic volume deposited at the various stations in the United States. During the
1990s, the adjusted migration network sent more migrants to previously
lower-ranked destinations, and fewer to Los Angeles. Over a decade,
that simple alteration deflected a million immigrants from Los Angeles
toward low-traffic destinations in which the rent-to-wages ratio was more
favorable.

If the automatic, market-linked deflection were the only process at
work, all immigrant-reception regions and cities would replay the same
deflection scenario. Indeed, there are marked points of interlocal similarity, as chapter 2 showed. Nonetheless, this volume has consistently
argued that, important as it is, automatic market adjustment was not the
only deflection process at work in the Los Angeles metropolitan region.
Deflection depended as well on local political mobilization in support of
poverty-intolerant law enforcement.[1] Lawlessness tolerated poverty; law
enforcement deflected it.[2] Los Angeles initially tolerated industrial and
housing lawlessness. However, when migrant networks had saturated
mainstream labor markets as well as the buffers, economic conditions
among Latino migrants in Los Angeles fell increasingly below the legal
and subjective threshold of minimal human decency. Most noticed was
the growth of slums and sweatshops. This alarming expansion set in
motion a corrective political reaction such that Los Angeles and many
regional cities became increasingly poverty intolerant. The essence of this
reaction was actual enforcement of previously unenforced local and state

laws governing housing, occupational safety, occupational health, and minimum wages. When enforced rather than ignored, such laws rendered it impossible for employer firms to remain internationally competitive in low-wage industries, or for slumlords to profit from dilapidated tenements. The obstacle was not that, economically speaking, sweatshops and slums could not have expanded any further if Los Angeles had left them alone; the obstacle was fines and jail time for their owners. Facing these deterrents, low-wage employers left Los Angeles, taking their substandard jobs with them, and slumlords brought their rat-infested tenements up to the legal mark. Reduced access to sweatshops and slums then deflected new migrants to second-settlement destinations. The sequential stages that culminated in deflection from Los Angeles (network maturation, migratory influx, mainstream saturation, buffer saturation, poverty intolerance, deflection) should generalize to second-reception areas as well.

Intermetropolitan Differences in Poverty Tolerance

Because these chapters have stressed the contribution of poverty intolerance to deflection of immigrants, it is appropriate to address in closing some noneconomic influences on local poverty intolerance, which is a continuous variable, not a discrete variable. That is, cities are more or less intolerant of poverty, not tolerant or intolerant. Even given buffer saturation, metropolitan areas probably differ in their tolerance for immigrant poverty for social, cultural, and political reasons, rather than only and narrowly economic ones. Precisely this intermetropolitan difference ultimately creates the quilt of jurisdictions that defines the aggregate national toleration for immigrant poverty at any moment. It is a fair inference that, given saturated buffers, a reception area's tolerance for immigrant poverty contracts, but how much and how fast? That is unknown.

When it comes to toleration of immigrant poverty, localities' prompt or retarded enforcement of housing, welfare, occupational, safety, and industrial legislation largely defines their agency. Enforcement of housing, safety, occupational, health, and minimum wage laws confers upon states and localities some ability to reduce unwanted immigration by deflecting it. Prompt enforcement is strong agency; slow enforcement is weak agency; no enforcement is no agency; and no agency is toleration.[3] Where there is no agency, a locality does not enforce minimal standards of human decency within its borders. Any indigent may enter, and live as wretchedly as circumstances warrant. No one will interfere. Los Angeles's Skid Row is such a place.[4] There is no bottom to human misery on Los Angeles's Skid Row.

Law enforcement is the vehicle through which a locality's underlying intolerance for poverty finds expression, but law enforcement is not the only or even the main source of that intolerance. Cultural characteristics of cities influence their subjective threshold of intolerance for poverty, but the subjective threshold mainly operates through the political system of which police are the arm. For example, in Los Angeles, the Roman Catholic Church endorsed slum and sweatshop abatement, but its influence depended upon Catholic voters. Its program worked because many Catholics lived in Los Angeles. But one would not expect Catholic influence to be equally great where few Catholics live. All by itself, the diocese of Los Angeles's well-intentioned intervention against slums and sweatshops helped deflect poor immigrants to other cities and even to other countries, thus foreclosing for some migrants the cheerless option of living in a slum and working in a sweatshop in Los Angeles. Lacking so many Catholics, but awash in poverty-tolerant Baptists, Atlanta might tolerate more immigrant poverty than did Los Angeles. This is just a guess. Nonetheless, the guess suggests the wide possibilities for intermetropolitan difference in subjective tolerance for poverty that might exist in the face of comparable squalor.

Political Structure and Poverty Intolerance

All interlocal differences in tolerance for poverty do not arise from cultural sources. Sometimes the political system itself influences whether or how quickly a locality's intolerance for poverty finds political expression. Municipalities in California did not enjoy much direct control over occupational, safety, health, wages, and housing law enforcement. They relied instead on the California Department of Industrial Relations and the U.S. Department of Labor to enforce labor law.[5] When municipalities rely on outsiders to enforce economic laws, they of course enjoy less agency than when they enforce their own codes.[6]

Thus tethered to California's lackadaisical enforcement effort, Los Angeles's numerous justice movements mobilized and informed voters in order to influence state officeholders. Testifying before the California State Assembly, Victor Narro represented the Coalition for Humane Immigrant Rights of Los Angeles, a social justice movement. In addition to asking California to grant more law enforcement resources to the labor commissioner, Narro declared that the Los Angeles city attorney's office should become "more active" in initiating criminal prosecutions of sweatshop owners.[7] Narro's request exposed the tension that Los Angeles-based justice movements perceived between local and state enforcement authority. Unfortunately for the movements, California's officials had the authority to enforce California's laws. The political success of the anti-sweatshop movement therefore required mobilizing Los Angeles-based political pressure on state officeholders. This requirement placed a buffering layer between citizens and law enforcers that made it harder for Los

Angeles to control its own industrial environment. That said, the pressure of the movements caused state authorities to take action, less than requested, but more than previously, and more than other states were taking.

In contrast, housing code enforcement was the direct and immediate responsibility of mayors and municipal police departments. A suburban mayor could order police to prevent indigents from living in garages, and the city's police would enforce that order. In the realm of housing state and federal officials manipulated incentives to obtain local compliance with their growth-oriented policies, but did not politically control the localities. For this reason, in Los Angeles and the regional cities, nonimmigrant voters exercised more direct influence over housing code enforcement than they did over occupational and industrial code enforcement. If we consider living wage, antislum, antisweatshop, and higher minimum wage agitation as left-wing political movements, and nimbyism as a right-wing movement, then southern California municipalities more easily enforced right-wing anti-immigrant policies than left-wing. Policies are deemed anti-immigrant in a restricted sense when, if implemented, the policies reduce the number of immigrants who can inhabit the locality. If states passed local housing codes, then state police and state office holders would have had the responsibility for enforcing housing regulations in Los Angeles County's eighty-eight jurisdictions as, in fact, they enforced industrial regulations. This jurisdictional change would have weakened nimbyism in southern California, rendering right-wing anti-immigrant politics harder to empower.

Relative Power of the Growth Regime

A third political condition affecting local intolerance for poverty is the power of the municipal growth regime, and its pro-growth ideology. The growth regime was weak in Los Angeles as early as 1980. An urban growth regime consists of a ruling growth coalition, which dispenses its successful pro-growth message to the voters.[8] Urban growth regimes prefer unimpeded high-influx immigration. They are also extremely tolerant of the economic inequalities that sustained immigration brings. First, employers of low-wage immigrant labor are charter members of growth regimes. Their economic interest requires that they tolerate low-wage immigration and the slums the low-wage immigrants inhabit. They also seek to impose some of their wages bill on taxpayers by passing along to them the cost of immigrants' medical care. Second, immigrant influx promotes population growth, thus raising property values, the raison d'être of urban growth regimes. In this sense, the weakened political and ideological stature of Los Angeles's growth regime, and the regional emergence of no-growth politics, discussed in chapter 3, strengthened the ability of metropolitan voters to deflect immigration. Thanks to the existing weakness of the central city's growth regime, antisweatshop and living wage campaigns were more politically effective than would otherwise have been possible. Thanks also to the weakness of Los Angeles's regional growth regime, suburban nimbyism and suburban city councils more successfully defied state and federal incentives to build affordable housing in suburbs.[9] Nimbyism's grass roots strength in Los Angeles[10] reflected simultaneously the diffusion of no-growth and slow-growth ideas among the voters, and the political incapacity of pro-growth politicians and business elites to overpower suburban voters, who ringed the metropolitan core with a "no go zone" of housing inaccessible to poor people, including but not limited to immigrants.[11]

Rejecting the growth ideology was a condition of poverty intolerance in Los Angeles. The ideology proclaims that population growth is always desirable and resonates strongly during network-driven migrations because of the growth-produced problems that additional growth solves. Writing about suburban Santa Ana, a densely populated immigrant suburb, the *Los Angeles Times* put this dilemma this way: How could Santa Ana "enforce health and safety laws without forcing thousands of residents onto the street?"[12] If Santa Ana enforced its own housing code, today's garage-dwelling immigrants would become tomorrow's homeless. Similarly, if Los Angeles enforced industrial and occupational laws, the today's "working poor" would become tomorrow's beggars. Therefore, in the short run, enforcing housing, industrial, and occupational codes worsens the poverty that intolerance is intended to reduce. It requires not only extra police work but hiring more police as well. It is, furthermore, inhumane in its immediate results. It also contradicts the growth imperative. Realizing all this, police and public officials in Los Angeles's metropolitan cities were often reluctant to enforce housing, industrial, and occupational codes against hapless immigrant families.

Inversion of Public Policy Debate

Network-driven migration of Mexican and Central Americans thus created an ironic inversion of the usual policy debate about poverty. In the usual debate, carried on in the usual pro-growth context, vigorous enforcement of occupational safety, health, and wage laws looks unsound. If, it is argued, these laws are enforced or (even worse) strengthened and enforced, then the enforcing locality drives away the worst jobs, leaving precisely the most vulnerable teenage and ethnic minority workers more unemployed than before. It is better to keep the low-paying jobs than to strip the most vulnerable workers of low-wage employment. The same considerations apply to antislum legislation. If enforced, such laws reduce the most "affordable housing" available to the locality's poorest residents, increasing their homelessness. Conversely, toleration of slums and sweatshops (nonenforcement of existing law) buys time for economic growth that will provide better jobs tomorrow for today's low-wage slum dwellers. These jobs will absorb the sweatshops' impoverished labor force into the mainstream, and permit the better-paid workers of tomorrow to afford satisfactory housing. The same logic applies to unionizing low-wage workers: if encouraged, the long-term counterproductive result would include egress of low-wage industries to lower wage localities. If permitted to unionize, poor workers unionize themselves right out of a job, becoming welfare recipients rather than earners.

However, in the context of long-term, network-driven migration, the conventional policy discourse arrives at inverted conclusions. That is, confronting saturated buffers, the moment of truth for poverty intolerance, cities and states can raise the minimum wage above national levels, intending thereby to drive sweatshops out of town and with them the low-wage immigrants they employ. Similarly, as the Los Angeles experience shows, more aggressive enforcement of occupational safety, health, and wage legislation prevents sweatshop employers from competing in international industries, such as garment manufacture, that require substandard wages. When they moved their firms out of town, sweatshop owners reduced by approximately fifty-seven thousand the number of immigrant workers who could live in Los Angeles. Required to provide standard housing or go to jail, slumlords upgraded their tenements, benefiting seated tenants but reducing Los Angeles's supply of the most affordable housing, slums. In tandem with deflecting low-wage jobs from town, reducing slums also deflected low-wage immigrants still abroad to other destinations, benefiting the Los Angeles metropolitan region.

Likewise, when nimby political power prevented the legal debasement of suburban housing standards, which was the goal of regional housing authorities, selfish nimbies erected an iron ring of unaffordable housing around Los Angeles's metropolitan core. Nimby political power thus neutralized the poor immigrants' two economic weapons, overpaying and overcrowding. Prevented by law from overcrowding, the poorest immigrants could not expand their housing access into the metropolitan suburbs. Prices of housing in the metropolitan core therefore rose as more immigrants arrived and the immigrants' rent-to-wages ratio declined. In Los Angeles, aggressive nimbyism thus deflected, by dint of unaffordable housing prices, migrants who had not yet arrived.

Here is the irony of policy formation in the context of network-driven migration: bad policy becomes good policy. Good policy here means policy that narrowly benefits the policymaking locality, not policy that benefits the state, the nation, the poor, the elderly, immigrants, or humanity. California's high minimum wage deflected unwanted immigrants to states with lower minimum wages. Cities that enforced high industrial standards deflected unwanted immigrants to cities that did not enforce labor law. Cities that prosecuted slumlords deflected unwanted immigrants to cities that did not prosecute them. Cities that refused to debase housing quality deflected unwanted immigrants to cities that did. Bad policy had become good policy. Possibly this reversal explains the intellectual fog in which Los Angeles and the metropolitan region's planning and municipal authorities constructed immigrant policy in the last decades of the twentieth century. When following the rulebook degrades conditions rather than improves them, cities have to muddle through until the rulebook is rewritten. Muddling through, Los Angeles city governments lacked a firm concept of what justified the nameless policy that this volume has called absorption and deflection. Nonetheless, what proved true in the Los Angeles region should prove equally true in second-settlement regions— save that the process of rewriting the rulebook is already under way.

Local Intolerance for Poverty

The concept of "local intolerance for poverty" appears in these pages as a capsule description of a real condition that arises in first-reception cities and regions, even including European cities.[13] Localities move toward poverty intolerance when the saturation of economic buffers necessitates political intervention to prevent further degradation of living conditions among immigrants. In calling attention to local intolerance for poverty, this volume neither recommends intolerance nor endorses human meanness. Local poverty intolerance is an external social fact or it is nothing. Consider the obverse, local toleration of poverty. Toleration sounds friendly and humane. However, localities tolerate poverty when they ignore vast slums and sweatshops, overcrowded housing, child labor, truancy, epidemics, high infant mortality, ubiquitous beggars, bankrupt hospitals, overcrowded schools, teeming informal sectors, degraded ethnic economies, freeloading sweatshop owners, and massive tax evasion. Third World cities tolerate poverty because they have no alternative, but even they are not averse to deflecting poor residents to other cities or even to other countries whenever possible.[14]

Now that, thanks to globalization, Third World poverty has reached First World cities, Los Angeles faced the choice of how much immigrant poverty to tolerate. If cities, regions, and states really regulate slums and sweatshops, really reject child labor, really require employers to provide health care to employees, and really regulate the informal economy, then they raise some residents out of poverty and reduce the percentage of those in poverty. Local intolerance of poverty is an exact description of their policy, not a value judgment. It reduces but does not eliminate poverty in the locality, much less in the world. However, it does stabilize a locality's standard of living and quality of life by making it more difficult to inhabit the locality without the minimum acceptable income. Such a policy brings some poor residents up to the standard, reducing their squalor, but deflects others elsewhere. Therefore, although local poverty intolerance does not abolish world poverty, it reduces the real incidence in the locality, not just its visibility. These accomplishments improve the quality of life in the locality and very slightly decrease the volume of poverty in the world. After all, those who are deflected are no worse off than they were and those upgraded are better off.

In the absence of effective national regulation of immigration, possibly a result of national incapacity to regulate immigration, first-reception towns, cities, and regions receive more poor immigrants than, after a longer or shorter time, they will or can absorb so they move toward poverty intolerance. Writing for an international readership of urban experts, Willem Van Vliet defines a "livable city" as one in which "residents can find jobs that pay a living wage."[15] Retaining livability thus defined is impossible when a city is at the receiving end of a sustained, high-volume immigration of impoverished persons. Therefore, in Van Vliet's sense of the word, municipal "livability" is restored when municipalities bring some residents up to the local minimum standard even if the same policies deflect others. Restoration requires time, but as it is accomplished, the towns, cities, regions, and states deflect some unwanted immigrants into other towns, cities, and regions. Immigration first saturates the mainstream economy, then, becoming network-driven, throws out economic buffers, which permit the immigration to continue past the saturation of the mainstream. When later the twin buffers of the informal economy and the ethnic economy are themselves saturated, the stage is set for a municipal regime of poverty intolerance to emerge. This regime enforces laws restricting slums and sweatshops, stabilizing the locality, but deflecting some future migration.

Naming the Nameless Policy

At some risk of overconfidence, I can identify the theoretical conclusion toward which this case study of Los Angeles heads. The unique case of Los Angeles is possibly not unique, but it does typify how all or most cities deal with protracted immigration of low-income people. If so, the case of Los Angeles exposes an existing national immigrant policy that has yet received no name. That is, the United States has a policy of having no national immigrant policy, and in its absence, cities make a de facto immigrant policy, which becomes the nation's by default. This policy deserves a name. Let us call it sequential absorption and deflection. This is the process whereby first-reception towns, cities, regions, and states receive immigrants, absorb as many as they can or, strictly speaking, are willing to absorb, and then deflect others. Second-reception cities repeat the process. Sequential absorption and deflection becomes national policy when destination countries admit more poor immigrants than first-reception centers can decently house or employ and thus begin to deflect the surplus to second-settlement reception localities.

Some evidence already indicates that the same conditions that accompanied Latino migration in Los Angeles are coming into existence in the second-reception areas. In Nebraska, Mexican immigrants cluster in the slaughterhouse industry, and sustain high unemployment. Hoping to lift them out of poverty, the governor of Nebraska introduced a meatpacking workers' bill of rights, the objective of which was to reduce slaughterhouse employers' rampant violation of state wages, hours, and safety laws.[16] Because Virginia enforces industrial laws more effectively than North Carolina does, Mexican labor contractors refuse to take their North Carolina crews into Virginia.[17] In Kennett Square, Pennsylvania, neighbors complained that Mexican immigrants parked too many cars and trucks in front of their houses, violated zoning laws, and lived in illegally overcrowded homes.[18] Police in the Chesapeake Bay region have harassed Latino drivers, who lacked car insurance and driver's licenses but needed cars to get to work. Neighbors complained that Latino immigrants inhabited "overcrowded subdivided apartments, old houses and trailers that were not well maintained and typically overpriced."[19] The mayor of Georgetown, Delaware, declared that Mexican immigrants were "lowering the region's standard of living."[20] Mexicans in Lexington, Kentucky, are "quite poor" and earn wages below the poverty level. Nonetheless, a proposal to build a community center for them brought out nay-saying nimbies.[21] Unable to find another charge, police in New Hampshire charged illegal immigrants with "trespassing" into the United States.[22] These are symptoms of sequential deflection already in process in second-reception areas. If it be true, as James Hollifield claims, that liberal democracies cannot control their borders, then sequential deflection is unavoidable in liberal democracies.[23] If liberal democracies could control borders, but fail to do so, then sequential deflection is simply the product of a failed national immigration policy.[24] Either way, sequential absorption and deflection is the name of America's hitherto nameless immigrant policy.

Sequential Deflection as Process

What happened to Los Angeles, this volume has argued, was a gradual drift toward poverty intolerance without formally acknowledging the drift. Deflection was a de facto policy, not official policy. It roped together a number of independent and ad hoc policies of specific immigration-linked evils. Moreover, it was only partly successful. Between 1980 and 2000, the city of Los Angeles reduced its share of national immigrant population by 28.5 percent. In the same time, the Los Angeles metropolitan area reduced its share of the nation's foreign-born Mexican population by

36.7 percent. These reductions measure the decline in the percentage share of Los Angeles relative to the national populations of foreign born and foreign-born Mexicans respectively. Turning the statistics around, we observe that Los Angeles did not deflect 71.5 percent of the foreign born and it did not deflect 63.3 percent of foreign-born Mexicans. More were not deflected than deflected. Nonetheless, the ability of Los Angeles to reduce its immigrant population improved the quality of life in Los Angeles and also displayed municipal agency. In Los Angeles, real immigrant deflection emerged from a multistrand social process that involved many different actors, few of whom were consciously hostile to Latinos, immigrants, or to the poor.[25]

In respect to sequential deflection, intent is not essential but effect is. The three prongs of the deflection process were the automatic and spontaneous reaction of housing and labor markets to long-term migration networks, social movements, and law enforcement. The left-wing social movements mobilized political power to enforce housing, industrial, and occupational laws and, in some cases, even to raise existing standards.[26] By raising the state minimum wage, California assisted deflection in that its high minimum wage in the 1980s and 1990s reduced its attractiveness to low-wage employers. Strengthened enforcement of the California workers' compensation law had the same result. By sealing suburbs from affordable housing, homeowner nimbyism raised rents in the metropolitan core. By attacking sweatshops and slums, justice crusades reduced the supply of dilapidated tenements and degraded jobs without increasing the supply of good housing and good jobs. Taken together, strengthened law enforcement made it ever harder to work or live in Los Angeles as an impoverished person.

Los Angeles's political passage toward poverty intolerance took two decades. The process accompanied a gradual realization that the metropolitan region should not tolerate the worsening squalor associated with sustained, high-volume immigration. The high rents and declining wages of the 1980s did much to persuade Latino immigrants that other regions and other cities offered more congenial living conditions in the 1990s.[27] This much was automatic. Somehow, through a process still little understood, the migration network assimilated the market's message, and redirected Latino immigrants to nontraditional destinations. Chapter 2 tells that story.

But the market's automatic judgment was by no means the only poverty-intolerant authority. Had suburbs been opened to affordable housing, as federal and state planners wished to open them, unwanted immigrants would have transformed portions of the Los Angeles suburbs into a West Coast version of Queens.[28] Queens enables its residents to move about effectively on fixed-rail mass transit and houses them decently and inexpensively at high density. Queens works well in this sense, and has excellent restaurants and, unlike Los Angeles, interesting street life to boot. However, it does not offer the suburban Los Angeles life style, so relished by Angelinos, nor does it have a political base of homeowner nimbies. As it was, only some towns and neighborhoods of metropolitan Los Angeles were thus transformed, because many of those whose unmet material needs would have compelled this transformation were deflected. Home-owning residents of the Los Angeles suburbs did not want their neighborhoods to become Queens. Protected in their fragmented metropolis, nimbies frustrated regional planners, newspapers, and business elites,[29] and unwittingly compelled thousands of Latino immigrants to seek housing in other regions.[30] By reducing pressure on the housing supply, this deflection slightly improved the housing circumstances of Latino immigrants who stayed.

Similarly, during the 1990s, minimum wage, antislum, and antisweatshop crusades cranked up the legal pressure against slumlords and sweatshop owners. These ethnic entrepreneurs had provided impoverished immigrants with the slums in which they could afford to live and with the sweatshops that employed them. By repeatedly raising the minimum wage above federal levels, California and Los Angeles increased the legal pressure on sweatshop employers to upgrade or shut down. This was sometimes their intent.[31] Affiliated political crusades mobilized intolerance for poverty, strengthened law enforcement, and improved pay and working conditions for low-wage employees in California and in Los Angeles. These crusades successfully pulled thousands out of poverty and reduced the poverty of others. Wages and working conditions in Los Angeles improved. The city and region became more livable. This was the manifest goal of the antipoverty political mobilization. However, the same mobilizations that benefited some Latinos deflected others to new settlement areas where substandard wages, housing conditions, and health care were still tolerated. Most of those thus deflected did not live in the Los Angeles metropolitan area when deflected. Some had not even decided to emigrate.[32] In effect, social movements partly pulled up the metropolitan drawbridge, enabling Los Angeles to stabilize its internal status quo and deflect unwanted immigrants at the same time.

In this connection, Los Angeles's large garment manufacturing industry did not decline because of the North American Free Trade Agreement, as is commonly believed. Certainly, NAFTA subjected the Los Angeles industry to intensified wage competition from China and Mexico.[33] But Los Angeles garment factories could easily have met this threat by lowering wages to internationally competitive levels. That outcome was not permitted. The Los Angeles industry declined because, thanks to the newly installed poverty-intolerant regime, garment contractors were legally prevented from paying abundant, willing, and available immigrant workers wages low enough to enable the contractors to compete with China and Mexico. Had Los Angeles garment factories offered Mexican wages and found no takers, then we could conclude that Mexico's competition shut down the Los Angeles garment factories. That did not happen. Rather, contractors were legally prevented from lowering wages and working conditions to Mexican levels. Of course, had permission had been granted, the result would have been shantytowns inhabited by thousands of garbage-picking immigrant children. There is no other way families could live in Los Angeles on Mexican wages. The same shantytowns existed in Mexico, and could easily have existed in Los Angeles as well. However, Los Angeles would not tolerate the shantytowns that an internationally competitive garment industry required—so a third of garment industry jobs left the region, and with them the region's support capacity for thousands of low-wage immigrants.

Globalization, and Immigration Policy

A policy regime of sequential absorption and deflection appears superficially to support the globalization arguments critiqued in chapter 1. After all, as immigrants exhaust the demand for their labor in one metropolitan area, sequential deflection moves them to others that offer untapped demand for their low-wage labor. In this manner, it might be argued, immigrants unlock a host country's demand for their labor city by city rather than all at once. If so, sequential absorption and deflection is the serial process whereby immigrants access a nation's aggregate demand for cheap labor. Demand, however, is still what causes immigration.

True enough, as far as it goes, this defense of the demand side encounters four rejoinders. First, when deflected immigrants went to Butte, Tuscaloosa, or Wheeling, they did not go there because these provincial cities had become "world cities." Globalization theorists expected low-wage immigration to stay in world cities rather than to spill down the urban hierarchy. Neither did the low-wage immigrants, once in the provinces, perform household-supporting functions for affluent professional couples in need of nannies, gardeners, and maintenance workers. The demand that attracted deflected immigrants to provincial cities was hard, gritty jobs in manufacturing, retail, slaughterhouses, and construction. This is not the rosy scenario that globalization theorists had painted.

Second, when they migrated to provincial cities, Latino immigrants had already exhausted the target-hardened job supply in first-reception cities like Los Angeles. Such cities had developed poverty-intolerant urban regimes as a result of protracted exposure to declining social and economic conditions associated with network-driven immigration. That is precisely why the newest Latinos could build no more substandard niches in them. In contrast, according to the optimistic globalization scenario, low-wage immigrants would never exhaust the gardening, nanny, housemaid, and roofer jobs that affluent professionals offered them in Los Angeles, much less push first-reception cities into poverty intolerance that deflected immigrants to the second-settlement areas.

Third, unlike the Latinos, high-skilled Asian immigrants continued to earn high wages in their original niches, which expanded enough to absorb the influx of additional immigrants. This is the scenario that globalization theorists promised for low-wage immigrants as well, though it materialized only for the highly skilled portion of the immigrant wave. Globalization theorists were right about the highly skilled immigrants, but wrong about the unskilled.

Finally, the demand-driven migration that the globalization theorists promised increasingly denoted effective demand that could not attain the tougher legal standards enforced in first-reception cities. As demand for low-wage labor declined without ever disappearing, initially low wages dropped even lower. Satisfaction of declining demand for labor required more squalor and more local tolerance for poverty. Enough was finally enough. Declared intolerable, this continuous expansion of toleration for poverty turned into intolerant urban regimes that deflected at least some immigrants. This indictment convicts the globalization theorists of having peddled an optimistic and saccharine expectation that developed countries could expect eternally painless immigration from the Third World. They promised a party that would never end.

How Obnoxious Is Sequential Absorption and Deflection?

That said, once people look past the arguments about immigration, and focus instead on how to handle network-driven immigrants whom national borders cannot stop, then the indictment of unofficial policy of sequential absorption and deflection is far less obnoxious than it might initially appear. Local poverty intolerance sounds inhumane. It is not far-sighted; it relies on police repression; and it evokes gloomy Malthusian reflections about spaces in the urban lifeboat. A policy of intolerance is indeed unhappy, but deflecting cities should not be blamed. They reacted to the national policy context that generated local circumstance; they did not create the context. Yes, someone should reduce the world's problems, but no one does. Given the world's increasingly unequal distribution of income; given raging war, overpopulation, famine, genocide, and pestilence in the Third World; given ineffective federal immigration laws, and given lack of interest in immigration reform from non-reception states, the policy of immigrant deflection that Los Angeles cities followed had some advantages.

Above all, deflection distributed the burden of low-wage immigration more evenly among the nation's large, medium, and small cities. Appendix figure A.2 shows the severe regional clustering of immigrant Mexicans that still existed in 2000 even after two decades of deflection. Nonetheless, thanks to deflection, somewhere in Georgia now live and work immigrant Latinos who, but for deflection, would have been living and working in Los Angeles instead. How tragic is that? It is good for Georgia, which gains hard-working, family-loving new citizens so compatible with the state's ultraconservative ideology. Latino migration also provides cultural benefits of value to the native population. Neglected elsewhere in this volume, these are many, but consider cuisine first. Georgia is ground zero for America's obesity epidemic. Latino immigrants teach Georgia's native-born citizens to eat vegetables, beans, rice, and peppers instead of their current diet of fried pork rinds and Big Macs. This cultural reeducation might lower rates of hypertension in Georgia. How tragic is that?

Deflection was also good for the Los Angeles region. There is no valid reason that the citizens of Los Angeles or any first-reception city should experience tumultuous and wholesale disruption of their life world as a result of sustained, high-volume low-wage immigration while provincial cities escape any impact. Deflection equalizes the impact of immigration among the regions.

Now, as in the past, when the immigrants were Europeans, absorbing many low-wage immigrants is costly in the historical short run even if beneficial in the long-run.[34] In 2002, the top six immigrant reception states housed 39 percent of the United States' population, but they contained 52 percent of immigrant adults who had not completed high school, 70 percent of immigrants without health insurance, and 75 percent of immigrant households receiving welfare.[35] This imbalance was costly as well as unfair.[36] Without immigrant deflection, these regional imbalances would have been even greater in 2002 than they actually were. Absorbing immigration is a national responsibility, and all of a nation's citizens should arguably discharge it, not just those who happen to reside in first-reception cities and traditional settlement regions.[37] To this extent, the default policy of sequential absorption and deflection achieves a regional equalization of immigration's burden that the U.S. Congress could not.

As for Latino immigrants in Los Angeles, the region's new poverty-intolerant urban regime improved their welfare. They earned higher wages, worked in safer plants, and paid lower rents. The schools they attended had fewer children per classroom teacher. Their hospital emergency rooms had fewer indigent users. Prospects for social mobility improved. Deflection worked to their advantage.

But what about the million Latinos who were deflected from Los Angeles in the 1990s? Deflection did not shut down their migration networks and terminate their options. After 2000, people continued to emigrate from Mexico and Central America to the United States in the same numbers as before.[38] They simply ended up in different cities and states.

Deflection Encourages Police Harassment

Unfortunately, to find those new homes, deflected migrants had frequently to endure harassment by local police intent on deflecting them again.[39] Police harassment is the nastiest part of sequential deflection, and it is an essential aspect of this policy. When localities embrace deflection, they are tempted to subject poor immigrants to harassing surveillance from local police, who may seize any excuse to charge them.[40] In the southern California cities of Glendale and Redondo Beach, for example, esquineros sought casual work on street corners. Mostly illegal immigrants, they lounged on the corners as they waited for potential employers—the usual practice everywhere in southern California. Street corner labor markets had their own social organization; everyone knew that the esquineros were neither lawless nor dangerous.[41] Esquineros worked hard. But, seeking to rid themselves of unwanted street corner labor markets, which were something of an eyesore, the southern California cities of Redondo Beach and Glendale enforced municipal ordinances that prohibited anyone from soliciting employment on public streets. All those arrested for this crime were immigrant Latinos. Finally, a judge ruled that neither city could prohibit adults from soliciting employment on public streets.[42] This is a constitutional right—even of illegal immigrants. This ruling signaled that both cities had exceeded their legal rights in their frantic efforts to deflect immigrants.

Deflection Benefits the Deflected

On the positive side, once deflected to low-wage, poverty tolerant states and cities, Latino immigrants could still find work—albeit at lower wages and under worse working conditions than Los Angeles would have tolerated. In that sense, deflection even benefited the deflectees because getting something inferior is better than getting nothing. Without deflection to second-reception states and cities, the end of the poverty-tolerant regime in first-reception cities like Los Angeles would have ended Latino immigration then and there. In the long run, the nation's existing, de facto policy of sequential absorption and deflection expands the number of low-wage migrants that the United States can and will absorb—and thus benefits the deflected.

═ Appendix ═

Figure A.1   **The Foreign-Born from Mexico in the United States as Percentage of Total County Population, 2000**

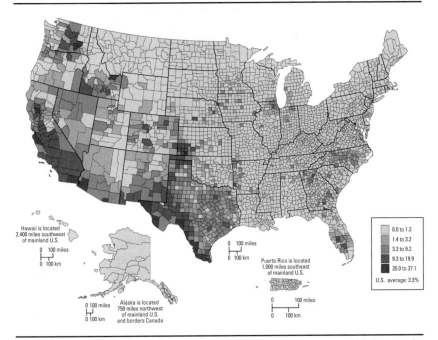

Source: U.S. Census Bureau, Census 2000, Summary File 3. Originally published on the Migration Information Source (www.migrationinformation.org), a project of the Migration Policy Institute.

Figure A.2   Overcrowding in the United States, 2000

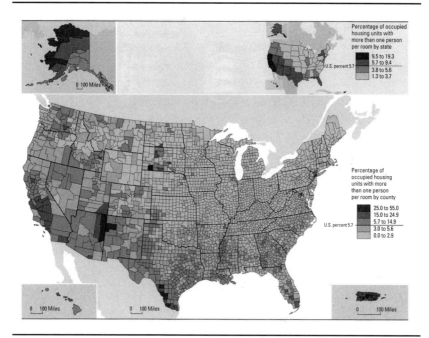

Source: U.S. Census Bureau, Census 2000, Summary File 3. American Factfinder at factfinder.census.gov provides census data and mapping tools.
Note: Data based on sample. For information on confidentiality protection, sampling error, nonsampling error, and definitions, see www.census.gov/prod/cen2000/doc/sf3.pdf.

$=$ Notes $=$

Chapter 1

1. Sassen 1990b, 484–85; Sassen-Koob 1989, 70; Moore and Pinderhughes 1993, xxvii; see also Sassen-Koob 1985, 255. For a critical evaluation of the polarization thesis, see Hamnett 1994, 401–24.
2. "The expansion of the high-income work force . . . has led to a process of high-income gentrification, which rests, in the last analysis, on the availability of a vast supply of low-wage workers" (Sassen 1991, 279, see also 281, 282).
3. Wrigley 1997, 17–139.
4. Waldinger 1996[0], 12–29.
5. "The presence of large immigrant communities then can be seen as mediating in the process of informalization rather than directly generating it: The demand side of the process of informalization is therewith brought to the fore" (Sassen 1991, 282).
6. Sassen 1991, 282; see also Frey 1996–1997, 26.
7. Massey and Denton 1993, 446.
8. Bonstein and Dettmer 2004, 58–60; see also "Arbeitsmarkt: für mehr legale Beschäftigung! Gegen Schwarzarbeit!" Bonn, Germany: Federal Ministry of Finance. http://www.bundesfinanzministerium.de; Cyrus 2001, 209–11; for eastern Europe, see Sik 1995.
9. Sensing precisely demand theory's declining popularity, Krissman (2005) rallied support for the demand-driven explanation of immigration to the United States.
10. See review in Light, Kim, and Hum 2000, 2002.
11. Sassen 2000, 91, 113.
12. Hamnett 1994, 408; Ong and Blumenberg 1996; Light 2000; Light, Kim, and Hum 2000, 2002.
13. Durand, Massey, and Malone 2002, 20.
14. They follow Gunnar Myrdal, who originated the concept of cumulative causation: "In the normal case a change does not call forth countervailing changes but, instead, supporting changes, which move the system in the same direction as the first change but much further. Because of such circular causation a social process tends to become cumulative and often to gather speed at an acceleration rate" (Myrdal 1957, 3).

175

15. "Immigration may begin for a variety of reasons, but the forces that initiate international movement are quite different from those that perpetuate it" (Massey, Durand, and Malone 2002, 18).

16. Williamson 1990, 102–4; "This process of labor transfer is typically viewed analytically as a one-stage phenomenon, that is, a worker migrates from a low productivity job to an urban industrial job. The question is rarely asked as to whether or not the typical unskilled rural migrant can indeed find higher-paying regular urban employment. The empirical fact of widespread and chronic urban unemployment and underemployment attests to the implausibility of such a simple view of the migration process" (Todaro 1969, 139).

17. Todaro 1969, 1984.

18. Mayhew 1885, 5.

19. Light 1983, 1933–36; Williamson (1990, 123) agrees: "Male immigrants into Britain's cities did not exhibit lower earnings than non-immigrants. Nor did they exhibit higher unemployment rates. They also exhibited the same age-earnings experience. . . . What we do have seems to be inconsistent with the view that migrants entered the city in response to expected future high earnings, suffering unemployment or underemployment in the traditional low-wage service sectors while they waited for the better jobs. Rather, they appear to have been motivated by current job prospects, and those prospects appear to have been confirmed."

20. Hart 1973.

21. Bromley 1988.

22. "In the largest and most rapidly growing cities of the periphery (such as Mexico City, Lima, Bombay, Istanbul, Cairo, and Lagos), large portions of the population . . . live in 'illegal' housing. New immigrants are the group most likely to be living illegally. The definition of illegal in this context is not always clear: it refers to not being properly regulated by the prevailing state rules, but the range of meaning may be wide. In some cases the 'illegal' dwellings have been constructed on public land or on land belonging to private owners, and a de facto squatting is the result. In others, construction has violated zoning regulations, by building on farmland or what has been reserved as park space (green area); or construction has been carried out without regard to municipal ordinances, proper inspection and permits, or the engineering, sanitary, and aesthetic norms set by the authorities" (Keyder 2000, 120; see also Nientied and van der Linden 1988).

23. Josef Gugler (1988) reviews the overurbanization literature, and concludes the term is still satisfactory when interpreted to mean more urbanized than optimal. This is not the original meaning of the term.

24. Gonzalez and Cota 2003.

25. Light 1983, 133–36; "We may well be witnessing a phase in the global convergence, between the core and the periphery, of the content and patterns of informality" (Keyder 2000, 132).

26. Bruecker et al. 2002, 23.

27. "The massive growth of Third World cities implied by this level of rural to urban migration is likely to lead to a collapse of the social, economic and political systems which govern these cities. This collapse, in turn, will drive those with capacity to move to seek refuge in other countries" (Stahl 1995, 216).

28. Massey and Taylor 2004a, 2.
29. International Organization for Migration 2003.
30. The usual question is what causes immigration. Hatton and Williamson (1998, 31) suggest that we ask why immigration is not stopped: "But shouldn't we be asking why immigrant countries remained so open for so long? Liberal democracies might be expected to have enacted pro-labor policies sooner and with more drama than they in fact did—immigration restrictions being one such policy."
31. Bade 2003, 4: "As in the past, newcomers today are flocking to cities, heading for the very largest—Los Angeles, New York, San Francisco, Chicago—where their compatriots have already put down roots" (Waldinger and Lichter 2003, 6).
32. Money 1999, 23; The Mexican village of Santa Maria de Arriba has become a ghost town as a result of three decades of migration to the United States. See "Village borders on extinction," *Orange County* [California] *Register*, August 3, 2003.
33. Massey and Taylor 2004b, 386.
34. Heer 2002, 34; also Goldin 1994, 224.
35. Gugler 1988, 80–81; Dixon 2005.
36. Bean and Stevens 2003, 70.
37. Borjas 1996, 72–80; see also Clark 1998b; Camarota 1999.
38. *Statistics Norway* 2003. www.ssb.no/english/subjects/. Estimates were obtained by multiplying per family social allowances by number of families with no correction for number of children. This method slightly inflates the immigrant share of social allowances and unemployment relief.
39. Bean and Stevens 2003, table 4.1 pl. 69 and table 4.5, 77; Camarota 2004b, 8.
40. Boeri 2002, xi.
41. Freeman 1992, 1161.
42. "Between the 1960s and 1990s, it became apparent that the number of immigrants receiving public assistance was rising rapidly" so Congress made it harder for immigrants to qualify for welfare (Borjas 2002, 11).
43. Light and Gold 2000, 9–25.
44. "French state policy towards self-employed immigrants is to regulate (and restrict) access to the trades: immigrants are not entitled to open independent businesses" (Ma Mung and Lacroix 2003, 174; see also Haberfellner 2003; Wilpert 2003).
45. Schmalz-Jacobson 1994, 31, and table 13. For a fuller explanation, see the articles in Kloosterman and Rath, eds. 2003.
46. "Ethnic economies constitute a relatively rewarding option in the North American context, whereas, in the continental European model, achieving socioeconomic success implies finding a well-paid and well-protected job as an employee. . . . If ethnic economies are so important and useful for minorities in the United States, it is not only because of the crucial role of ethnicity, group cohesion, or ethnic resources. It is also because the American context constitutes a favorable background for ethnic economies" (Pécoud 2000, 453).
47. The term "ethnic ownership economy" refers to regulated businesses owned by immigrants; the term "ethnic economy" refers as well to the informal sector,

and to ethnic-controlled economies (Light 2005, 651; Light and Gold 2000; Hum 1997, 44).

48. Kindleberger 1967.

49. Believing this, Fischer and Straubhaar (1996, 37), optimistically conclude that "There is little ground to fear mass-immigration from third countries because the potential consists mainly of people who will find it hard to migrate, due to a lack in demand for their labour."

50. "As migrants flood the urban job markets, unemployment and underemployment grow" (Todaro 1984, 17).

51. Baldwin-Edwards 1999, 2.

52. Pécoud 2002, 494–96.

53. Bean and Stevens 2003, 30.

54. "In Germany, self-employment among immigrants has been growing regularly. In 1970, less than 2% of non-German workers were self-employed but by 1998, this figure had climbed to 8.8%. This is still below the proportion of self-employment among German workers while the second is declining, so that one can expect that non-Germans will soon be proportionally more represented among independent workers than Germans" (Pécoud 2002, 494–96).

55. "As immigrant entrepreneurs arrive, concentrate geographically, and establish new business enterprises that rely on immigrant labor for their survival, immigration can, quite literally, generate its own demand" (Massey 1999, 39).

56. Dickerson 2005.

57. Light and Gold 2000, 52.

58. "The apparently insatiable underground economy is still healthy and still attracting migrants from across the globe" (Baldwin-Edwards 1999, 13).

59. "Relative immigrant wages were dramatically lower in labor markets where new immigration flows were largest" (Lalonde and Topel 1991, 174; see also Borjas 2003).

60. "Even if wages fall in the richer country, there could still be a greater likelihood of finding a job there, so migration could continue to increase" (Stalker 2000, 24).

61. Actually, immigrant shantytowns have already come into brief existence on Long Island (see Schienberg 2004).

62. Duneier 1999.

63. Keyder 2000, 128.

64. Velez 2003, 165.

65. Hatton and Williamson (1998, 247–48) attribute the restrictionist immigration policy of the early twentieth century to rising inequality. "What changed immigration policy most, however, were changes in inequality. Rising inequality, manifested by an increasing gap between unskilled workers and the average citizen, caused more restrictive immigration policy. Rising equality, manifested by a declining gap between unskilled workers and the average citizen, created more open immigration policy."

66. "The long-term patterns of immigration control tend to be cyclical: periods of openness followed by periods of closure generated by the ultimate political victory of those who incur the costs associated with immigration" (Money 1999, 222).

67. Bean and Stevens 2003, 206.

68. Hanson et al. 2002, 221.
69. "Over the last three decades, there have been more applicants for immigration into advanced industrial countries than these have been willing to admit, either temporarily, permanently or as refugees" (Stahl 1995, 227).
70. Bruecker et al. 2002, tables 1.1 and 1.2.
71. U.S. Bureau of the Census 1980b, table 46; 1997, table 55.
72. Only 40 percent of illegals enter without inspection; the rest are visa abusers, whom no border controls could prevent.
73. Massey 1999, 50.
74. Peterson 1981, 4.
75. Zimmerman and Fix 1994, 287.
76. Money 1999, 23.
77. "While in theory immigration policy has been solely a federal responsibility, in fact, its outcomes are influenced signally by the concerns and strategies of local actors" (Wells 2004, 1337–38).
78. "Immigration policy . . . is by and large failed policy" (Freeman 1997, 49).
79. At least in North America, cities compete to exclude the poor, and immigrants are the poorest of the poor (Dreier, Mollenkopf, and Swanstrom 2001, 175).
80. Borjas 1999, 206.
81. Obdeijn 203, 48; also Krissman 2005, 37.
82. Money 1999, 9–10.
83. Martin and Taylor 2001, 95, 103.
84. "25 Held after Police Clear Encampment." *Los Angeles Times*, January 17, 2004, section B, p.1.
85. Cantanzarite and Aguilera 2002, 101.
86. "Immigrants are often exploited by employers, employees, the government, or taxpayers, as well as by the growing group of licit and illicit labor brokers. But that exploitation comes at a cost of inequality in democratic societies that pride themselves on equality of opportunity, if not equality of outcomes" (Money 1999, 21).
87. Edwards 2003.
88. Police in New Hampshire charged illegal Mexican immigrants with "trespassing" into the United States, but courts rejected the case, arguing that local trespassing laws do not apply to unlawful entry into the United States (WMUR 2005).
89. Lewis 2002, 13.
90. "El color amarillo los identifica como taxis. Trahen taximetro y radios de onda corta. Recogen a los pasajeros en cualquier parte de la ciudad, pero se esconden cuando aparece una patrulla de la policia porque no tienen licencia para ser taxistas" (Gonzalez-Portillo 2000, 4A).
91. "As one would expect, undocumented migrants are more likely than legal immigrants to be working informally" (Massey, Durand, and Malone 2002, 123).
92. Fix and Hill 1990, 8, 87, 117; Schienberg 2004; see also: "Bossing the big Tortilla." *The Economist.* 375(8426), May 14, 2005: 29–30.
93. "Pervasive disregard for the immigration laws may have its own impact. Such laws are routinely violated by those who enter illegally or overstay their permits . . . and by employers who willingly hire undocumented workers, community organizations that help unauthorized migrants escape detection,

and ordinary citizens who avail themselves of cheap migrant labor to clean their houses, mow their lawns, and take care of their children. Massive disregard for particular laws may well breed contempt for the law and for government in general" (Freeman 1997, 50).

94. Gordon 2005.
95. Rath 2002.
96. Hanson et al. 2002, 201.
97. "Despite the whole body of employment, health and safety regulations, illegal practices are still common at some of Britain's small clothing enterprises. Poor working conditions are a feature of many firms in the West Midlands clothing industry, and the West Midlands Low Pay Unit found clothing firms operating from 'Disused factories, old warehouses, back street rooms above shops and peoples front rooms.' People are working in cramped conditions, with inadequate lighting, ventilation and sanitation facilities. Health and safety aspects were unsatisfactory, there were no emergency fire procedures and the exit doors were blocked" (Ram, Jerrard, and Husband 2001, 82).
98. Raes et al. 2001.
99. Bader 2005.
100. Rekers and van Kempen 2000, 66.
101. "With the disappearance of extra market opportunities in appropriation of land and settlement, the attraction of the city for potential immigrants will decrease—not only because shelter now has to be rented, but also because of the diminished likelihood of capturing part of the urban rent accruing to all property holdings in a growing metropolis" (Keyder 2000, 130–31).
102. Kelly 2005.
103. Hanson et al. 2002, 283.
104. Hernández-León and Zúñiga 2002, 4; "The spread of emigration to new regions presumably means that new chains were being created. The fall in emigration from northern Italy to Argentina presumably means that some of the older chains must have been broken" (Baines 1991, 35).
105. "Desperate Mixtecans needed a place to go, but large American cities such as Los Angeles . . . already contained so many Mexicans that immigrants from different regions simply faced too much competition in the labor market to get a foothold." So they went to New York City! (Pape 2003, 22).
106. Massey, Durand, and Malone 2002, 127.
107. Kelly 2005.
108. Wells 2004, 1316.
109. Scott 2002, 177.
110. Frey and Liaw 1996; Suro and Singer 2002; Frey 2003; Gozdiak and Martin 2005; Zúñiga and Hernández-León 2005.

Chapter 2

1. Light 1983, 275–77; Baines 1991, 33–34; Fairchild 1925, 158–61.
2. MacDonald and MacDonald 1964; Tilly and Brown 1967.
3. Waldinger 1999, 228; Krissman 2005.
4. Massey et al. 1987.
5. Myrdal 1957, 50.

6. Portes and Rumbaut 1990, 32; Massey 1999, 45–47; Money 1999, 210.
7. Light, Bhachu, and Karageorgis 1993, 26.
8. Massey et al. 1987, 170.
9. Hagan 1998.
10. Light, Bhachu, and Karageorgis 1993; Light, Bernard, and Kim 1999; Light, Kim, and Hum 2000.
11. Kandel and Massey 2002, 1002.
12. Fussell 2004.
13. Stahl 1995.
14. Bartel 1989.
15. Bartel and Koch 1991.
16. Rauch and Hamilton 2001, 5.
17. Hatton and Williamson 1994.
18. "The group most clearly and severely disadvantaged by newly arrived immigrants is other recent immigrants who are, in the final analysis, the closest substitutes for newcomers" (Fix and Passel 1994, 50; see also Lalonde and Topel 1991, 177, 180, 190; Bean and Stevens 2003, 130; Borjas 1996; Bump, Lowell, and Pettersen 2005; Hagan 1998, 61; Borjas 1999, 201; Borjas 2003, 36; Camarota 2003, 7).
19. Williamson 1990, 237; Lipman 2003, 8; Lipman 2001, 36; White and Hurdley 2003; O'Hara 2002; Keil 1998.
20. Light 1983, 246–53; Light 2001.
21. Burgess and Bogue 1967.
22. See Light 1983, 242–58; Light 2001.
23. Bean and Stevens 2003, 130.
24. Bodnar 1985, 171; Graham 2004, 60.
25. Heer 2002, 49.
26. Bump, Lowell, and Pettersen 2005.
27. "Once emigration from a particular region was established, it tended to remain high. The continuity of high emigration rates can be explained by a phenomenon called chain migration. . . . Chain migration meant that the immigrants tended to settle in a relatively limited number of locations. As late as 1910, 70 percent of Norwegian immigrants in the USA were found in only six states" (Baines 1991, 34; see also Hatton and Williamson 1994, 534; on current immigration networks, see Waldinger and Lichter 2003, 6).
28. The six traditional destinations, in descending order of immigrant population, are: California, New York, Texas, Florida, Illinois, and New Jersey.
29. Bump, Lowell, and Pettersen 2005.
30. Frey 2003; Light and Bhachu 1993, 6–8.
31. Durand, Massey, and Capoferro (2005, table 1.2) estimate that the national share of the Mexican population of these three states declined from 87.3 in 1980 to 72.6 in 2000. California's share declined from 57.8 in 1990, its peak, to 47.8 percent in 2000.
32. Bump, Lowell, and Pettersen 2005, 33–34.
33. See Ellis 2001.
34. Originally, 1970 census data were to have been included, but this expansion proved impractical because so few Asian Indians were in the United States in 1970.

35. Smith and Edmonston 1997, 183–87.
36. Because of their heavy concentration in technological industries, Asian Indians clustered most heavily in Silicon Valley (see Hill and Hayes 2003).
37. Johnson, Johnson-Webb, and Farrell 1999; Bump, Lowell, and Pettersen 2005; Suro and Singer 2002; Frey 2003; Grieco 2003; Schachter 2003; Heer 2002.
38. Heer noticed Patrick McDonnell's 2001 article in the *Los Angeles Times* that said as much.
39. Heer 2002, 42.
40. Heer 2002, 47.
41. Additionally, they argue that federal legislation changed the character of Mexican immigration, tending to replace sojourners with settlers, and thereby increasing the Mexican origin population of the United States. Again, in their view, the federal legislation made the situation worse because, left to themselves, many Mexicans would finally have repatriated who, thanks to federal intervention, have decided instead to settle permanently in the United States (see Massey, Durand, and Malone 2002, 126).
42. "Thus the early 1990s witnessed an unusual coincidence of conditions" (Durand, Massey, and Capoferro 2005, 12, emphasis added).
43. Hondagneu-Sotelo 2003, 677.
44. Borjas 2003; Ong and Zonta 2001; Reed 1999; Levine 2001; Friedberg and Hunt 1999; Rosenfeld and Tienda 1999, tables 2.5 and 2.6; Levine 2001, table 5; Camarota 2003, 7.
45. Thus, objecting to a one-sided emphasis upon regional labor market saturation Levine (2001, 6), insisted upon adding (not substituting) equal attention to structural economic changes.
46. Massey, Durand, and Malone 2002, 121.
47. Massey, Durand, and Malone 2002, 120.
48. "Latino immigrants in general and Mexican immigrants in particular suffer substantially lower earnings than other groups" (Bean and Stevens 2003, 121).
49. "Hispanics lost ground from the early 1970s to the late 1990s. The unadjusted Hispanic/White wages gap grew from 28 to 45 percent in this period" (Ong and Zonta 2001, 48).
50. "In 1960, the average immigrant man living in the United States actually earned about 4 percent more than the average native man. By 1998, the average immigrant earned about 23 percent less. . . . As a result of this growing disadvantage in human capital, the relative wage of successive immigrant waves also fell. At the entry, the newest immigrants in 1960 earned 13 percent less than natives; by 1998, the newest immigrants earned 34 percent less" (Borjas 1999, 8; see also Ellis 2001, 117; Bean and Stevens 2003, 121).
51. von Scheven and Light 2005.
52. The eight new settlement states were Massachusetts, Virginia, North Carolina, Georgia, Arizona, Nevada, Oregon, and Washington.
53. Bean and Stevens 2003, 126.
54. Relative immigrant wages were dramatically lower in labor markets where new immigration flows were largest. . . . Weekly wages of recent immigrants . . . fell by over 20 percent relative to white natives in cities with the highest immigrant rates (Lalonde and Topel 1991, 174, 177; see also Bartel and Koch 1991).

55. Massey, Durand, and Malone 2002, 126.
56. Gorman 2005.
57. Fuentes-Salinas 2004.
58. "Residential overcrowding historically has been a prominent feature of the immigrant experience in the United States" (Myer and Lee 1996, 63).
59. Compare Money's similar approach (1999, 210): "Immigrant networks are important social and economic networks that dramatically reduce the costs of immigration. They promise food and shelter to newly arrived immigrants until they can become self-sustaining, thereby reducing the connection between labor market demands and immigration and further straining the capacity of the local community to cope with the growing population."
60. Zolberg 2001, 10.
61. Massey 1999, 43–47; see also, Light 1983, 271–301.
62. Light 1981; Light 2001.
63. Alexander et al. 2003, 25.
64. Durán 2004.
65. De La Torre-Jimenez 2004.
66. Gurak and Caces 1992, 158.
67. The entire analysis was also replicated with a different measure of economic welfare called disposable income. Disposable income was obtained by subtracting average rents in a metropolitan area from average wages there. The larger the amount remaining, the larger the disposable income. The disposable income measure yielded the same results as the rent to wage ratio so it is not shown separately.
68. Bump, Lowell, and Pettersen 2005, 33.
69. Hernández-León and Zúñiga 2002; see also Zook 2003.

Chapter 3

1. Pieterse 1994, 161.
2. Petras 1983, 48–49; and Zolberg 1991.
3. Bornschier and Stamm 1990.
4. Massey et al. 1993, 446.
5. Sassen 1991, 2002.
6. Savitch 1990, 151; Scott and Storper 1993, 3–4, 11.
7. Sassen 1988, 22–23, 136; Sassen 1991, 329; also Häusermann and Krämer-Badoni 1989, 344. For a critical evaluation of the polarisation thesis, see Hamnett 1994.
8. O'Loughlin and Friedrichs 1996.
9. "The world economy is managed from a relatively small number of urban centers in which banking, financing, administration, professional services, and high-tech production tend to be concentrated. . . . Poorly educated natives resist taking low-paying jobs at the bottom of the occupational hierarchy, creating a strong demand for immigrants. . . . Native workers with modest educations cling to jobs in the declining middle, migrate out of global cities, or rely on social insurance programs for support" (Massey et al. 1993, 447).
10. Sassen 2000, 101.
11. Moore and Pinderhughes 1993, xxvii.

12. Sassen 1988, 484–85; see also Sassen-Koob 1985, 255.
13. Griswold 2002, 9.
14. Light and Gold 2000, 39–44.
15. Sassen 2000, 93.
16. Sassen 2000; Bonstein and Dettmer 2004.
17. Massey, Durand, and Malone 2002, 123–4.
18. Demand-driven explanations are not new. Harry Jerome explained immigration to the United States on the basis of demand in 1926. What is novel about contemporary globalization theory is the identification of a changed income structure in the reception countries as the source of the demand. That view identifies increased income inequality as the cause of the original demand, and also the consequence of the resulting immigration. Globalization theorists do not investigate the possibility that, when it passes some threshold, inequality also sets in motion immigration-restriction, but Hatton and Williamson (1998, 247–48) have concluded that increased inequality caused the political restriction that ended the European migration in 1924.
19. "The informal economy, in turn, emerges as a mechanism for reducing costs, even for firms and households that do not need the informal economy for survival, and as a mechanism for providing flexibility when this is essential or advantageous" (Sassen 2000, 112).
20. Sassen 2000, 94.
21. "The presence of large immigrant communities then can be seen as mediating in the process of informalization rather than directly generating it: The demand side of the process of informalization is therewith brought to the fore" (Sassen 1991, 282).
22. "As immigrant entrepreneurs arrive, concentrate geographically, and establish new business enterprises that rely on immigrant labor for their survival, immigration can, quite literally, generate its own demand" (Massey 1999, 39).
23. See Fligstein 1998; and Fernandez-Kelly and Garcia 1989, 250.
24. Dicken 1992, 121.
25. Logan and Swanstrom 1990; for someone who says exactly this, see Peterson 1981.
26. Logan and Swanstrom 1990, 5–6.
27. Kloosterman 1996, 468.
28. Gottdiener and Komninos 1989, 8; see also Ward 2004, 153, 183.
29. See also Talwar, 2001, 121
30. Waldinger 1996; Waldinger and Lichter 2003, 218–19.
31. "African Americans' social support networks often lag behind those of other racial and ethnic groups in terms of expressive aid, such as advice-giving, and instrumental aid, such as money lending/giving" (Smith 2003, 1035).
32. Simon 1995, 220; see also Light 1999.
33. Reyneri 1997.
34. "As immigrant entrepreneurs arrive, concentrate geographically, and establish new business enterprises that rely on immigrant labor for their survival, immigration can, quite literally, generate its own demand" (Massey 1999, 39).
35. Cornelius 1998.

36. "Of course, it is U.S. employers who create" the demand for immigrant labor (Krissman 2005, 29).
37. Massey et al. 1993, 448.
38. Gurak and Caces 1992, 157.
39. Martin and Taylor 2001, 98.
40. Light 1999.
41. "The polarisation thesis . . . may be contingent on the existence of large-scale ethnic immigration and a cheap labour supply" (Hamnett 1994, 408).
42. Goldin 1994, 225. See also: Blau 1980, 37; Fraundorf 1978, 219; Hill 1975, 58–59; Shergold 1976, 459–60.
43. Harrison 1991, vii.
44. Trotter and Lewis 1996, 251; Groh 1972, 60.
45. Groh 1972, 113; Henri 1975.
46. Walton 1994, 38.
47. Groh 1972, 60.
48. Krissman, 2005, 29.
49. Fischer and Straubhaar 1996, 14.
50. Krissman 2005, 29.
51. "The market-driven perspective on immigration is passé" (Camarota 2004a, 8).
52. Stark 1991, 315.
53. Light 2005.

Chapter 4

1. Allen and Turner 1997, 185.
2. Soja, Morales, and Wolff 1983; also Soja 1989.
3. Scott 1988, chapters 6–9.
4. Ellis 2001, 151–2.
5. Clark 1998a, 22.
6. Mumford Center, State University of New York at Albany. Available: http://mumford1.dyndns.org/cen2000/NewAmericans.
7. However, the likelihood that immigrants would receive public assistance rose between 1970 and 1998 (Borjas 1999, 11).
8. McConville and Ong 2003, 1, 10.
9. Dickey 2003; Reed 1999; Cleeland 2002; Wedner 2003; Sanchez 2003; Dickerson 2004.
10. Levine 2001, 26.
11. Lindo 2004.
12. Myers, Pitkin, and Park 2004, 5.
13. Los Angeles Alliance for a New Economy 2003, 19.
14. Gottlieb, Vallianatos, Freer, and Dreier 2005, 44.
15. California Department of Industrial Relations, Industrial Welfare Commission http://www.dir.ca.gov available December 12, 2004.
16. On anti-poverty social movements in New York City, see: Gordon (2005, 199).
17. http://www.chirla.org/programs.htm.
18. Gottlieb, Vallianatos, Freer, and Dreier 2005, 95.
19. http://www.laane.org/lw/index.htm; see also Reich 2003.

20. "Both the City and the County of Los Angeles . . . face an across-the-board crisis of poverty, inadequate housing and lack of health-care coverage that is one of the worst in the nation" (Range 2004, 2).
21. http://www.justiceforjanitors.org.
22. Erickson, Fisk, Milkman, Mitchell, and Wong 2002, 564.
23. Chinchilla and Hamilton 2001, 105; see also: Gottlieb, Vallianatos, Freer, and Dreier 2005, 96.
24. More et al. 2000, 15.
25. Catanzarite and Aguilera, 2002.
26. McCarthy and Vernez 1997, 89.
27. McConville and Ong 2003, 14.
28. Hagan 1998, 61.
29. Reed 1999, xviii.
30. Vernez 1993, 150.
31. Light and Roach 1996.
32. Lopez, Popkin, Telles 1996, 299.
33. Ong and Blumenberg 1996; Schimek 1989.
34. Ortiz 1996, 257.
35. "A significant number of immigrants in California and the United States currently have very low wages, and the evidence suggests that their wages will not improve substantially throughout their working lives. This evidence, combined with the fact that more-recent immigrants have had lower . . . wages relative to earlier immigrants, has substantial ramifications for public-service usage and tax revenues into the future" (Schoeni, McCarthy, and Vernez 1996, 67).
36. Ellis 2001, 129, 132.
37. Clark 1998a, 80.
38. Smith and Edmonston 1997, 180.
39. Levine 2001, 111–2, 185.
40. Stalker 2000, 108.
41. A globalization enthusiast, Griswold even claims that "demand for less-skilled will continue to *grow* [my italics] in the years to come" (2002, 9). However, demand has been declining for decades already so how can it continue to grow?
42. Sell 1972.
43. Marcelli 2001, 88.
44. López-Garza 2001, 148, 158.
45. Hamilton and Chinchilla 2001, 102.
46. Cited in Brown, Domenzain, and Villoria-Siegert 2002, 67.
47. Chinchilla and Hamilton 2001, 196–7.
48. Chinchilla and Hamilton 2001, 201.
49. Sanchez 1987.
50. Chinchilla and Hamilton 2001, 208.
51. Light, Har-Chvi, and Kan 1994.
52. Chinchilla and Hamilton 2001, 208.
53. Joassart-Marcelli and Flaming 2002, 6.
54. Joassart-Marcelli and Flaming 2002, 6.

55. Baldwin-Edwards estimates the extent of informal economy participation in 13 European countries. Highest was Greece, 29 percent; the lowest was Finland, 2 percent. The median was Ireland, 16.5 percent. By this standard, Los Angeles' informal economy would be medium to large in size. "The underground economy . . . has, it seems, been expanding in almost all European countries. A European Commission report of 1990 concluded that in most northern European countries (except France and Belgium) the black economy was about 5 percent of declared work compared with 10–20 percent in southern countries" (Baldwin-Edwards 1999, 5).

56. Cleeland 2002.

57. "There is already substantial evidence of an intersection of poverty and immigration in Europe and the U.S. . . . . Much of the growth of the poverty population in inner cities in the U.S. was from immigration. Approximately 20 percent of the growth of the poverty population in Los Angeles was from immigration" (Clark 1998b, 373).

58. Joassart-Marcelli and Flaming 2002, 18.

59. They recommended three other measures as well: teaching English to Latino workers, thus improving their access to mainstream employment; acknowledging that union organizing formalizes employment conditions, thus encouraging unionization; conferring amnesty on workers "who have tenure" in the Los Angeles economy, thus reducing their susceptibility to employers' intimidation. Of these proposals, the last would require federal legislation, and is thus beyond the power of local authorities to effectuate.

60. "I favor vigorous enforcement of laws, ensuring fair and safe working conditions to eradicate sweatshop operations. This requires more vigilant oversight by the state . . . in the enforcement of existing labor laws as well as health and safety codes and regulations" (López-Garza 2001,161).

61. In Chicago, Hispanic- and Asian-owned business experienced a four-fold growth between 1982 and 1997 (see Tienda 2002, 90).

62. Light and Gold 2000, 28.

63. Romney 1996, 1998.

64. Hum 2000, 287; also: Hum 2001, 83–93.

65. This Los Angeles result corresponds to what Bean and Stevens say about Mexican ownership economies nationally (2001, 130).

66. Light and Roach 1996, table 7.4.

67. "Internal competition among co-ethnics within an enclave economy happens when there is an excess of similar types of business cashing in on a similar ethnic niche and competing for a limited pool of customers. . . . Ethnic enterprise often finds itself caught in an unending vicious circle of cost cutting and operating long unsocial hours—competitive behaviour soon feeds on itself" (Bun and Hui 1995, 527).

68. Light and Roach 1996, 196.

69. Light and Roach 1996, 201.

70. Borjas 1990, 231–32.

71. Lipman 2005, 10.

72. Light 1985, 81.

73. O'Hara 2002, figure 1.

74. "Cisneros: Dream of owning a home still eludes most Hispanics." Agencia EFE, http://www.quepasa.com/content/?c=105&id=164750.
75. Myers and Lee 1996, 57; see also Hill and Hayes 2003, 8.
76. Moore 2004.
77. McGreevey 2005.
78. Mena 2003.
79. Pitkin 2002, 7.
80. Guerra, Marks, and Brackman 2001, 6–13.
81. Mexican American Legal Defense and Education Fund. No date. "Latinos and the State Earned Income Tax Credit (EITC): Poverty Despite Work." Available: www.maldef.org/publications.pdf.
82. Gottlieb, Vallianatos, Freer, and Dreier 2005, 46.
83. Deering's California Codes Annotated. California Vehicle Code § 12801.5 operative March 1, 1994.
84. Mohan and Hoffman 2003.
85. Fausset 2002.
86. Pally and Wilson 2000, 11.
87. Pitkin 2002, 6.
88. See http://www.cesinaction.org/ceshistory.html.
89. "Richard Riordan, downtown lawyer-developer-banker, who engineered the overthrow of California's liberal Supreme Court majority in 1986" (Davis 1990, 134).
90. Tobar 1997.
91. Stewart 2003.
92. Pitkin 2002, 7.
93. Stewart 2001.
94. Pape, Eric. 2003. "So far from God, So Close to Ground Zero." *Los Angeles Times Magazine,* Aug 3: 20ff.
95. "The dynamics that converge in the global city produce a strong demand for low-wage workers" (Sassen 2002, 256). But readers learn that "a gathering trend toward informalization" (257) also exists in these cities. How can both statements be true?
96. "California has been very slow to expand housing, transportation, or other services to accommodate the needs of its growing population. Most alarming is the low level of housing construction during the decade of the 1990s" (Myers 2001, 387–88).
97. Massey, Durand, and Malone 2002.

Chapter 5

1. Gurak and Caces 1992, 159.
2. Gregory 1989, 17.
3. Waldinger 1996, 310.
4. Grieco 1987, 40; Waldinger 1995, and Waldinger 1996, 310.
5. Sequeira and Rasheed 2004.
6. Light and Bonacich 1988, 205–25.
7. Wong 1987.
8. Light and Karageorgis 1994; Light and Gold 2000, chapter 2.

9. "Only non-whites are 'ethnic' and rely on 'ethnic' resources. White workers . . . are not 'ethnic' simply because they belong to the majority" (Pécoud 2000, 456).

10. Liu 2004.

11. Light 1983, 367–68.

12. Massey 1988.

13. Massey 1988, 398.

14. "Immigrants and US Business," *Migration News*, 3, June, 1996.

15. Waldinger 1995, and Waldinger 1996, 310.

16. Cornelius 1998.

17. Kloosterman and Rath 2003.

18. Ram, Singhera, Abbas, Barlow, and Jones 2000, 496.

19. Villar 1994.

20. Hamilton and Chinchilla 1995, 32.

21. Raijman and Tienda 2003.

22. Kim 1999.

23. "Not surprising, virtually all immigrant employers hire primarily co-ethnics" (Hum 1997, 44).

24. Gold 1994.

25. Kim 1999.

26. Kim 1999.

27. Gurak and Caces 1992, 165.

28. Wilson 1998.

29. Heer 2002.

30. Sanders, Nee, and Sernau 2002, 306.

31. Brown, Domenzain, and Villoria-Siegert 2002, 128.

32. Compare Uzzi 1996; Zhou 1992, 169.

33. Sarmiento 1996, 38–39.

34. Brown, Domenzain, and Villoria-Siegert 2002, chapter 5.

35. The extent of compliance with this law is uncertain. The California Safety Compliance Corporation estimated that 40 percent of garment contractors did not register. The Corporation also estimated that the industry employed 158,000 workers compared with the estimate of 98,000 that Lee (1996) offered. The largest enforcement sweep in history found only 20 percent of firms unregistered, not 40 percent (Silverstein and Lee 1996).

36. Levy 1997, 8–10.

37. Bonacich 1993, 65; Bonacich 1994, 152–53.

38. Lee 1992.

39. Hess 1990, 94.

40. Appelbaum 1997.

41. Light, Bernard, and Kim 1999.

42. Garment manufacturing industries were defined as "apparel and accessories, except knit," and "miscellaneous fabricated textile products." These are U.S. census categories.

43. Waldinger 1996, 298.

44. Lee (1992) found that Korean garment factories in Los Angeles employed an average of thirty sewers. Assuming that all employers hired 21 employees, we underestimate the share of labor that Korean factories hired, but that underestimate might not affect final estimation of the aggregate share of coethnic

and non-coethnic employees in the various garment factories. To assess the robustness of our conclusion, Richard Bernard recalculated our estimate on the assumption that Korean firms hired thirty employees whereas all non-Korean employers hired only nineteen. He found that 29.7 percent of all garment factories employed coethnics and 70.3 percent employed non-coethnics. Even though the underlying assumptions differed, these estimates approximate those obtained in table 4.2.
45. Hess 1990; also Light, Jung-Kwuon, and Zhong 1990.
46. Kim 1999.
47. Light, Har-Chvi, and Kan 1994.

Chapter 6

1. For a personal account of the early garment industry in Los Angeles, see: Orfalea 1999.
2. Kessler 1999a.
3. Scott 1996.
4. California Fashion Association 1999.
5. Sarmiento 1996, 38–3.
6. Light 1988, 61.
7. Dickerson 1999, 1. On social capital in garment manufacturing, see: Uzzi 1996 especially, 677–83.
8. Zhou 1992, 169.
9. Orrenius 1999, 5.
10. Light 1988, 61. James Lewis finds that immigrant workers in Chicago had comparable problems: "significant health and safety problems, routine violation of overtime, wage and hour regulations," failure to schedule breaks, violation of anti-discrimination laws, and fear of migration authorities (2002, 13).
11. Bonacich and Appelbaum 2000, 224.
12. Other authorities confirm this estimate (see Lee 1996).
13. Bonacich and Appelbaum 2000, 235.
14. Lee 1994.
15. Sarmiento 1996, 37–41.
16. Fix and Hill 1990, 87.
17. Bonacich and Appelbaum 2000, 235–36.
18. Bar-Cohen and Carrillo 2002, 138.
19. Gambetta and Reuter 1995; Petras 1992, 77.
20. Haller 1990, 209–10.
21. A federal sting operation disclosed widespread corruption among immigration police on the U.S. side of the U.S.-Mexico border. This operation explained how tons of cocaine had crossed the border undetected for years previously ("Temptation along the Border." *Los Angeles Times,* June 8, 2005, p. B12)
22. Bonacich and Appelbaum 2000, 125.
23. Bar-Cohen and Carrillo 2002, figure 5.1; Cleeland and Dickerson 2001.
24. "Since the 1980s labor law enforcement has faced significant challenges stemming primarily from the budget cuts and low staffing levels that were perva-

sive during the 16 years under the Deukmejian and Wilson administrations" (Bar-Cohen and Carrillo 2002, 135).

25. John Logan and Harvey Molotch (1987) are the basic source on the growth ideology in American cities.
26. Bonacich and Appelbaum 2000, 181.
27. These substandard wages are not necessarily illegal because workers may not have worked full-time for an entire year.
28. Bonacich and Appelbaum 2000, 2.
29. Bonacich and Appelbaum 2000, chapter 10.
30. Manufacturing industries in Los Angeles have been in decline for thirty years (see Scott 1996, 224; Ong and Blumenberg 1996, 310–14).
31. Soja 1996, 439.
32. Kessler 1999b, 573.
33. Lee 1998a; Kessler 1999a.
34. Wong 1998.
35. *Apparel Industry Magazine* 1999.
36. Lee 1998a.
37. Esbenshade 2004, 37; Liebhold and Rubenstein 1999, 9.
38. Hemphill 1999.
39. U.S. Department of Labor 1997.
40. California Department of Labor Standards and Enforcement 2002.
41. California Department of Industrial Relations 1994.
42. Kessler 1999b, 585.
43. Milkman and Appelbaum 2004, 51.
44. Esbenshade 2004, 117.
45. California Department of Labor Standards and Enforcement 2002.
46. "Workers' Compensation in California." Institute of Governmental Studies, University of California, Berkeley, April 2005. http://www.igs.berkeley.edu/library/htWorkersCompensation.
47. Wong 1998.
48. Weil 2003.
49. Dickerson and Cleeland 2000; Cleeland 1999.
50. Visit the website of SaveOurState, California's right-wing anti-immigrant movement: www.saveourstate.org.
51. Opera fans recall that in *La Bohème*, Puccini's overworked and underpaid heroine, Mimi, dies tragically of tuberculosis, even then a common complaint among garment employees.
52. Silverstein and White 1996
53. Ojeda 1996
54. "IIPPs must have one of more persons responsible for the workplace safety program, a system for ensuring worker compliance with safety rules, a system for communicating safety issues to workers, worksite safety inspections, procedures for investigating injuries and illnesses after they occur, methods for correcting hazards, worker training and instructions in the appropriate languages, and related record keeping requirements" (Brown, Domenzain, and Villoria-Siegert 2002, 36–37).
55. Loucky, Soldatenko, Scott, and Bonacich 1994, 356.

56. The Los Angeles restaurant industry had comparable substandard working conditions (see Kang 1998a, 1998b).
57. Bonacich and Appelbaum 2000, 173.
58. Hiltzik 1995. Helen Schlauffler and colleagues (2000, 12) estimate that only one-third of people less than sixty years of age in Los Angeles County had no health insurance in 1999.
59. "A big savings for Wal-Mart comes in health care, where Wal-Mart pays 30 percent less for coverage for each insured worker than the industry average. An estimated 40 percent of employees are not covered by its health plan" (Greenhouse 2003b, 3).
60. "Construction and manufacturers such as furniture and garment makers have added thousands of jobs in recent years, but most do not offer health benefits" (Lee 1998b; see also Nazario and Shutt 1995).
61. Market-based solutions also started to appear. Storefront clinics sprang up to offer medical care to poor Latinos in Spanish at bargain prices. Offering the service were Mexican doctors, unlicensed to practice medicine in California (Mena 2004).
62. Bonacich and Appelbaum 2000, 183.
63. "I'll tell you who gets the free ride in this . . . county," says Jonathan Friedman, chief of staff to Burt Margolin, the county health czar. "When two-thirds of the uninsured work or are dependents of full-time employees, small business is getting a free ride" (Hiltzik 1995, 11).
64. "Wal-Mart officials said that the raid surprised them, and that they had no idea the company's cleaning contractors used illegal immigrants" (Greenhouse 2003a, 2).
65. Brown, Valdez, Wyn, Yu, and Cumberland 1994, 1.
66. Governor Wilson did not point out that the garment retailers and manufacturers were the main beneficiaries of this public subsidy. "Thirty percent to 60% of all apparel manufacturing in Southern California is done by unregistered, untaxed, cash-paying shops," says Robert Walter, vice president of Frank Walter Sportswear, a sewing contractor that produces girls' clothing. "If all the sewing contractors and apparel manufacturers were registered and paid taxes, we wouldn't be having this health care problem" (Hiltzik 1995, 11).
67. Freedberg and Russell 1999. Immigrant parents even resist state-subsidized medical insurance programs for which their children are eligible because they fear that accepting public welfare will result in denial of their citizenship application. The operative law is a 100-year-old federal law that denies citizenship to aliens who have received public welfare.
68. Although 77 percent of the Latino voters opposed this measure, Latinos were only 8 percent of the voters.
69. Skelton 1999
70. For example, 70,000 illegal immigrant women in California received free prenatal care in 1999 (Lindlaw 1999).
71. Silverstein and Lee 1996
72. Wal-Mart is the major distributor of this line (Silverstein and Lee 1996).
73. Bonacich and Appelbaum 2000, 165–66; White 1996; Cleeland 1999.

74. "Regulating the Immigrant Labor Market." *Migration News*, 2. September, 1995. http://migration.ucdavis.edu/mn/more.php?id=1028_0_2_0.
75. Bar-Cohen and Carrillo 2002, 151–2.
76. Brown, Domenzain, and Villoria-Siegert 2002, 129.
77. California State Assembly 2001.
78. Barstow 2003.
79. Ingram, Levin, and Jones 2003, 1.
80. Dickerson 2003.
81. Esbenshade 2004, 11.
82. "The implementation of NAFTA roughly coincided in time with a crackdown on sweatshops at both the state and federal levels, which brought the issue of industry compliance to the fore. Both NAFTA and increased state and federal enforcement roughly coincided with an increase in the minimum wage, which was primarily absorbed by contractors who own the sewing factories and their employees, who are often illegally underpaid. . . . Faced with increasingly fierce competition, threatened by joint compliance legislation, a higher minimum wage, and pressure by retailers, who, along with the marketers, drive the commodity chain, manufacturers increasingly began to turn to Mexico for garment assembly" (Kessler 1999b, 576–77).
83. Light and Roach 1996.
84. Bonacich and Appelbaum 2000, 154.
85. Wong 1998.
86. Kessler 1999a.
87. Wolff 1995.
88. "Wherever the garment industry has taken root in the U.S., unlicensed, substandard sewing shops have sprung up by the hundreds. They are illegal, off-the-books, pay no minimum wages, unemployment insurance, or health benefits and ignore child-labor laws or overtime pay regulations" (Petras 1992, 77).
89. Polanyi 1957, chapter 7.
90. The issue has now become national, not just regional. Health coverage is an important part of the entire reception context for immigrants. "Many immigrants hold jobs that do not offer health insurance, and their comparatively low incomes make it very difficult for them to purchase insurance on their own" (Camarota and Edwards 2000).
91. "The availability of a large pool of immigrant labor and the presence of highly skilled workers, in the context of economic restructuring, have made it possible to compete with foreign production by combining First World funding and management with Third World Southern California-based immigrant labor" (Zentgraf 2001, 64).

Chapter 7

1. Hanson et al. 2002, 178.
2. White and Hurdley 2003, 687–88.
3. Light 1981.
4. Barbara Lal (1990) documents and interprets ably Robert Park's role in the Chicago School.

5. "And we leave to private enterprise . . . the task of determining the city's limits and the location of its residential and industrial districts" (Park 1925, 579; for a lengthier discussion of The Chicago School's lack of appreciation of real property production, see Light 2001).

6. "Policy-makers and scholars seem to believe property development is a simple response to economic opportunity. . . . According to this reasoning, if there is a demand for office or residential space, then developers will come along and fill it" (Fainstein 1994, 18; see also Fong and Shibuya 2000, 139; Fong and Gulia 2000, 168).

7. Lingering in sociology like the ghost of forgotten ancestors, the production of supply by demand is an old error that, destroyed in another area of study, still beclouds and befuddles this one (see Light 1978, 475).

8. Massey 1985, 319.

9. Continuing the practice, Massey and Denton (1993) do not list developer, realtor, entrepreneur, self-employment, or real property in their index.

10. De Magalhaes 2001,104.

11. Molotch 1976.

12. Logan and Molotch 1987.

13. Jonas and Wilson 1999, 3.

14. True, Logan and Molotch distinguish between growth bloc entrepreneurs on the basis of their agency. At one extreme, "structural speculators" aggressively promote growth, and mobilize political pressure to assure it. At the other, "serendipitous entrepreneurs" have come into ownership of land, but do nothing to promote its development. However, this useful distinction does not strip even the serendipitous entrepreneurs from membership in an urban growth bloc (1987, 29–31).

15. Light 1984, 111–12.

16. Molotch 1988, 31.

17. Higham 1988, 16.

18. The nineteenth-century memoirs of Henry Villard make it clear that American real estate companies in Milwaukee actively recruited German- and French-speaking real estate agents in order to penetrate immigrant markets (1999, 125). In this sense, the immigrant realtors had joined Milwaukee's growth bloc in the nineteenth century. Note that this development does not amount to an immigrant-owned real estate development sector.

19. For a textbook view of how to do property development, see: McMahan 1988.

20. Richard Platkin 1972.

21. Light, Bhachu, and Karageorgis 1993.

22. Fairchild 1925, 151–63.

23. Palm 1985, 66.

24. Rose Helper's 1969 survey of the real estate industry in Chicago paid only the briefest of attention to black realtors.

25. Fong and Wilkes 1999, 598.

26. Teixeira 1997.

27. Teixeira 1998, 273.

28. Teixeira 1998, 270.

29. Smith 2000.

30. For more, visit: littleindia.com/January2004/passagetoOak.htm.
31. Visit the New Jersey Indian Business Association at their website: www. njindia.com/njassoc.htm.
32. Visit: www.ontrackrealty.com.
33. For histories and descriptions of Los Angeles, see: Light 1988; Klein 1990; Laslett 1996; Soja and Scott 1996; Hise 1997.
34. Hise 1997, 11.
35. Fulton 1997, 7.
36. Purcell 2000, 86.
37. Hise 1997, 21.
38. Hise 1997, 14.
39. Hise 1997, 16.
40. Hise 1997 17; see also Pincetl 1999b, 233–34.
41. Purcell 2000, 94.
42. Purcell 2000.
43. Pincetl 1999b; also Strickland 2001; See also stories in the *Los Angeles Times* that spotlight anti-growth sentiment in Southern California: Wedner 2001; Strickland 2001.
44. "The extent to which Los Angeles was literally invented by the *Los Angeles Times* and by its owners . . . in the Chandler family, remains hard for people in less recent parts of the country to apprehend" (Didion 1992, 222).
45. Miller 2000.
46. Dear 2001.
47. "Growth networks often work behind the scenes, in a corrupt manner, to exploit rapid development" (Gottdiener 1985, 225).
48. "Place entrepreneurs can so completely control the local land-use planning process that they capture the local elected officials and bureaucracy entirely" (Pincetl 1999a, 210). To learn more about the land use plan for the Santa Monica mountains, see the Los Angeles County Department of Regional Planning website at http://planning.co.la.ca.us/drp_smm.html.
49. Purcell 2000.
50. Sabagh and Bozorgmehr 1996, 82.
51. International corporations that invest in Los Angeles real estate join the growth machine from abroad in that their return on investment depends on metropolitan growth. But these international corporations have not been shown earlier to promote immigration to the region to support their investment (see Davis 1987).
52. Even William Clark's 1996 excellent review of residential patterns in Los Angeles, very carefully crafted, shows no awareness of real estate development as a guiding process.
53. Strickland 2001.
54. Goldberg 1985, 44–51.
55. Many rich immigrants came to the San Gabriel Valley from Taiwan with fortunes to invest in real estate, but they were suspicious of American developers so they welcomed the opportunity to work with coethnic promoters, who swindled them. John Chi's Trinity Valley Investment Corporation swindled hundreds of Chinese investors out of their property investment in what investigators called, "one of the nation's largest affinity scams" (see Dunn 1993).

56. Wong 1979, 26.
57. For biographies of Hsieh, visit http://en.wikipedia.org/wiki/Frederic_Hsieh and http://forums.yellowworld.org/archive/index.php.
58. "Fred Hseih, a canny real-estate promoter with offshore banking connections, conceived the idea of selling Monterey Park as the Chinese version of the California Dream. Beguiled by slick speakers from Taiwan and Cantonese-speakers from Hong Kong and Indonesia, he transformed Monterey Park into North America's first Chinese-majority suburb by 1985" (Davis 1990, 207).
59. Horton 1995, 29.
60. Allen and Turner declare that the Chinese push into the San Gabriel Valley is attributable to "a single Chinese immigrant, Frederic Hsieh" (1997, 122).
61. Fong 1994, 29; Allen and Turner 1997, 122; Tseng 1994, 172.
62. "In the 1970s Monterey Park was the major port of Chinese entry into the [San Gabriel] Valley. At that time the city held many attractions for the newcomers: a location near the old, congested Chinatown, an established Asian population, and relatively new and affordable residential and commercial property—all vigorously marketed in Taiwan and Hong Kong by enterprising Chinese real estate and business interests who saw a future in a convenient, pleasant, and affordable suburb" (Horton 1995, 15).
63. Horton 1995, 28.
64. Wong 1979, 277.
65. Wong 1979, 285.
66. Horton 1995, 29.
67. Fong 1994, 51.
68. Horton 1995, 30; Chinese in Toronto studied and imitated the shopping center methodology that Monterey Park initiated. In 2001, there were fifty-two Chinese shopping centers in Toronto, all suburban. In outer suburbs, Chinese developers introduced Chinese shopping centers "to attract more Chinese immigrants to move into surrounding areas" (Wang 1999, 177).
69. King 2002. On-line: http://www.findarticles.com/p/articles.
70. Li 1998, 511.
71. For a list of leading Asian American entrepreneurs in Los Angeles, visit the website of the RM Institute for the Study of Entrepreneurship and Business Incubation, http://researchmethods.org/aaentre-list.htm.
72. Horton 1995, 31.
73. Zhou 1998, 548.
74. Lee 1969, 51.
75. Min 1996, 35, declares Los Angeles "unique" among American cities because of its Koreatown.
76. Kim 1986, 60.
77. Abelmann and Lie 1995, 100–1.
78. Light 2001.
79. Kim 1986, 57.
80. Keil 1998, 101, 144.
81. "[Koreatown] is a new model—a healthy financial dynamic not controlled by Anglo elites or their banks" (Dymski and Veitch 1992, 151).
82. Oh 1983.

83. Koreatown was founded in 1973 "by nine Korean merchants who wanted to draw the Korean immigrants into the community." Gene Kim was the first president of the Korean Association of Southern California. His idea was "a brilliant promotional stroke. They offered to put up signs, free, for any Korean business establishments that wanted them. That was in February, 1973. They had soon erected 60 signs and suddenly Korea Town existed" (Smith 1976, 35).

84. Quinones 2001, 22. Hyunsun Choi (2004, 136) says that Lee was a congregant of a nearby Korean Baptist church, and attracted many parishioners to his first business—which was a grocery store. Lee's restaurant opened in 1975.

85. Light and Bonacich 1988, 200.

86. Sherman 1979.

87. "Efforts to promote Koreatown had involved concentrated investments by Korean real estate operators in one neighborhood" (Light and Bonacich 1988, 308).

88. Light and Bonacich 1988, 201.

89. Kim 1975.

90. Light and Bonacich 1988, 309.

91. Miller 1988.

92. Light and Bonacich 1988, 311.

93. Allen and Turner 1997, 149–150; see also Choi 2004, 58–83.

94. Millican 1992.

95. Pinsky 1994.

96. Kim 1986, 56.

97. Lee and Sanchez 1999.

98. Light, Har-Chvi, and Kan 1994.

99. Stemfel 1992; also Berry 2004.

100. Vincent 2001.

101. Kang 2004.

102. Fulmer 1999.

103. Kotkin and Friedman 1993; Furlong 1988.

104. Keil 1998, 146.

105. Real estate "has been increasingly absorbed into the international system as foreign entrepreneurs buy up significant blocks of U.S. land and buildings" (Molotch 1988, 29).

106. Helper 1969; Molotch 1972.

107. Ottley 1943, 34.

108. Myrdal 1944, Appendix 7, 1125–26.

109. "My first opportunity came as a result of a dispute between two landlords in West 134th Street. To 'get even' one of them turned his house over to me to fill with colored tenants. I was successful in renting and managing this house, and after a time I was able to induce other landlords to . . . give me their houses to manage." Philip Payton (http://.www.mapsites.net/gotham/Docs/PaytonQuotes.htm). Edward O'Donnell (2004) provides a capsule history.

110. For a brief biography, see "Philip Payton: Harlem Realtor" at http://www.issues-views.com/index.php?article=1011.

111. RealEstateEspanol is an internet site of the National Association of Hispanic Real Estate Professionals in 2001 that permits searches for a Spanish-

speaking realtor, property for sale, or a search of new listings (http://www.
realestateespanol.com).
112. Krivo 1995.

Chapter 8

1. They did have the East Los Angeles Community Union (TELACU), a four-hundred-million-dollar conglomerate politically connected to Mexican American politicians. However, TELACU was a jobs machine whose product sometimes included affordable housing for seniors. It did not build affordable housing for working-class families (see http://www.telacu.com; Martin 2004).
2. Even in a laissez-faire housing market like the United States, inter-group housing competition can become openly political (see Cuomo 1974).
3. Burgess 1925, 53–62; Hawley 1971, 99–103; Light 1981.
4. Mutchler and Krivo 1989.
5. Sabagh and Bozorgmehr 1996.
6. Dawes et al. 2000, 73. On the concept of growth machine, see Molotch 1976 and 1988.
7. Laslett 1996.
8. Hise 1997; Pincetl 1999.
9. Soja and Scott 1996.
10. Light 1983, 210.
11. Bottles 1988, 22–52. For a discussion of the Los Angeles growth machine, see Light 1983, 206–212.
12. For a critical history of suburbanization in the United States, see: Gottdiener 1985, 241–50.
13. Light 1988, 56–58.
14. Sabagh and Bozorgmehr 1996.
15. The average single-family home in Los Angeles County occupied two-tenths of an acre in 2001.
16. Zeman 1944.
17. Blank and Torrecilha 1998, 15.
18. Lerner 2003.
19. Crouch and Dinerman 1963, especially 283–88; Davis 1990, 170–81.
20. "Local governments use zone laws . . . to segregate land uses and to limit access of potential unwanted new residents and land use" (Dreier, Mollenkopf, and Swanstrom 2001, 101). American states also have "an uninterrupted legacy" of discriminating against resident non-citizens in respect to land ownership and land use (Plascencia, Freeman, and Setzler 2003, 6).
21. Fogelson 1964.
22. Krivo 1995; Allen and Turner 1997, 93; Keil 1998, 121; Wedner 2001a, b, c.
23. Overpayment was defined by SCAG as paying more than one-third of the household income in rent.
24. In 2003, the National Low-Income Housing Coalition reported that a worker in Los Angeles County had to earn $22 an hour in order to afford the rent on a standard two-bedroom apartment. That sum was three times more than the state minimum wage, which 14 percent of the labor force actually earned (Wedner 2003).

25. Pitkin 2002, 7; also, Pally and Wilson 2000, 10.
26. Chavez and Quinn 1987, 1.
27. Moore 2004.
28. Hugo 1997.
29. Marti, 2003.
30. Guerra, Marks, and Brackman 2001, 8.
31. Gold 2001a.
32. Strickland 1999.
33. Lipman, Harkness, and Newman 2005, Appendix B; Harkness and Newman 2005, 55.
34. Garcia and Clarke 2001, 3.
35. Stewart 2001a.
36. Alexander et al. 2003, 23.
37. Fulton 1997
38. Purcell 2000.
39. "The problems created by runaway development are eroding the California dream and threatening the state's economic vitality" (*Los Angeles Times* 1988, II, 6; on slow-growth movements in Los Angeles suburbs, see Horton 1995, 88–92).
40. "For our city and our region to grow and prosper," the mayor of Los Angeles said, the city requires affordable housing. The statement suggests that the mayor innocently adhered to the ideology of growth. In fact, the city of Los Angeles need not grow to prosper (Mattea Gold 2001).
41. But the growth machine is still in power in outlying Riverside and San Bernardino Counties (see Scott Gold 2001).
42. Davis 1990, 156.
43. Guerra, Marks, and Brackman 2001, 16, 54.
44. In 1998 Sierra Club members voted against adding any anti-immigration plank to its slow-growth program, but the vote was close.
45. Dear 2001.
46. Wedner 2001c.
47. Burgess 1928.
48. Indeed, this transition is slowly underway despite resistance documented in this paper (Stewart 2001c). The rate of home ownership in Los Angeles declined from 40.9 percent in 1970 to 38.6 percent in 2000.
49. See Stromber 2005.
50. McKibben 2005.
51. Davis 1990, 104.
52. See http://www.api.ucla.edu/rhna, http:/api.ucla/edu/rhna/Regional HousingNeedsAssessment/WhatisRHNA/Main.htm (accessed December 24, 2005). See also http://www.planningcenter.com/pdf/9.2.3/Housethe Region/pdf (accessed December 24, 2005).
53. "The existing need assessment simply examines key variables from the most recent Census to measure ways in which the housing is not meeting the needs of current residents. These variables include the number of low-income households paying more than 30% of their income for housing, as well as severe overcrowding" (see SCAG website http://www.scag.ca.gov).
54. On zoning enforcement in suburbs, see Baumgartner 1988, 18, 80–89.

55. SCAG: "Higher densities can improve the affordability of housing because per unit land costs are lower and construction can be performed more efficiently."
56. Government Code Section 65915.
57. SCAG: "Politically, changing the general plan and rezoning surplus industrial and/or commercial land can be an effective way to make a significant amount of land available for housing."
58. "Her three neighbors also rent rooms to strangers. This is how they cobble together the $1,100 monthly rent. In all, the four 950 square foot houses on a one-third of an acre lot are home to 42 people who put up with mice, cockroaches, broken windows, and faulty plumbing. Before the city kicked families out of the garages, there were 55 people" (Mena 2003).
59. Bodnar 1985, 82–83.
60. "In some neighborhoods, converted garages and illegal units are the only housing that poor families can afford. When those units are eliminated, many renters can be thrown into a tight housing market with little assistance" (Stewart 2001b).
61. Zorbaugh 1929, 69–86, 109, 129–130.
62. Davis 1990, 24.
63. Although the acronym is recent, nimbyism has a long history in American cities (see Light 1977).
64. Visit Silver's website: www.sf-valley.org/Encino. See also Liu 2003.
65. Guerra, Marks, and Brackman 2001, 21.
66. Takahashi 1997.
67. Tamaki, 2003.
68. "Going Past 'No' on Housing." Editorial, *Los Angeles Times,* May 11, 2004, section B, p. 14.
69. For example, Gene Lassers's website (http://www.dangerouspath.com) criticizes the safety, security, and noise pollution that could accompany Boeing Realty Corporation's proposed PacifiCenter Project. None of the representative nimby websites accessible in August 2003 address immigration: El Toro: http://www.eltoroairport.org; Ventura County: http://www.rallyfortheranch.com; Garden Grove, http://www.cggna.org; Westwood, http://www.savewestwood-village.org; Claremont, http://www.cc4claremont.tripod.com, and http://www.coyote-hills.org; Long Beach: http://www.carso-park.org; Mission Viejo: http://www.friendsofthefoothills.org, http://www.ocheartandsoul.org, and http://www.ranchomissionviejo.com. Property developers counter with their own websites (see http://www.pacificenter.com and http://www.newhallland.com).
70. "Many homeowners have made their largest financial investment in a community with certain characteristics, and their local government is expected to reflect their concerns. New infill development can increase traffic congestion, overwhelm the capacity of local public facilities, and require an increased tax burden on current residents" (Johnson, Moller, and Dardia 2004, 84).
71. "Many suburban communities continue to pass affordable housing restrictions, make the approval process increasingly complicated, use exclusionary zoning practices, impose excessive subdivision controls, and put in place tactics to delay project approval." They are "still NIMBY in the suburbs" (Engel et al. 2005, 5).

72. Finnegan and Barabak 2005.
73. Myers 2001, 395.
74. Johnson, Johnson-Webb, and Farrell 1999.
75. See also Myers and Lee 1996.
76. Bump, Lowell, and Pettersen 2005, 33–34.
77. Myers 2001, 387–88.
78. Myers and Park 2002.
79. Gibson 2005.
80. For reviews of this extensive literature, see: Schill 2005; and Quigley and Rosenthal 2005
81. Molotch 1972, 216–17.
82. To get rid of its homeless, the City of Santa Clarita shut down its homeless shelter, then bought 175 homeless persons one-way bus tickets to neighboring towns (Rivera 2004; see also Hymon 2004).
83. Di Massa and Winton 2005.
84. "With the most crowded households of any large U.S. city and many of its dwellings substandard, Santa Ana faces an intractable dilemma: how to enforce health and safety laws without forcing thousands of residents onto the street" (Mena 2003).
85. San Marino and Palos Verdes Estates house many rich immigrant homeowners; they house few poor immigrant renters.

Chapter 9

1. Acuna 1996.
2. Gregory 1989, 80.
3. Stein 1973, 73.
4. "Keep Moving." Band 7, Songs from the Depression, by Mike Seeger, John Cohen, and Tom Paley. Folkways Record FH 5264.
5. Federal Writer's Project 1939, 65.
6. Chavez 1997, 66–69.
7. Hymon 2004.
8. See www.saveourstate.org.
9. Fox 2004, 615.
10. Hanson 2003, xiv.
11. Visit the CRA website: www.saveourlicense.com; see also Mohan and Hoffman 2003.
12. Southern Poverty Law Center, *Intelligence Report*, Spring, 2004, 36–37.
13. Hernandez 2003, 6; see also: Hernández-León and Zúñiga 2005, 264.
14. Harwood 1986; Lapinski, Peltola, Shaw, and Young 1997; Fox 2004.
15. Feagin 1997, 38.
16. American cities compete to attract the wealthy and exclude the poor, a practice that tends to lock the poor into central cities (Dreier, Mollenkopf, and Swanstrom 2001, 175).
17. http://www.maldef.org/publications/pdf/2002-2003_AnnualReport.pdf, 6.
18. Edwards 2003; Walker 2004.
19. Skejskal 2003.
20. Edwards 2003.

21. Zavella 1997, 156.
22. Here's more of Jimmy Cox's song, composed in 1923: "When in your pocket, not one penny; Then your friends, you haven't any!"
23. Chavez 1997, 66–69.
24. Doty 2003, 19–23.

Chapter 10

1. "The City of Los Angeles should step up enforcement of housing safety laws, and do more to expose slumlords" (Gottlieb et al. 2005, 199).
2. Bean and Spener 2004, 368.
3. If cities wait for migrants themselves to notice how wretched local economic conditions have become, and then to go elsewhere in search of greener pastures, the cities have not exhibited agency.
4. Lopez 2005.
5. California Employment Development Department 2001,31.
6. "Sure it's a federal matter, but nobody at that level is doing anything, and the driver's license flap is a symptom. . . . We can't decide whether to enforce existing laws or completely throw open the floodgates to cheap labor. We won't end policies that drive foreigners to the United States, and we won't stop griping about the cost of having them here" (Lopez 2004). This is the problem to which sequential deflection is the solution.
7. Narro 2001, 22.
8. Mossberger and Stoker 2001, 812.
9. "Going Past 'No' on Housing." Editorial, *Los Angeles Times*, May 11, 2004, B14.
10. Tamaki 2003.
11. "Since the 1980s, residential developers have been on the defensive, and growth opponents have been on the offensive" (Guerra, Marks, and Brackman 2001, 44).
12. Mena 2003.
13. "[Rotterdam's] local government is to publish a plan in December aimed at limiting the number of poor immigrants and refugees settling in Rotterdam." "Rotterdam Considers Ban on Refugees." *Expatica News*, Nov. 12, 2003. http://www.expatica.com/main.asp?pad=2,18,&item_id=35646.
14. "The legal order represented by the state, emerging concretely in the law and regulations affecting real property, comes to be seen as a burden that can be avoided, circumvented, battled, or bribed aside" (Keyder 2000, 128).
15. Van Vliet, 2002, p. 34
16. Gouveia, Carranza, and Cogua 2005, 38–43.
17. Griffith 2005, 50.
18. Shutika 2005, 114–16.
19. Dunn, Aragones, and Shivers 2005, 174–75.
20. Dunn, Aragones, and Shivers 2005, 177.
21. Rich and Miranda 2005, 202, 205.
22. Belluck 2005.
23. Hollifield 1992.
24. "The current US policy mix of heavy border enforcement, light interior enforcement, and low levels of temporary immigration of manual labourers

appears to be ineffective at stemming the tide of illegal immigrants" (Hanson et al. 2002, 283; on the Immigration Reform and Control Act of 1986, see also Graham 2004, 108).

25. But some were. A right-wing social movement, SaveOurState opposed immigration. But their anti-immigrant rallies did not start until well into the second millennium; they were poorly attended; and they actually attracted 15 pro-immigration opponents for every anti-immigration protestor (see http://www.saveourstate.org; on their unsuccessful rally, see Thermos 2005).
26. Gottlieb et al. 2005, 96.
27. Vincent and Lee 2004.
28. Myers 2001, 395; McKibben 2005.
29. Southern California's original nimby is Gerald A. Silver, founder of Home Owners of Encino. Silver's ideology: "Our goal is to preserve the single-family habitability and lifestyle of Encino" (Liu 2003; see also http://www.sf-valley.org/encino).
30. However, sometimes the Mexican Americans were the nimbys. Mexican American women in East Los Angeles prevented the building of a prison in their neighbourhood (Takahashi 1997, 911).
31. "The intent is to drive these businesses into the legitimate economy or to put them out of business" (California Employment Development Department 2001, 32).
32. "As new migrants entered the binational labor market, they naturally sought to avoid the difficult and radically changed circumstances in California" (Durand, Massey, and Capoferro 2005, 12).
33. Kessler 1999, 573.
34. "Our foreign residents add to the burden of public and private relief an amount largely out of proportion to their relative numbers in the general population" (Fairchild 1925, 324).
35. Camarota 2004, table 3.
36. Money 1999, 212.
37. Money 1999, 219.
38. Camarota 2004.
39. Walker 2004.
40. Police from Gretna, Louisiana, blockaded the bridge over the Mississippi River, and fired upon refugees from neighboring New Orleans who attempted to cross it after the hurricane Katrina disaster in September 2005. This callousness shocked the nation, but Gretna's police were only following orders they received from the Gretna city council (Riccardi 2005).
41. Malpica 2002.
42. Shackelford 2004; Shields 2005.

= References =

Abelmann, Nancy, and John Lie. 1995. *Blue Dreams: Korean Americans and the Los Angeles Riots.* Cambridge, Mass.: Harvard University Press.

Acuña, Rodolfo F. 1996. *Anything But Mexican: Chicanos in Contemporary Los Angeles.* London: Verso.

Alexander, Barbara, Martha Andrews, William Apgar, Kermit Baker, Pamela Baldwin, Michelle Barnes, and Eric Belsky. 2003. *The State of the Nation's Housing.* Cambridge, Mass.: Joint Center for Housing Studies of Harvard University.

Allen, James P., and Eugene Turner. 1997. *The Ethnic Quilt: Population Diversity in Southern California.* Northridge: California State University Press.

Apparel Industry Magazine. 1999. "Sewn Products Expo." Atlanta, Ga.

Appelbaum, Richard P. 1997. "Using Religion's Suasion in Garment Industry." *Los Angeles Times*, February 16, p. M1.

Bade, Klaus J. 2003. "L'Europe, Continent d'Immigration: Migrations et Intégration à la Fin du XXe Siècle." In *Les Migrations du Travail en Europe*, edited by Klaus Morgenroth, Paul Vaiss, and Joseph Farré. Bern, Switz.: Peter Lang.

Bader, Veit. 2005. "Dutch Nightmare? The End of Multiculturalism?" *Canadian Diversity* 4(1): 9–11.

Baines, Dudley. 1991. *Emigration from Europe 1815–1930.* London: Macmillan.

Baldwin-Edwards, Martin. 1999. "Where Free Markets Reign: Aliens in the Twilight Zone." In *Immigrants and the Informal Economy in Southern Europe*, edited by Martin Baldwin-Edwards and Joaquin Arango. London: Frank Cass.

Bar-Cohen, Limor, and Deana Milam Carrillo. 2002. "Labor Law Enforcement in California, 1970–2000." In *State of California Labor*, edited by Paul Ong and James R. Lincoln. Los Angeles: University of California Institute for Labor and Employment.

Barstow, David. 2003. "California Leads Prosecution Of Employers in Job Deaths." *New York Times*, December 23, 2003, p. A1.

Bartel, Anne P. 1989. "Where Do the New U.S. Immigrants Live?" *Journal of Labor Economics* 7(4): 371–91

Bartel, Anne P., and Marianne Koch. 1991. "Internal Migration of U.S. Immigrants." In *Immigration, Trade, and the Labor Market*, edited by John M. Abowd and Richard B. Freeman. Chicago: University of Chicago Press.

Baumgartner, M. P. 1988. *The Moral Order of a Suburb.* New York: Oxford University Press.

Bean Frank D., and David A. Spener. 2004. "Controlling International Migration through Enforcement: The Case of the United States." In *International*

Migration: Prospects and Policies in a Global Market. Oxford: Oxford University Press.

Bean, Frank D., and Gillian Stevens. 2003. *America's Newcomers and the Dynamics of Diversity.* New York: Russell Sage Foundation.

Belluck, Pam. 2005. "Town Uses Trespass Law to Fight Illegal Immigrants." *New York Times,* July 13, section A, p. 14.

Berry, Kate. 2004. "Fueling the Koreatown Boom." *Los Angeles Business Journal,* July 26, 2004. Available at: http://www.findarticles.com/p/articles/mi_m5072/is_30_26/ai_n6154361.

Blank, Susan, and Roman S. Torrecilha. 1998. "Understanding the Living Arrangements of Latino Immigrants: A Life Course Approach." *International Migration Review* 32(1): 3–19.

Blau, Francine D. 1980. "Immigration and Labor Earnings in Early Twentieth Century America." *Research in Population Economics* 2(1980): 21–41.

Bodnar, John. 1985. *The Transplanted: A History of Immigrants in Urban America.* Bloomington: Indiana University Press.

Boeri, Tito. 2002. "Preface." In *Immigration Policy and the Welfare System,* edited by Tito Boeri, Gordon Hanson, and Barry McCormick. Oxford: Oxford University Press.

Bonacich, Edna. 1993. "Asian and Latino Immigrants in the Los Angeles Garment Industry: An Exploration of the Relationship between Capitalism and Racial Oppression." In *Immigration and Entrepreneurship: Culture, Capital, and Ethnic Networks,* edited by Ivan Light and Parminder Bhachu. New Brunswick: Transaction Publishers.

———. 1994. "Asians in the Los Angeles Garment Industry." In *The New Asian Immigration in Los Angeles and Global Restructuring,* edited by Paul Ong, Edna Bonacich, and Lucie Cheng. Philadelphia: Temple University Press.

Bonacich, Edna, and Richard P. Appelbaum. 2000. *Behind the Label.* Los Angeles: University of California Press.

Bonstein, Julia, and Markus Dettmer. 2004. "Schwarzarbeit: Wenn der Postmann Klingelt." *Der Spiegel* 3: 58–60.

Borjas, George J. 1990. *Friends or Strangers: The Impact of Immigrants on the U.S. Economy.* New York: Basic Books.

———. 1996. "The New Economics of Immigration." *The Atlantic Monthly* 278(November): 72–80.

———. 1999. *Heaven's Door: Immigration Policy and the American Economy.* Princeton, N.J.: Princeton University Press.

———. 2002. "The Impact of Welfare Reform on Immigrant Welfare Use." Washington, D.C.: Center for Immigration Studies.

———. 2003. "The Labor Demand Curve is Downward Sloping: Reexamining the Impact of Immigration on the Labor Market." Working Paper No. 9755. Cambridge, Mass.: National Bureau of Economic Research.

Bornschier, Volker, and Hanspeter Stamm. 1990. "Transnational Corporations." In *Economy and Society,* edited by Alberto Martinelli, and Neil J. Smelser. Newbury Park: Sage Publications.

Bottles, Scott. 1988. *Los Angeles and the Automobile.* Berkeley: University of California Press.

Bromley, Ray. 1988. "Working in the Streets: Survival Strategy, Necessity, or Unavoidable Evil?" In *The Urbanization of the Third World*, edited by Josef Gugler. Oxford: Oxford University Press.

Brown, E. Richard, R. Burciaga Valdez, Roberta Wyn, Hongjian Yu, and William Cumberland. 1994. "Who are California's Uninsured?" Los Angeles: UCLA Center for Health Policy Research.

Brown, Marianne P., Alejandra Domenzain, and Nelliana Villoria-Siegert. 2002. "Appendix VI: Industry Profiles and Expanded Findings." In *Voices From the Margins: Immigrant Workers' Perceptions of Health and Safety in the Workplace*. Los Angeles: UCLA-LOSH. Available at: http://www.losh.ucla.edu.

Bruecker, Herbert, Gil S. Epstein, Barry McCormick, Gilles Saint-Paul, Allesandra Venturini, and Klaus Zimmerman. 2002. "Managing Migration in the European Welfare State." In *Immigration Policy and the Welfare System*, edited by Tito Boeri, Gordon Hanson, and Barry McCormick. Oxford: Oxford University Press.

Bump, Micah, Lindsay Lowell, and Silje Pettersen. 2005. "The Growth and Population Characteristics of Immigrants and Minorities in American's New Settlement States." In *New Immigrant Communities: Addressing Integration Challenges*, edited by Elzbieta Gozdziak and Susan F. Martin. Lanham, Md.: Lexington Books.

Bun, Chan Kwok, and Ong Jin Hui. 1995. "The Many Faces of Immigrant Entrepreneurship." In *Cambridge Survey of World Migration*, edited by Robin Cohen. Cambridge: Cambridge University Press.

Burgess, Ernest W. 1925. "The Growth of the City: An Introduction to a Research Project." In *The City*, edited by Robert E. Park, Ernest W. Burgess, and Roderick D. McKenzie. Chicago: University of Chicago.

———. 1928. "Residential Segregation in American Cities." *Annals of the American Academy of Political and Social Science* 140(November): 105–15.

Burgess, Ernest W., and Donald J. Bogue. 1967. "Research in Urban Society: A Long View." In *Urban Sociology*, edited by Ernest W. Burgess and Donald J. Bogue. Chicago: University of Chicago.

California Department of Industrial Relations. 1994. "Targeted Industries Partnership Program Issues First Yearly Report." Sacramento, Calif.: State Printing Office. Available at: http://www.dir.ca.gov/DIRNews/1994/94-13.html.

———. 2004. Industrial Welfare Commission. "History of California Minimum Wage." Available at: www.dir.ca.gov/iwc/iwc.html (accessed December 28, 2005).

California Department of Labor Standards and Enforcement. 2002. *Annual Report on the Effectiveness of the Bureau of Field Enforcement*. Sacramento, Calif.: State Printing Office. Available at: http://www.dir.ca/gov/dlse/BOFEO1.htm.

California Employment Development Department. 2001. "Joint Enforcement Strike Force on the Underground Economy: A Report to the California Legislature." In California. Assembly Committee on Labor and Employment, and Assembly Budget Subcommittee No. 4. *Overview of the Enforcement Activities of the Department of Industrial Relations*. Sacramento, Calif.: State Printing Office.

California Fashion Association. 1999. *Fact Sheet—Los Angeles County*. Los Angeles: California Fashion Association.

California State Assembly, Committee on Labor and Employment. 2001. *Overview of the Enforcement Activities of the Department of Industrial Relations*. Sacramento, Calif.: State Printing Office.

208   Deflecting Immigration

Camarota, Steven A. 1999. "Importing Poverty: Immigration's Impact on the Size and Growth of the Poor Population in the United States." Center Paper 15. Washington, D.C.: Center for Immigration Studies. Available at: http://www.cis.org/articles/poverty_study/povstudy.pdf.

———. 2003. "The Impact of Immigration on American Workers." Testimony prepared for the U.S. House of Representatives Committee on the Judiciary Subcommittee on Immigration, Border Security, and Claims. 108th Cong., 1st sess. Washington, D.C.: Center for Immigration Studies. Available at: http://www.cis.org/articles/2003/stevetestimony103003.html.

———. 2004a. "Economy Slowed, But Immigration Didn't: The Foreign-Born Population, 2000–2004." Backgrounder 12–04. Washington, D.C.: Center for Immigration Studies. Available at: http://www.cis.org/articles/2004/back1204.pdf.

———. 2004b. "The High Cost of Cheap Labor: Illegal Immigrants and the Federal Budget." ISBN 1-881290-43-3. Washington, D.C.: Center for Immigration Studies. Available at: http://www.cis.org/articles/2004/fiscal.pdf.

Camarota, Steven A., and James R. Edwards, Jr. 2000. "Without Coverage: Immigration's Impact on the Size and Growth of the Population Lacking Health Insurance." ISBN 1-881290-03-4. Washington, D.C.: Center for Immigration Studies. Available at: http://www.cis.org/articles/2000/coverage/uninsured.pdf.

Catanzarite, Lisa, and Michael Bernabe Aguilera. 2002. "Working with Co-Ethnics: Earnings Penalties for Latino Immigrants at Latino Jobsites." *Social Problems* 49(1): 101–127.

Chavez, Leo R. 1997. "Immigration Reform and Nativism." In *Immigrants Out!* edited by Juan F. Perea. New York: New York University Press.

Chavez, Stephanie, and James Quinn. 1987. "Substandard Housing Garages: Immigrants In, Cars Out." *Los Angeles Times,* May 24, 1987, p. A1.

Chinchilla, Norma Stoltz, and Nora Hamilton. 2001. "Doing Business: Central American Enterprises in Los Angeles." In *Asian and Latino Immigrants in a Restructuring Economy,* edited by Marta López-Garza and David R. Diaz. Stanford, Calif.: Stanford University Press.

Choi, Hyunsun. 2004. "Social Capital and Community Economic Development in Los Angeles Koreatown: Faith-Based Organizations in Transitional Ethnic Community." Ph.D. diss., University of Southern California. Available at: http://www.kccd3300.org/researchdocs/pdf/dissertation_hyunsunChoi.pdf.

Clark, William A. V. 1996. "Residential Patterns: Avoidance, Assimilation, and Succession." In *Ethnic Los Angeles,* edited by Roger Waldinger and Mehdi Bozorgmehr. New York: Russell Sage Foundation.

———. 1998a. *The California Cauldron: Immigration and the Fortunes of Local Communities.* New York: Guilford Press.

———. 1998b. "Mass Migration and Local Outcomes: Is International Migration to the United States Creating a New Urban Underclass?" *Urban Studies* 35(3): 371–83.

Cleeland, Nancy. 1999. "Garment Jobs: Hard, Bleak, and Vanishing." *Los Angeles Times,* March 11, 1999, p. A1.

———. 2002. "Off-the-Books Jobs Growing in Region." *Los Angeles Times,* May 6, 2002, p. C1.

Cleeland, Nancy, and Marla Dickerson. 2001. "Davis Cuts Requested Labor Law Funding." *Los Angeles Times,* July 27, 2001, p. C1.

Cornelius, Wayne. 1998. "The Structural Embeddedness of Demand for Immigrant Labor: New Evidence from California." In *Crossings: Mexican Immigration in Interdisciplinary Perspective*, edited by Marcelo Suarez-Orozco. Cambridge, Mass.: Harvard University Press.

Crouch, Winston W., and Beatrice Dinerman. 1963. *Southern California Metropolis*. Los Angeles: University of California Press.

Cuomo, Mario. 1974. *Forest Hills Diary: The Crisis of Low-Income Housing*. New York: Random House.

Cyrus, Norbert. 2001. "Schattenwirtschaft und Migration." In *Migration und Integration in Berlin*, edited by Frank Gesemann. Berlin: Leske and Budrich.

Davis, Mike. 1987. "Chinatown, Part Two? The Internationalization of Downtown Los Angeles." *New Left Review* 164(July/August): 65–86.

———. 1990. *City of Quartz: Excavating the Future in Los Angeles*. London: Verso.

Dawes, Amy, Michael Diehl, Carla Lazzareschi, and Stacey R. Strickler. 2000. *Imagining Los Angeles*. Los Angeles: The Los Angeles Times.

De La Torre-Jimenez, Lilian. 2004. "Inland Empire Crece con el Impulse de los Latinos." *La Opinión* [Los Angeles]. May 3, 2004, p. 18.

De Magalhaes, Claudio Soares. 2001. "International Property Consultants and the Transformation of Local Markets." *Journal of Property Research* 18(2): 99–121.

Dear, Michael. 2001. *Sprawl Hits the Wall: Confronting the Realities of Metropolitan Los Angeles*. Los Angeles: Southern California Studies Center.

Dicken, Peter. 1992. *Global Shift: The Internationalization of Economic Activity*. New York: The Guilford Press.

Dickerson, Marla. 1999. "L.A. Trade Cut from New Cloth." *Los Angeles Times*, July 21, 1999, p. A1.

———. 2003. "Is California Climate Getting Too Chilly for Business?" *Los Angeles Times*, February 9, 2003, p. C1.

———. 2004. "Poverty Rate in State Fell in 1990s." *Los Angeles Times*. February 2, 2004, p. C1.

———. 2005. "Mexico Runs on Sidewalk Economy." *Los Angeles Times*, May 9, 2005, p. A1.

Dickerson, Marla, and Nancy Cleeland. 2000. "Employment in L. A. Garment Industry Trade Continues to Shrink." *Los Angeles Times*, August 18, 2000, p. C1.

Dickey, Fred. 2003. "Undermining American Workers." *Los Angeles Times Magazine*, July 20, 2003, p. 12ff.

Didion, Joan. 1992. *After Henry*. New York: Simon & Schuster.

DiMassa, Cara Mia, and Richard Winton. 2005. "Four Suburbs Said to Have Dumped Homeless in L.A." *Los Angeles Times*, September 24, 2005, p. B1.

Dixon, Robyn. 2005. "Zimbabwe Slum Dwellers are Left With Only Dust." *Los Angeles Times*, June 21, 2005, p. A1.

Doty, Roxanne Lynn. 2003. *Anti-Immigrantism in Western Democracies*. London: Routledge.

Dreier, Peter, John Mollenkopf, and Todd Swanstrom. 2001. *Place Matters: Metropolitics for the Twenty-First Century*. Lawrence: University Press of Kansas.

Duneier, Mitchell. 1999. *Sidewalk*. New York: Farrar, Straus & Giroux.

Dunn, Ashley. 1993. "Immigrants Lose Large Sums in Investment Deals." *Los Angeles Times*, February 9, 1993, p. A1.

Dunn, Timothy J., Ana Maria Aragones, and George Shivers. 2005. "Recent Mexican Migration in the Rural Delmarva Peninsula." In *New Destinations: Mexican Immigration in the United States*, edited by Victor Zúñiga and Rubén Hernández-León. New York: Russell Sage Foundation.

Durán, Agustín. 2004. "Afirman que los Alquileres Seguiran Subiendo en Los Angeles." *La Opinión* [Los Angeles] March 31, 2004, p. 3A.

Durand, Jorge, Douglas S. Massey, and Chiara Capoferro. 2005. "The New Geography of Mexican Immigration." In *New Destinations: Mexican Immigration in the United States*, edited by Victor Zúñiga and Rubén Hernández-León. New York: Russell Sage Foundation.

Dymski, Gary A., and John M. Veitch. 1992. "Race and the Financial Dynamics of Urban Growth: L.A. as Fay Wray." In *City of Angels*, edited by Gerry Riposa and Carolyn G. Dersch. Dubuque, Iowa: Kendall/Hunt Publishing.

The Economist. 2005. "Bossing the Big Tortilla." Vol. 375, No. 8426. May 14, 2005, pp. 29–30.

Edwards, James R. 2003. "Officers Need Backup: The Role of State and Local Police in Immigration Law Enforcement." Backgrounder, April 2003. Washington, D.C.: Center for Immigration Studies. Available at: http://www.cis.org/articles/2003/back703.pdf

Ellis, Mark. 2001. "A Tale of Five Cities? Trends in Immigrant and Native-Born Wages." In *Strangers at the Gates: New Immigrants in Urban America*, edited by Roger Waldinger. Berkeley: University of California Press.

Engel, David, Trent Frazier, Peter Lawrence, Jeffrey Lubbell, Konrad Schlater, and Edwin Stromberg. 2005. *Why Not in Our Community? Removing Barriers to Affordable Housing*. Washington: U.S. Department of Housing and Urban Development.

Erickson, Christopher L., Catherine L. Fisk, Ruth Milkman, Daniel J. B. Mitchell, and Kent Wong. 2002. "Justice for Janitors in Los Angeles: Lessons from Three Rounds of Negotiations." *British Journal of Industrial Relations* 40: 543–67.

Esbenshade, Jill. 2004. *Monitoring Sweatshops*. Philadelphia, Pa.: Temple University Press.

Fainstein, Susan S. 1994. *The City Builders*. Oxford: Blackwell.

Fairchild, Henry Pratt. 1925. *Immigration*. New York: Macmillan.

Fausset, Richard. 2002. "Yards So Ugly They're a Crime." *Los Angeles Times*, August 26, 2002, p. B3.

Feagin, Joe R. 1997. "Old Poison in New Bottles." In *Immigrants Out!* edited by Juan F. Perea. New York: New York University Press.

Federal Writer's Project. Works Progress Administration. 1939. *California: A Guide to the Golden State*. New York: Hastings House.

Fernandez-Kelly, M. Patricia, and Anna M. Garcia. 1989. "Informalization at the Core: Hispanic Women, Homework, and the Advanced Capitalist State." In *The Informal Economy*, edited by Alejandro Portes, Manuel Castells, and Lauren A. Benton. Baltimore, Md.: The Johns Hopkins University Press.

Finnegan, Michael, and Mark Z. Barabak. 2005. "Villaraigosa's Support Goes Beyond Latinos." *Los Angeles Times*, May 19, 2005, p. A1.

Fischer, Peter A., and Thomas Straubhaar. 1996. "Is Migration into EU Countries Demand Based?" In *Economics and European Union Migration Policy*. London: Institute for Public Policy Research.

References   211

Fix, Michael, and Paul T. Hill. 1990. *Enforcing Employer Sanctions*. Santa Monica: RAND Corporation.

Fix, Michael, and Jeffrey S. Passel. 1994. *Immigration and Migrants*. Washington, D.C.: The Urban Institute.

Fligstein, Neil. 1998. "Is Globalization the Cause of the Crises of Welfare States?" European University Institute, Florence, Political and Social Sciences, Working Paper SPS No. 98/5. Available at: www.iue.it.sps/wp-abs/sps98-5.html (accessed December 28, 2005).

Fogelson, Robert M. 1964. *The Fragmented Metropolis: Los Angeles, 1850–1930*. Cambridge, Mass.: Harvard University Press.

Fong, Eric, and Milena Gulia. 2000 "Neighborhood Change within the Canadian Ethnic Mosaic, 1986–1991." *Population Research and Policy Review* 19(2): 155–77.

Fong, Eric, and Kumiko Shibuya. 2000. "Suburbanization and Home Ownership: The Spatial Assimilation Process in U.S. Metropolitan Areas." *Sociological Perspectives* 43(1): 137–57.

Fong, Eric, and Rima Wilkes. 1999. "The Spatial Assimilation Model Reexamined: An Assessment by Canadian Data." *International Migration Review* 33(3): 594–620.

Fong, Timothy P. 1994. *The First Suburban Chinatown*. Philadelphia, Pa.: Temple University Press.

Fox, Cybelle. 2004. "The Changing Color of Welfare? How Whites' Attitudes toward Latinos Influence Support for Welfare." *American Journal of Sociology* 110(3): 580–625.

Fraundorf, M. N. 1978. "Relative Earnings of Native and Foreign–Born Women." *Explorations in Economic History* 15(2): 211–20.

Freedberg, Louis, and Sabin Russell. 1999. "Immigrants' Fears Leave Children Without Insurance." *San Francisco Chronicle*. January 15, 1999, p. A3.

Freeman, Gary. 1992. "Migration Policy and Politics in the Receiving States." *International Migration Review* 26(4): 1144–67.

———. 1997. "Immigration as a Source of Political Discontent and Frustration in Western Democracies." *Studies in Comparative International Development* 32(3): 42–64.

Frey, William H. 1996/97. "Immigration and the Changing Geography of Poverty." *Focus* 18(2): 24–28.

———. 2003. "Metropolitan Magnets for International and Domestic Migrants." *Living City Census Series*. Washington, D.C.: Center on Urban and Metropolitan Policy, Brookings Institution.

Frey, William, and Kao-Lee Liaw. 1996. "The Impact of Recent Immigration on Population Redistribution within the United States." Working Paper 96–376. Ann Arbor: Population Studies Center of the University of Michigan.

Friedberg, Rachel M., and Jennifer Hunt. 1999. "Immigration and the Receiving Economy." In *The Handbook of International Migration: The American Experience*, edited by Charles Hirschman, Philip Kasinitz, and Josh DeWind. New York: Russell Sage Foundation.

Fuentes–Salinas, José. 2004. "Crónica: La Pasión de MacArthur Park." *La Opinión* [Los Angeles] March 8, 2004.

Fulmer, Melinda. 1999. "Mid-Wilshire Making a Comeback: A Surge of Korean-American Investing is Breathing New Life into the Ailing, Once-Grand Stretch of L.A.'s Boulevard." *Los Angeles Times*, April 16, 1999, p. A1.

212   Deflecting Immigration

Fulton, William. 1997. *The Reluctant Metropolis: The Politics of Urban Growth in Los Angeles.* Point Arena, Calif.: Solano Books.

Furlong, Tom. 1988. "Growing Influence of Asians on California Real Estate." *Los Angeles Times,* August 14, 1988, p. D1.

Fussell, Elizabeth. 2004. "Migrant's Origin Nations and Communities and the Cumulative Causation of Migration." Paper presented at the Annual Meeting of the American Sociological Association, San Francisco, California (August 15, 2004).

Gambetta, Diego, and Peter Reuter. 1995. "Conspiracy among the Many: The Mafia and Legitimate Industries." *The Economics of Organized Crime,* edited by Gianluca Fiorentini, Sam Peltzman. Cambridge: Cambridge University Press.

Garcia, Norma Edith, and Patrick Clarke. 2001. *Housing in Southern California: A Decade in Review.* Los Angeles: Southern California Association of Governments.

Geospatial and Statistical Data Center of the University of Virginia Library. N.d. Available at: http://fisher.lib.virginia.edu/collections/stats/cbp (accessed December 27, 2005).

Gibson, Campbell, and Emily Lennon. 1999. "Nativity of the 50 Largest Urban Places, 1870 to 1990." Washington: U.S. Census Bureau, Population Division. Available at: http://www.census.gov/population/www/documentation/twps0029/tab19.html.

Gibson, Timothy A. 2005. "NIMBY and the Civic Good." *City and Community* 4: 381–401.

Gold, Mattea. 2001. "Fannie Mae Allots $50 Billion to Ease Area's Housing Crunch." *Los Angeles Times,* November 10, 2001, p. B1.

Gold, Scott. 2001. "Paying the Price of Growth in Inland Empire." *Los Angeles Times,* November 25, 2001, p. A1.

Gold, Steven. 1994. "Patterns of Economic Cooperation among Israeli Immigrants in Los Angeles." *International Migration Review* 28(1): 114–35.

Goldberg, Michael. 1985. *The Chinese Connection: Getting Plugged in to Pacific Rim Real Estate, Trade, and Capital Markets.* Vancouver: University of British Columbia Press.

Goldin, Claudia. 1994. "The Political Economy of Immigration Restriction in the United States." In *The Regulated Economy: A Historical Approach to Political Economy,* edited by Claudia Goldin and Gary D. Libecap. Chicago: University of Chicago Press.

Gonzalez, Eliseo Diaz, and Eduardo Mendoza Cota. 2003. "La Velocidad de Ajuste de los Salarios en Mexico: El Mercado de Trabajo Despues de la Crisis de 1995." Paper presented at 6th Congreso de la Associacion Mexicana de Estudios del Trabajo, Hermosillo, Sonora (April 9, 2003).

Gonzalez-Portillo, Patricia. 2000. "Un Viaje Peligroso." *La Opinión* [Los Angeles], February 27, 2000, p. 4A.

Gordon, Jennifer. 2005. *Suburban Sweatshops.* Cambridge, Mass.: Harvard University Press.

Gorman, Anna. 2005. "Employers of Illegal Immigrants Face Little Risk of Penalty." *Los Angeles Times,* May 29, 2005, p. A1.

Gottdiener, Mark. 1985. *The Social Production of Urban Space.* Austin: University of Texas Press.

Gottdiener, Mark, and Nicos Komninos. 1989. "Introduction." In *Capitalist Development and Crisis Theory: Accumulation, Regulation and Spatial Restructuring*, edited by Mark Gottdiener and Nicos Komninos. New York: St. Martin's Press.

Gottlieb, Robert, Mark Vallianatos, Regina M. Freer, and Peter Dreier. 2005. *The Next Los Angeles*. Berkeley: University of California Press.

Gouveia, Lourdes, Miguel A. Carranza, and Jasney Cogua. 2005. "The Great Plains Migration: Mexicanos and Latinos in Nebraska." In *New Destinations: Mexican Immigration in the United States*, edited by Victor Zúñiga and Rubén Hernández-León. New York: Russell Sage Foundation.

Gozdziak, Elzbieta and Susan F. Martin, eds. 2005. *New Immigrant Communities*. Lanham, Md.: Rowman and Littlefield.

Graham, Otis L. 2004. *Unguarded Gates: A History of America's Immigration Crisis*. Lanham, Md.: Rowman and Littlefield.

Greenhouse, Steven. 2003a. "Cleaner at Wal-Mart Tells of Few Breaks and Low Pay." *New York Times*, October 25, 2003, p. A10.

———. 2003b. "Wal-Mart, Driving Workers and Supermarkets Crazy." *New York Times*, October 19, 2003, p. D3.

Gregory, James N. 1989. *American Exodus*. New York: Oxford University Press.

Gregory, Peter. 1989. "The Determinants of International Migration and Policy Options for Influencing the Size of Migration Flows." Working Paper No. 2. Washington, D.C.: Commission for the Study of International Migration and Comparative Economic Development.

Grieco, Elizabeth. 2003. "Foreign Born Hispanics in the United States." Migration Information Source. Washington, D.C.: Migration Policy Institute. Available at: http://www.migrationinformation.org/feature/display.cfm?ID=95.

Grieco, Margaret. 1987. "Family Networks and the Closure of Employment." In *The Manufacture of Disadvantage*, edited by Gloria Lee and Ray Loveridge. Milton Keynes, UK: Open University Press.

Griffith, David C. 2005. "Rural Industry and Mexican Immigration and Settlement in North Carolina." In *New Destinations: Mexican Immigration in the United States*, edited by Victor Zúñiga and Rubén Hernández-León. New York: Russell Sage Foundation.

Griswold, Daniel T. 2002. "Willing Workers Fixing the Problem of Illegal Mexican Migration to the United States." "Publication No. 19." Washington, D.C.: Center for Trade Policy Studies of the Cato Institute.

Groh, George W. 1972. *The Black Migration*. New York: Weybright and Talley.

Guerra, Fernando, Mara A. Marks, and Harold Brackman. 2001. "Rebuilding the Dream: A New Housing Agenda for Los Angeles." Los Angeles: The Center for the Study of Los Angeles of Loyola Marymount University.

Gugler, Josef. 1988. "Overurbanization Reconsidered." In *The Urbanization of the Third World*, edited by Josef Gugler. Oxford: Oxford University Press.

Gurak, Douglas T., and Fe Caces. 1992. "Migration Networks and the Shaping of Migration Systems." In *International Migration Systems*, edited by Mary M. Kritz, Lin Lean Lim, and Hania Zlotnik. Oxford: Clarendon Press.

Haberfellner, Regina. 2003. "Austria: Still a Highly Regulated Economy." In *Immigrant Entrepreneurs: Venturing Abroad in the Age of Globalization*, edited by Robert Kloosterman and Jan Rath. Oxford: Berg Publishers.

Hagan, Jacqueline Maria. 1998. "Social Networks, Gender, and Immigrant Incorporation: Resources and Constraints." *American Sociological Review* 63(1): 55–67.

Haller, Mark. 1990. "Illegal Enterprise: A Theoretical and Historical Interpretation." *Criminology* 28(2): 207–35.

Hamilton, Nora, and Norma Chinchilla. 1995. "Central Americans in California: Transnational Communities, Economies and Cultures." Occasional Papers No. 1. Los Angeles: Center for Multiethnic and Transnational Studies, University of Southern California.

———. 2001. *Seeking Community in a Global City: Guatemalans and Salvadorans in Los Angeles.* Philadelphia, Pa.: Temple University Press.

Hamnett, C. 1994. "Social Polarisation in Global Cities: Theory and Evidence." *Urban Studies* 31(3): 401–24.

Hanson, Gordon H., Kenneth F. Scheve, Matthew J. Slaughter, and Antonio Spilimbergo. 2002. "Immigration and the US Economy: Labour-Market Impacts, Illegal Entry, and Policy Choices." In *Immigrant Policy and the Welfare System,* edited by Tito Boeri, Gordon Hanson, and Barry McCormick. Oxford: Oxford University Press.

Hanson, Victor Davis. 2003. *Mexifornia.* San Francisco: Encounter Books.

Harkness, Joseph M., and Sandra J. Newman. 2005. *The Housing Landscape for America's Working Families 2005.* Washington, D.C.: Center for Housing Policy.

Harrison, Alferdteen. 1991. *Black Exodus.* Jackson: University Press of Mississippi.

Hart, Keith. 1973. "Informal Income Opportunities and Urban Employment in Ghana." *Journal of Modern African Studies* 11(1): 61–89.

Harwood, Edwin. 1986. "American Public Opinion and U.S. Immigration Policy." *Annals of the American Academy of Political and Social Science* 487(September): 201–12.

Hatton, Timothy J., and Jeffrey G. Williamson. 1994. "What Drove the Mass Migrations from Europe in the Late Nineteenth Century?" *Population and Development Review* 20: 533–59.

———. 1998. *The Age of Mass Migration.* Oxford: Oxford University Press.

Häusermann, Hartmut, and Thomas Krämer-Badoni. 1989. "The Change of Regional Inequality in the Federal Republic of Germany." In *Capitalist Development and Crisis Theory: Accumulation, Regulation and Spatial Restructuring,* edited by Mark Gottdiener and Nicos Komninos. New York: St. Martin's Press.

Hawley, Amos H. 1971. *Urban Society.* New York: Ronald Press.

Heer, David. 2002. "When Cumulative Causation Conflicts with Relative Economic Opportunity." *Migraciones Internacionales* 1(3): 32–53.

Helper, Rose. 1969. *Racial Policies and Practices of Real Estate Brokers.* Minneapolis: University of Minnesota.

Hemphill, Thomas A. 1999. "The White House Apparel Industry Partnership Agreement: Will Self-Regulation Be Successful?" *Business and Society Review* 104(2): 121–37.

Henri, Florette. 1975. *Black Migration: Movement North, 1900–1920.* New York: Anchor Books.

Hernandez, Antonia. 2003. "MALDEF: 35 Years of Promoting a Fair Chance for All Latinos." Los Angeles: Mexican American Legal Defense and Educational Fund.

Hernández-León, Rubén, and Victor Zúñiga. 2002. "Mexican Immigrant Communities in the South and Social Capital: The Case of Dalton, Georgia." Working Paper No. 64. San Diego: The Center for Comparative Immigration Studies, University of California.

———. 2005. "Appalachia Meets Aztlan: Mexican Immigration and Intergroup Relations in Dalton, Georgia." In *New Destinations: Mexican Immigration in the United States*, edited by Victor Zúñiga and Rubén Hernández-León. New York: Russell Sage Foundation.

Hess, Darrel. 1990. "Korean Garment Manufacturing in Los Angeles." Master's thesis. University of California, Los Angeles.

Higham, John. 1988. *Strangers in the Land*, 2nd ed. New Brunswick, N.J.: Rutgers University Press.

Hill, Laura E., and Joseph M. Hayes. 2003. "California's Newest Immigrants." *California Counts: Population Trends and Profiles* 5(2): 1–19.

Hill, Peter J. 1975. "Relative Skill and Income Levels of Native and Foreign-Born Workers in the United States." *Explorations in Economic History* 12(1): 47–60.

Hiltzik, Michael A. 1995. "Dependence on Employer Leaves Many Uncovered." *Los Angeles Times*. October 30, 1995, p. A11.

Hise, Greg. 1997. *Magnetic Los Angeles: Planning the Twentieth Century Metropolis.* Baltimore, Md.: The Johns Hopkins University Press.

Hollifield, James F. 1992. *Immigrants, Markets and States: The Political Economy of Postwar Europe.* Cambridge, Mass.: Harvard University Press.

Hondagneu–Sotelo, Pierrette. 2003. "Review of Beyond Smoke and Mirrors: Mexican Immigration in an Era of Economic Integration." *Contemporary Sociology* 32: 677–78.

Horton, John. 1995. *The Politics of Diversity.* Philadelphia, Pa.: Temple University Press.

Hugo, Martin. 1997. "War on Illegal Garage Units Softened." *Los Angeles Times,* June 5, 1997, p. B1.

Hum, Tarry. 1997. "The Economics of Ethnic Solidarity: Immigrant Ethnic Economics and Labor Market Segmentation in Los Angeles." Ph.D. dissertation. University of California, Los Angeles.

———. 2000. "A Protected Niche? Immigrant Ethnic Economies and Labor Market Segregation." In *Prismatic Metropolis: Inequality in Los Angeles*, edited by Lawrence D. Bobo, Melvin H. Oliver, James H. Johnson, and Abel Valenzuela. New York: Russell Sage Foundation.

———. 2001. "The Promises and Dilemmas of Immigrant Ethnic Economies." In *Asian and Latino Immigrants in a Restructuring Economy*, edited by Marta López–Garza and David R. Diaz. Stanford, Calif.: Stanford University Press.

Hymon, Steve. 2004. "Homeless Told to Pack Up as LAPD Sweep Continues." *Los Angeles Times,* January 1, 2004, p. B1

IGS Library. 2005. "Workers' Compensation in California." Berkeley: Institute of Governmental Studies, University of California. Available at: http://www.igs.berkeley.edu/library/htWorkersCompensation.

Ingram, Carl, Myron Levin, and Gregg Jones. 2003. "Legislature OKs Small Business Health Coverage." *Los Angeles Times,* September 14, 2003, p. A1.

International Organization for Migration. 2003. *World Migration Report 2003.* No. 861. Geneva: United Nations.

Joassart-Marcelli, Pascale, and Daniel Flaming. 2002. "Workers Without Rights: The Informal Economy in Los Angeles." Los Angeles, Calif.: Economic Roundtable.

Johnson, Hans P., Rosa M. Moller, and Michael Dardia. 2004. *In Short Supply? Cycle and Trends in California Housing.* Sacramento: Public Policy Institute of California.

Johnson, James H., Jr., Karen D. Johnson-Webb, and Walter C. Farrell, Jr. 1999. "Newly Emerging Hispanic Communities in the United States: A Spatial Analysis of Settlement Patterns, In-Migration Fields and Social Receptivity." In *Immigration and Opportunity,* edited by Frank D. Bean and Stephanie Bell-Rose. New York: Russell Sage Foundation.

Jonas, Andrew E. G., and David Wilson. 1999. "The City as a Growth Machine: Critical Reflections Two Decades Later." In *The Urban Growth Machine: Critical Perspectives, Two Decades Later,* edited by Andrew E. G. Jonas and David Wilson. Albany: State University of New York Press.

Kandel, William, and Douglas S. Massey. 2002. "The Culture of Mexican Migration: A Theoretical and Empirical Analysis." *Social Forces* 80(3): 981–1004.

Kang, K. Connie. 1998a. "41 Restaurants Violated Labor Laws." *Los Angeles Times,* August 22, 1998, p. B1.

———. 1998b. "Ex-workers' Suit Seeks Back Wages." *Los Angeles Times,* August 5, 1998, p. B1.

———. 2004. "An Ethnic Center's New Pull." *Los Angeles Times,* December 15, 2004, p. A1.

Keil, Roger. 1998. *Los Angeles: Globalization, Urbanization, and Social Struggles.* Chichester: John Wiley & Sons.

Kelly, David. 2005. "Illegal Immigration Fears Have Spread." *Los Angeles Times,* April 25, 2005, p. A1.

Kessler, Judy. 1999a. *Tying the Global to the Local: The LA Apparel Industry in Transition.* Los Angeles: Los Angeles Trade-Technical College.

———. 1999b. "The North American Free Trade Agreement, Emerging Apparel Production Networks and Industrial Upgrading: The Southern California/ Mexico Connection." *Review of International Political Economy* 6(4): 565–608.

Keyder, Caglar. 2000. "Liberalization from Above and the Future of the Informal Sector." In *Informalization: Process and Structure,* edited by Faruk Tabak and Michaeline A. Crichlow. Baltimore, Md.: The Johns Hopkins University Press.

Kim, Dae Young. 1999. "Beyond Co-ethnic Solidarity: Mexican and Ecuadorean Employment in Korean-Owned Businesses in New York City." *Ethnic and Racial Studies* 22(3): 581–605.

Kim, David. 1975. *Korean Small Businesses in the Olympic Area.* Los Angeles: School of Architecture and Urban Planning, University of California.

Kim, Hak-Hoon. 1986. "Residential Patterns and Mobility of Koreans in Los Angeles County." Master's thesis. California State University, Los Angeles.

Kindleberger, Charles P. 1967. *Europe's Post-War Growth: The Role of Labor Supply.* Cambridge, Mass.: Harvard University Press.

King, Danny. 2002. "Grocery Chain Wields Influence on Real Estate Scene." *Los Angeles Business Journal,* January 21, 2002. Available at: http://www.findarticles. com/p/articles/mi_m5072/is_3_24/ai_82323392.

Klein, Norman M. 1990. "The Sunshine Strategy: Buying and Selling the Fantasy of Los Angeles." In *Twentieth Century Los Angeles: Power, Promotion and Social Conflict*, edited by Norman M. Klein and Martin J. Schiesl. Claremont, Calif.: Regina Books.

Kloosterman, Robert C. 1996. "Double Dutch: Polarization Trends in Amsterdam and Rotterdam After 1980." *Regional Studies* 30(5): 467–76.

Kloosterman, Robert, and Jan Rath, eds. 2003. *Immigrant Entrepreneurs: Venturing Abroad in the Age of Globalization*. Oxford: Berg Publishers.

Knight, Richard V. 1989. "The Emergent Global Society." In *Cities in a Global Society*, edited by Richard V. Knight and Gary Gappert. Newbury Park, Calif.: Sage Publications.

Kotkin, Joel, and David Friedman. 1993. "California Portfolio: A New Gold Rush." *Los Angeles Times*, April 4, 1993, p. A4.

Krissman, Fred. 2005. "Sin Coyote ni Patron: Why the 'Migrant Network' Fails to Explain International Migration." *International Migration Review* 39: 4–44.

Krivo, Lauren J. 1995. "Immigrant Characteristics and Hispanic-Anglo Housing Inequality." *Demography* 32(4): 599–615.

Lal, Barbara Ballis. 1990. *The Romance of Culture in an Urban Civilization. Robert E. Park on Race and Ethnic Relations*. London: Basil Blackwell.

Lalonde, Robert J., and Robert H. Topel. 1991. "Labor Market Adjustments to Increased Immigration." In *Immigration, Trade, and the Labor Market*, edited by John M. Abowd and Richard B. Freeman. Chicago: The University of Chicago Press.

Lapinski, John S., Pia Peltola, Greg Shaw, and Alan Young. 1997. "Trends: Immigrants and Immigration." *The Public Opinion Quarterly* 61(2): 356–83.

Laslett, John. 1996. "Historical Perspectives: Immigration and the Rise of a Distinctive Urban Region, 1900–1970." In *Ethnic Los Angeles*, edited by Roger Waldinger and Mehdi Bozorgmehr. New York: Russell Sage Foundation.

Lee, Don. 1994. "Orange County Home Garment Work Targeted in Crackdown." *Los Angeles Times*, September 30, 1994, p. D5.

———. 1996. "Task Force in Tatters: State-Federal Tensions Hinder Garment Industry Crackdown." *Los Angeles Times*, August 4, 1996, p. D1.

———. 1998a. "Fashion Forward: Southern California's Niche Role in the Garment Industry has Helped Local Manufacturers Thrive Despite Job Losses Elsewhere and a Production Shift to Mexico." *Los Angeles Times*, April 26, 1998, p. D1.

———. 1998b. "An Anemic Rate of Health Coverage." *Los Angeles Times*, July 4, 1998, p. A1.

Lee, Don, and Jesus Sanchez. 1999. "A Trade-up Market for Home Buyers." *Los Angeles Times*, July 12, 1999, p. A1.

Lee, Dong Ok. 1992. "Commodification of Ethnicity." *Urban Affairs Quarterly* 28: 258–75.

Lee, Kyung. 1969. "Settlement Patterns of Los Angeles Koreans." Master's thesis. University of California, Los Angeles.

Lerner, Preston. 2003. "Whither the Lawn: What Southern California's Booming Population and Looming Water Crisis Mean for the Great Green Carpet of Suburbia." *Los Angeles Times Magazine*, May 4, 2003, p. 14ff.

Levine, Elaine. 2001. *Los Nuevos Pobres de los Estados Unidos: Los Hispanicos*. México, D.F.: Instituto de Investigaciones Económicas, Universidad Nacional Autónoma de México.

Levy, Steven. 1997. *California Economic Growth 1996–97*. Palo Alto: Center for Continuing Study of the California Economy.

Lewis, James. 2002. "Policy Implications of Immigrant Workers and Entrepreneurs: An Overview." In *Immigrant Workers and Entrepreneurs*. Chicago: Illinois Department of Human Services.

Lewis Mumford Center for Comparative Urban and Regional Research of the State University of New York at Albany. Various years. "Whole Population Segregation." Census Data for City of Los Angeles, 1980, 1990, and 2000.

———. 2002. "The New Americans." American Communities Project. Albany: State University of New York. Available at: http://www.albany.edu/mumford/activities/activities5.html; http://www.s4.brown.edu/S4/projects.htm.

Li, Wei. 1998. "Los Angeles's Chinese Ethnoburb: From Ethnic Service Center to Global Economy Outpost." *Urban Geography* 19(6): 502–17.

Liebhold, Peter, and Harry R. Rubenstein. 1999. *Between a Rock and a Hard Place: A History of American Sweatshops, 1820–Present*. Los Angeles: UCLA Asian American Studies Center and Simon Wiesenthal Center Museum of Tolerance.

Light, Ivan. 1978. "The Ethnic Vice Industry, 1880–1944." *American Sociological Review* 42(3): 464–79.

———. 1981. "Ethnic Succession." In *Ethnic Change*, edited by Charles Keyes. Seattle: University of Washington.

———. 1983. *Cities in World Perspective*. New York: Macmillan.

———. 1985. "Ethnicity and Business Enterprise." In *Making It in America*, edited by M. Mark Stolarik. Cranbury, N.J.: Bucknell University Press.

———. 1988. "Los Angeles." In *The Metropolis Era*, vol. 2, *Mega-Cities*, edited by Mattei Dogan and John D. Kasarda. Newbury Park, Calif.: Sage Publications.

———. 1999. "Globalization and Migration Networks." In *Immigrant Businesses*, edited by Jan Rath and Robert Kloosterman. Houndsmills, Basingstoke: Palgrave Macmillan.

———. 2001. "The Chicago School and the Ethnic Economy." In *Mirrors and Windows*, edited by Januscz Mucha, Dirk Kaesler, and Wlodzimierz Winclawski. Toruń: Copernicus University.

———. 2005. "The Ethnic Economy." In *The Handbook of Economic Sociology*, 2nd ed., edited by Neil J. Smelser and Richard Swedberg. New York: Russell Sage Foundation.

Light, Ivan, Richard Bernard, and Rebecca Kim. 1999. "Immigrant Incorporation in the Garment Industry of Southern California." *International Migration Review* 33(1): 5–25.

Light, Ivan, and Parminder Bhachu. 1993. "Introduction: California Immigrants in World Perspective." In *Immigration and Entrepreneurship*, edited by Ivan Light and Parminder Bhachu. New Brunswick, N.J.: Transaction.

Light, Ivan, Parminder Bhachu, and Stavros Karageorgis. 1993. "Migration Networks and Immigrant Entrepreneurship." In *Immigration and Entrepreneurship: Culture, Capital, and Ethnic Networks*, edited by Ivan Light and Parminder Bhachu. New Brunswick, N.J.: Transaction Publishers.

Light, Ivan, and Edna Bonacich. 1988. *Immigrant Entrepreneurs: Koreans in Los Angeles, 1965–1982*. Berkeley: University of California Press.

Light, Ivan, and Steven Gold. 2000. *Ethnic Economies*. San Diego, Calif.: Academic Press.

Light, Ivan, Hadas Har–Chvi, and Kenneth Kan. 1994. "Black/Korean Conflict in Los Angeles." In *Managing Divided Cities*, edited by Seamus Dunn. London: Keele University.

Light, Ivan, Im Jung-Kwuon, and Deng Zhong. 1990. "Korean Rotating Credit Associations in Los Angeles." *Amerasia* 16(1): 35–54.

Light, Ivan, and Stavros Karageorgis. 1994. "The Ethnic Economy." In *Handbook of Economic Sociology*, edited by Neil Smelser and Richard Swedberg. New York: Russell Sage Foundation.

Light, Ivan, Rebecca Kim, and Connie Hum. 2000. "Globalization, Vacancy Chains, or Migration Networks? Immigrant Employment and Income in Greater Los Angeles, 1970–1990." In *The Ends of Globalization*, edited by Don Kalb, Marco van der Land, Richard Staring, Bart van Steenbergen, and Nico Wilterdink. Boulder, Colo.: Rowman and Littlefield.

———. 2002. "Globalization Effects on Employment in Southern California, 1970–1990." In *Globalization and the New City*, edited by Malcolm Cross and Robert Moore. New York: Palgrave Macmillan.

Light, Ivan, and Elizabeth Roach. 1996. "Self–Employment: Mobility Ladder or Economic Lifeboat?" In *Ethnic Los Angeles*, edited by Roger Waldinger and Mehdi Bozorgmehr. New York: Russell Sage Foundation.

Light, Ivan, Georges Sabagh, Mehdi Bozorgmehr, and Claudia Der-Martirosian. 1994. "Beyond the Ethnic Enclave Economy." *Social Problems* 41(1): 601–16.

Lindlaw, Scott. 1999. "Davis to Decide on Cutting Prenatal Care for Illegal Immigrants." Associated Press release (May 12, 1999).

Lindo, Roger. 2004. "Trabajo y Pobreza Van de la Mano Para Muchos Inmigrantes." *La Opinión* [Los Angeles], May 19, 2004.

Lipman, Barbara J. 2001. "Paycheck to Paycheck: Working Families and the Cost of Housing in America." *New Century Housing* 2: 1–52.

———. 2003. "America's Newest Working Families: Cost, Crowding and Conditions for Immigrants." *New Century Housing* 4: 1–40.

———. 2005. *Something's Gotta Give: Working Families and the Cost of Housing.* Washington, D.C.: Center for Housing Policy.

Lipman, Barbara, Joseph M. Harkness, and Sandra J. Newman. 2005. *The Housing Landscape for America's Working Families, 2005.* Washington, D.C.: Center for Housing Policy.

Liu, Caitlin. 2003. "Valley's Silver Bullet Hits Mark." *Los Angeles Times*, June 8, 2003, p. B1.

Liu, Yujia. 2004. "Ethnic Economies and Women's Employment: A Causal Linkage?" Paper presented at the Annual Meeting of the American Sociological Association, San Francisco (August 18, 2004).

Logan, John R., and Harvey L. Molotch. 1987. *Urban Fortunes.* Los Angeles: University of California Press.

Logan, John R., and Todd Swanstrom. 1990. "Urban Restructuring: a Critical View." In *Beyond the City Limits: Urban Policy and Economic Restructuring in Comparative Perspective*, edited by John R. Logan and Todd Swanstrom. Philadelphia, Pa.: Temple University Press.

Lopez, David, Eric Popkin, and Edward Telles. 1996. "Central Americans: At the Bottom, Struggling to Get Ahead." In *Ethnic Los Angeles*, edited by Roger Waldinger and Mehdi Bozorgmehr. New York: Russell Sage Foundation.

Lopez, Steve. 2004. "This Idiocy is What Needs to be Terminated." *Los Angeles Times*, September 1, 2004, p. B1.

————. 2005. "Inhumanity Has Found a Home on Skid Row." *Los Angeles Times*, August 19, 2005, p. B1.

López–Garza, Marta. 2001. "A Study of the Informal Economy and Latina/o Immigrants in Greater Los Angeles." In *Asian and Latino Immigrants in a Restructuring Economy*, edited by Marta López-Garza and David R. Diaz. Stanford, Calif.: Stanford University Press.

Los Angeles Times. 1988. "Guide for Growth." Editorial. August 4, 1988.

Loucky, James, Maria Soldatenko, Gregory Scott and Edna Bonacich. 1994. "Immigrant Enterprise and Labor in the Los Angeles Garment Industry." In *Global Production: The Apparel Industry in the Pacific Rim*, edited by Edna Bonacich et al. Philadelphia, Pa.: Temple University Press.

Ma Mung, Emmanuel, and Thomas Lacroix. 2003. "France: The Narrow Path." In *Immigrant Entrepreneurs: Venturing Abroad in the Age of Globalization*, edited by Robert Kloosterman and Jan Rath. Oxford: Berg Publishers.

MacDonald, John S., and Leatrice D. MacDonald. 1964. "Chain Migration, Ethnic Neighborhood Formation, and Social Networks." *Milbank Memorial Fund Quarterly* 42: 82–97.

Malpica, Daniel Melero. 2002. "Making a Living in the Streets of Los Angeles: An Ethnographic Study of Day Laborers." *Migraciones Internacionales* 1: 124–48.

Marcelli, Enrico. 2001. "Informal Employment in California." In *The State of California Labor*, edited by Paul M. Ong and James Lincoln. Los Angeles: Institute of Industrial Relations of the University of California.

Martin, Hugo. 2003. "Southland Found Failing in Most Categories." *Los Angeles Times*, January 10, 2003, p. B6.

————. 2004. "A Savvy Housing Group Expands." *Los Angeles Times*, December 24, 2004, p. B1.

Martin, Philip L., and J. Edward Taylor. 2001. "Managing Migration: The Role of Economic Policies." In *Global Migrants, Global Refugees*, edited by Aristide R. Zolberg and Peter M. Benda. New York: Berghahn Books.

Massey, Douglas. 1985. "Ethnic Residential Segregation: A Theoretical Synthesis and Empirical Review." *Sociology and Social Research* 69: 315–350.

————. 1988. "Economic Development and International Migration in Comparative Perspective." *Population and Development Review* 14(3): 383–413.

————. 1999. "Why Does Immigration Occur? A Theoretical Synthesis." In *The Handbook of International Migration: The American Experience*, edited by Charles Hirschman, Philip Kasinitz, and Josh DeWind. New York: Russell Sage Foundation.

Massey, Douglas S., Rafael Alarcón, Jorge Durand, and Humberato González. 1987. *Return to Aztlan: The Social Process of International Migration from Western Mexico*. Berkeley: University of California Press.

Massey, Douglas S., Joaquín Arango, Graeme Hugo, Ali Kouaouci, Adela Pellegrino and J. Edward Taylor. 1993. "Theories of International Migration: A Review and Appraisal." *Population and Development Review* 19(3): 431–66.

Massey, Douglas S., and Nancy A. Denton. 1993. *American Apartheid*. Cambridge, Mass.: Harvard University Press.

Massey, Douglas S., Jorge Durand, and Nolan J. Malone. 2002. *Beyond Smoke and Mirrors: Mexican Immigration in an Era of Economic Integration.* New York: Russell Sage Foundation.

Massey, Douglas S., and J. Edward Taylor. 2004a. "Introduction." In *International Migration: Prospects and Policies in a Global Market,* edited by Douglas S. Massey and J. Edward Taylor. Oxford: Oxford University Press.

———. 2004b. "Back to the Future: Immigration Research, Immigration Policy, and Globalization in the Twenty–First Century." In *International Migration: Prospects and Policies in a Global Market,* edited by Douglas S. Massey and J. Edward Taylor. Oxford: Oxford University Press.

Mayhew, Henry. 1885/1995. *London Labour and the London Poor,* repr. ed. New York: Penguin Books.

McCarthy, Kevin F., and Georges Vernez. 1997. *Immigration in a Changing Economy: California's Experience.* Los Angeles: RAND Corporation.

McConville, Shannon, and Paul Ong. 2003. *The Trajectory of Poor Neighborhoods in Southern California, 1970–2000.* Washington, D.C.: Brookings Institution.

McDonnell, Patrick J. 2001. "State's Allure for Immigrants Wanes." *Los Angeles Times,* January 24, 2001, p. B1, 7. Available at: http://www.usc.edu/schools/sppd/futures/pdf/State's_alluretext.pdf.

Mcgreevy, Patrick. 2005. "Alleged Slumlords Donated to Delgadillo." *Los Angeles Times,* October 26, section A, p. 1.

McKibben, Dave. 2005. "A Low Cost Housing Idea Flops in Mission Viejo." *Los Angeles Times,* July 13, 2005, p. B6.

McMahan, John. 1988. *Property Development,* 2nd ed. New York: McGraw-Hill.

Mena, Jennifer. 2003. "In Housing Density, It's Too Close For Comfort." *Los Angeles Times,* September 15, 2003, p. B1.

———. 2004. "Storefront Clinics Surge in O.C. as Latinos Seek Low–Cost Care." *Los Angeles Times,* May 2, 2004, p. B6.

Mexican American Legal Defense and Education Fund. 2001. "Latinos and the State Earned Income Tax Credit (EITC): Poverty Despite Work." Los Angeles, Calif.: MALDEF. Available at: http://www.maldef.org/publications/pdf/EITC.pdf.

Migration Dialogue. 1995. "Regulating the Immigrant Labor Market." *Migration News* 2, September. Davis: University of California. Available at: http://migration.ucdavis.edu/mn/more.php?id=1028_0_2_0.

———. 1996. "Immigrants and US Business." *Migration News* 3, June. Davis: University of California. Available at: http://migration.ucdavis.edu/mn/more.php?id=967_0_2_0.

Milkman, Ruth, and Eileen Appelbaum. 2004. "Paid Family Leave in California: New Research Findings." In *The State of California Labor 2004.* Berkeley: University of California Institute for Labor and Employment.

Miller, Alan C. 1988. "Developer May Oppose Gallegly in the Primary." *Los Angeles Times,* January 6, 1998, p. B8.

Miller, Christian. 2000. "Head for the Hills." *The Amicus Journal* 22: 21–25.

Millican, Anthony. 1992. "Presence of Koreans Reshaping the Region." *Los Angeles Times,* February 2, 1992, p. B1.

Min, Pyong Gap. 1996. *Caught in the Middle: Korean Merchants in America's Multiethnic Cities.* Los Angeles: University of California Press.

Mohan, Geoffrey, and Allison Hoffman. 2003. "Campaign Building Against License Law." *Los Angeles Times*, October 18, p. A1.

Molotch, Harvey. 1972. *Managed Integration: Dilemmas of Doing Good in the City.* Berkeley: University of California Press.

———. 1976. "The City as a Growth Machine: Toward a Political Economy of Place." *American Journal of Sociology* 82(2): 309–32.

———. 1988. "Strategies and Constraints of Growth Elites." In *Business Elites and Urban Development*, edited by Scott Cummings. Albany: State University of New York Press.

Money, Jeannette. 1999. *Fences and Neighbors: The Political Geography of Immigration Control.* Ithaca, N.Y.: Cornell University Press.

Moore, Joan, and Raquel Pinderhughes. 1993. "Introduction." In *In the Barrios: Latinos and the Underclass Debate*, edited by Joan Moore and Raquel Pinderhughes. New York: Russell Sage Foundation.

Moore, Paul, Patrice Wagonhurst, Jessica Goodheart, David Runsten, Enrico Marcelli, Pascale Joassart-Marcelli, and John Medearis. 2000. "The Other Los Angeles: The Working Poor in the City of the 21st Century." Los Angeles: Los Angeles Alliance for a New Economy.

Moore, Solomon. 2004. "Fire Peril has Roots in Poverty." *Los Angeles Times*, October 2, p. B1.

More, Paul, Patrice Wagonhurst, Jessica Goodheart, David Runsten, Enrico Marcelli, Pascale Joassart-Marcelli, and John Medearis. 2000. *The Other Los Angeles: The Working Poor in the City of the 21st Century.* Los Angeles: Los Angeles Alliance for a New Economy. Available at: http://www.laane.org/research/reports.html#OtherLA.

Mossberger, Karen, and Gerry Stoker. 2001. "The Evolution of Urban Regime Theory." *Urban Affairs Review* 36(6): 810–35.

Mutchler, Jan E., and Lauren J. Krivo. 1989. "Availability and Affordability: Adaptation to a Housing Squeeze." *Social Forces* 68(1): 241–61.

Myers, Dowell. 2001. "Demographic Futures as a Guide to Planning: California's Latinos and the Compact City." *Journal of American Planning Association* 67(4): 383–97.

Myers, Dowell, and Seong Woo Lee. 1996. "Immigration Cohorts and Residential Overcrowding in Southern California." *Demography* 33(1): 51–65.

Myers, Dowell, and Julie Park. 2002. *The Great Housing Collapse in California.* Washington, D.C.: Fannie Mae Foundation.

Myers, Dowell, John Pitkin, and Julie Park. 2004. "California's Immigrants Turn the Corner." Policy Brief. Los Angeles: University of Southern California Urban Initiative.

Myrdal, Gunnar. 1944. *An American Dilemma*, 3rd ed. New York: Harper and Brothers.

———. 1957. *Economic Theory and Under-Developed Regions.* London: Duckworth.

Narro, Victor. 2001. "Statement of Victor Narro." In California. Assembly Committee on Labor and Employment. Paul Koretz, Chair, and Assembly Budget Subcommittee No. 4, George Nakano, Chair. *Overview of the Enforcement Activities of the Department of Industrial Relations.* Sacramento, Calif.: State Printing Office.

Nazario, Sonia, and Douglas P. Shutt. 1995. "Many in Middle Class Turn to County for Medical Help." *Los Angeles Times*, October 30, 1995, p. A1.

Nientied, Peter, and Jan van der Linden. 1988. "Approaches to Low–Income Housing in the Third World." In *The Urbanization of the Third World*, edited by Josef Gugler. Oxford: Oxford University Press.

Obdeijn, Herman. 2003. "Les migrations ver l'Europe: un Mouvement d'Émancipation du Tiers Monde." In *Les Migrations du Travail en Europe*, edited by Klaus Morgenroth, Paul Vaiss, and Joseph Farré. Bern: Peter Lang.

O'Donnell, Edward T. 2004. "A Neighborhood of Their Own." *New York Times*, June 6. Available at: http://query.nytimes.com/gst/fullpage.html?res=9C03E4DB1331F935A35755C0A9629C8B63&pagewanted=print.

Oh, M. David. 1983. *An Analysis of the Korean Community in the Mid-Wilshire Area*, pt. 2. Los Angeles: Mid-Wilshire Community Research Center Corporation.

O'Hara, Kate. 2002. *How Are We Housed? The Continuing Struggle for Decent, Affordable Housing in Los Angeles, 1990–2000*. Los Angeles: Southern California Association of Non-Profit Housing.

Ojeda, Victoria. 1996. *Mujeres y Salud Adelante*. Master's Thesis, University of California, Los Angeles.

O'Loughlin, John, and Juergen Friedrichs. 1996. "Polarization in Post–Industrial Societies: Social and Economic Roots and Consequences." In *Social Polarization in Post–Industrial Metropolises*, edited by John O'Loughlin and Juergen Friedrichs. New York: Walter de Gruyter.

Ong, Paul, and Evelyn Blumenberg. 1996. "Income and Racial Inequality in Los Angeles." In *The City: Los Angeles and Urban Theory at the End of the Twentieth Century*, edited by Allen J. Scott and Edward W. Soja. Los Angeles: University of California.

Ong, Paul M., and Michela Zonta. 2001. "Trends in Earnings Inequality." In *The State of California Labor*, edited by Paul M. Ong and James R. Lincoln. Los Angeles: University of California, Los Angeles, Institute of Industrial Relations.

Orfalea, Gregory. 1999. "A Kingdom of Rages." *Los Angeles Times Magazine*, April 18, pp. 14–15.

Orrenius, Pia. 1999. "The Role of Income Shocks and Family Networks in Migration and Migrant Self-Selection." Ph.D. dissertation. University of California, Los Angeles.

Ortiz, Vilma. 1996. "The Mexican-Origin Population: Permanent Working Class or Emerging Middle Class?" In *Ethnic Los Angeles*, edited by Roger Waldinger and Mehdi Bozorgmehr. New York: Russell Sage Foundation.

Ottley, Roi. 1943. *New World A–Coming*. Cleveland, Ohio: World Publishing.

Pally, Karen, and Becca Wilson. 2000. *In Short Supply: Recommendations of the Los Angeles Housing Crisis Task Force*. Los Angeles, Calif.: Los Angeles City Council.

Palm, Risa. 1985. "Ethnic Segmentation of Real Estate Agent Practice in the Urban Housing Market." *Annals of the Association of American Geographers* 75: 58–68.

Pape, Eric. 2003. "So Far from God, So Close to Ground Zero." *Los Angeles Times Magazine*, August 3, p. 20ff.

Park, Robert. 1925. "The City: Suggestions for the Investigation of Human Behavior in the City Environment." *American Journal of Sociology* 20(5): 577–612.

Pécoud, Antoine. 2000. "Thinking and Rethinking Ethnic Economics." *Diaspora* 9: 439–63.

———. 2002. " 'Weltoffenheit Schafft Jobs': Turkish Entrepreneurship and Multiculturalism in Berlin." *International Journal of Urban and Regional Research* 26(3): 494–508.

Peterson, E. Paul. 1981. *City Limits*. Chicago: University of Chicago Press.

Petras, Elizabeth McLean. 1983. "The Global Labor Market in the Modern World–Economy." In *U.S. Immigration and Refugee Policy: Global and Domestic Issues*, edited by Mary M. Kritz. Lexington, Mass.: Lexington Books.

———. 1992. "The Shirt on Your Back: Immigrant Workers and the Reorganization of the Garment Industry." *Social Justice* 19(1): 76–114.

Pieterse, Jan Nederveen. 1994. "Globalization as Hybridization." *International Sociology* 9(2): 161–84.

Pincetl, Stephanie S. 1999a. "The Politics of Influence: Democracy and the Growth Machine in Orange County, US." In *The Urban Growth Machine: Critical Perspectives, Two Decades Later*, edited by Andrew E. G. Jonas and David Wilson. Albany: State University of New York Press.

———. 1999b. *Transforming California*. Baltimore, Md.: The Johns Hopkins University Press.

Pinsky, Mark I. 1994. "Korean Americans Still Ponder Fate of Edward Cho." *Los Angeles Times*, May 23, p. A1.

Pitkin, Bill. 2002. "Did I Say Slums? Housing Reform in the City of Los Angeles." Paper presented at the Association of Collegiate Schools of Planning Conference, Baltimore, Maryland (November 23, 2002).

Plascencia, Luis F. B., Gary Freeman, and Mark Setzler. 2003. "The Decline of Barriers to Immigrant Economic and Political Rights in the American States: 1977–2001." *International Migration Review* 37(1): 5–23.

Platkin, Richard. 1972. "The Role of Ethnic Groups in Urban Real Estate: The Case of the Jews." Master's thesis. University of Washington.

Polanyi, Karl. 1957. *The Great Transformation*. Boston, Mass.: Beacon Press.

Portes, Alejandro, and Ruben Rumbaut. 1990. *Immigrant America*. Los Angeles: University of California Press.

Purcell, Mark. 2000. "The Decline of the Political Consensus for Urban Growth: Evidence from Los Angeles." *Journal of Urban Affairs* 22(1): 85–100.

Quepasa News. 2003. "Cisneros: Dream of owning a home still eludes most Hispanics." *Agencia EFE*. Phoenix, Ariz.: Quepasa.com. Available at: http://www.quepasa.com/content/?c=105&id=164750.

Quigley, John M., and Larry A. Rosenthal. 2005. "The Effects of Land Use Regulation on the Price of Housing: What Do We Know? What Can We Learn?" *Cityscape* 8(1): 69–110.

Quinones, Sam. 2001. "The Koreatown that Never Was." *Los Angeles Times Magazine*, June 3, p. 22ff.

Raes, Stephan, Jan Rath, Marja Dreef, Adam Kumcu, Flavia Reil, and Aslan Zorlu. 2001. "Stitched Up: The Rise and Fall of the Turkish Garment Industry in Amsterdam." In *Unraveling the Rag Trade: Immigrant Entrepreneurship in Seven World Cities*, edited by Jan Rath. Oxford: Berg Publishers.

Raijman, Rebeca, and Marta Tienda. 2003. "Ethnic Foundations of Economic Transactions: Mexican and Korean Immigrant Entrepreneurs in Chicago." *Ethnic and Racial Studies* 26(5): 783–80.

Ram, Monder, Bob Jerrard, and Joy Husband. 2001. "Still Managing to Survive: Asians in the West Midlands Clothing Industry." In *Unraveling the Rag Trade: Immigrant Entrepreneurship in Seven World Cities*, edited by Jan Rath. Oxford: Berg Publishers.

Ram, Monder, Balihar Singhera, Tahir Abbas, Gerald Barlow, and Trevor Jones. 2000. "Ethnic Minority Business in Comparative Perspective: The Case of the Independent Restaurant Sector." *Journal of Ethnic and Migration Studies* 26(3): 495–510.

Range, Peter Ross. 2004. "L.A. Confidential: How Community Activists are Making Big Developers Their Partners in Fighting Poverty." Ford Foundation Report. Winter 2004. Los Angeles: LAANE. Available at: http://www.laane.org/pressroom/stories/laane/laane04winterFordFound.html.

Rath, Jan, ed. 2002. *Unraveling the Rag Trade: Immigrant Entrepreneurship in Seven World Cities.* Oxford: Berg Publishers.

Rauch, James E., and Gary G. Hamilton. 2001. "Networks and Markets: Concepts for Bridging Disciplines." In *Networks and Markets,* edited by James E. Rauch and Alessandra Casella. New York: Russell Sage Foundation.

Reed, Deborah. 1999. *California's Rising Income Inequality: Causes and Concerns.* San Francisco: Public Policy Institute of California.

Reich, Michael. 2003. "Living Wage Ordinances in California." In *The State of California Labor.* Los Angeles: University of California Institute for Labor and Employment.

Rekers, Ans, and Ronald van Kempen. 2000. "Location Matters: Ethnic Entrepreneurs and the Spatial Context." In *Immigrant Businesses,* edited by Jan Rath. Houndsmills, Basingstoke, UK: Palgrave Macmillan.

Reyneri, E. 1997. "The Informalization of Migrant Labour: Oversupply of Illegal Migrants or Pull-Effect by the Underground Receiving Economy? The Italian Case." Paper presented at the University of Warwick International Conference on Globalization, Migration, and Social Exclusion. Coventry, UK (May 31, 1997).

Riccardi, Nicholas. 2005. "After Blocking the Bridge, Gretna Circles the Wagons." *Los Angeles Times,* September 16, p. A1.

Rich, Brian L., and Marta Miranda. 2005. "The Sociopolitical Dynamics of Mexican Immigration in Lexington, Kentucky, 1997 to 2002: An Ambivalent Community Responds." In *New Destinations: Mexican Immigration in the United States,* edited by Victor Zúñiga and Rubén Hernández-León. New York: Russell Sage Foundation.

Rivera, Carla. 2004. "Outsourcing of Homeless Stirs Inter-City Debate." *Los Angeles Times,* November 27, 2004, p. B3

Romney, Lee. 1996. "Hispanic Unemployment–Immigrant Self-Employment." *Migration News* 3, September. Davis: University of California. Available at: http://migration.ucdavis.edu/mn/more.php?id=1027_0_2_0.

Rosenfeld, Michael J., and Marta Tienda. 1999. "Mexican Immigration, Occupational Niches, and Labor–Market Competition: Evidence from Los Angeles, Chicago, and Atlanta, 1970–1990." In *Immigration and Opportunity: Race, Ethnicity, and Employment in the United States,* edited by Frank D. Bean and Stephanie Bell-Rose. New York: Russell Sage Foundation.

Sabagh, Georges, and Mehdi Bozorgmehr. 1996. "Population Change: Immigration and Ethnic Transformation." In *Ethnic Los Angeles,* edited by Roger Waldinger and Mehdi Bozorgmehr. New York: Russell Sage Foundation.

Saiz, Albert. 2003. "Room in the Kitchen for the Melting Pot: Immigration and Rental Prices." *The Review of Economics and Statistics* 85: 502–21.

Sanchez, Jesus. 2003. "Median Home Price Hits New High." *Los Angeles Times,* September 26, 2003, p. C2.

Sanchez, Raymond L. 1987. "Street Vendors Pay High Price for Unlicensed Trade in L.A." *Los Angeles Times,* October 26, 1987, p. B1.

Sanders, Jimy, Victor Nee, and Scott Sernau. 2002. "Asian Immigrants' Reliance on Social Ties in a Multiethnic Labor Market." *Social Forces* 81(1): 281–314.

Sarmiento, Socorro T. 1996. "Who Subsidizes Whom? Latina/o Immigrants in the Los Angeles Garment Industry." *Humboldt Journal of Social Relations* 22(1): 37–42.

Sassen, Saskia. 1988. *The Mobility of Labor and Capital.* Cambridge: Cambridge University Press.

———. 1990a. "Beyond the City Limits: A Commentary." In *Beyond the City Limits: Urban Policy and Economic Restructuring in Comparative Perspective,* edited by John Logan and Todd Swanstrom. Philadelphia, Pa.: Temple University Press.

———. 1990b. "Economic Restructuring and the American City." *Annual Review of Sociology* 16: 465–90.

———. 1991. *The Global City: New York, London, Tokyo.* Princeton, N.J.: Princeton University Press.

———. 2000. "The Demise of Pax Americana and the Emergence of Informalization as a Systemic Trend." In *Informalization: Process and Structure,* edited by Faruk Tabak and Michaeline A. Crichlow. Baltimore, Md.: The Johns Hopkins University Press.

———. 2002. "Global Cities and Survival Circuits." In *Global Woman: Nannies, Maids, and Sex Workers in the New Economy,* edited by Barbara Ehrenreich and Arlie Russell Hochschild. New York: Henry Holt.

Sassen-Koob, Saskia. 1985. "Capital Mobility and Labor Migration: Their Expression in Core Cities." In *Urbanization in the World Economy,* edited by Michael Timberlake. Orlando, Fla.: Academic Press.

———. 1989. "New York City's Informal Economy." In *The Informal Economy,* edited by Alejandro Portes, Manuel Castells, and Lauren A. Benton. Baltimore, Md.: The Johns Hopkins University Press.

Savitch, H. V. 1990. "Post–Industrialism with a Difference: Global Capitalism in World–Class Cities." In *Beyond the City Limits: Urban Policy and Economic Restructuring in Comparative Perspective,* edited by John R. Logan and Todd Swanstrom. Philadelphia, Pa.: Temple University Press.

Schachter, Jason P. 2003. "Migration by Race and Hispanic Origin: 1995 to 2000." *Census 2000 Special Reports CENSR–13.* Washington: U.S. Census Bureau, Economics and Statistics Administration.

Schienberg, Jonathan. 2004. "A Few Hundred Undocumented Immigrants are Living in Crude Shanties to Avoid Paying Rent." *Newsday,* April 14, 2004, p. A32.

Schill, Michael H. 2005. "Regulations and Housing Development: What We Know." *Cityscape* 8(1): 5–19

Schimek, Paul. 1989. "Earnings Polarization and the Proliferation of Low–Wage Work." In *The Widening Divide: Income Inequality and Poverty in Los Angeles,* edited by Eulalio Castellanos, Luz Echavarria, Ann Forsyth, Yvette Galindo, Paul M. Ong, Mary Richardson, and Sarah Rigdon Bensinger. Los Angeles: Graduate School of Architecture and Urban Planning of the University of California.

Schlauffler, Helen Halpin, Sara McMenamin, Hal Zawacki, and Jennifer Mordavsky. 2000. *The State of Health Insurance in California, 1999*. Los Angeles: Center for Health Policy Research of the University of California.

Schmalz-Jacobson, Cornelia. 1994. "Report by the Federal Government's Commissioner for Foreigners' Affairs on the Situation of Foreigners in the Federal Republic of Germany in 1993." Bonn: Bonner Universitäts–Buchdruckerei.

Schmidley, A. Dianne. 2001. *Profile of the Foreign-Born Population in the United States, 2000*. U.S. Census Bureau, Current Population Reports, Series P23-206. Washington: U.S. Government Printing Office.

Schoeni, Robert F., Kevin F. McCarthy, and Georges Vernez. 1996. *The Mixed Economic Progress of Immigrants*. Santa Monica, Calif.: RAND Corporation.

Scott, Allen J. 1988. *Metropolis*. Berkeley: University of California Press.

———. 1996. "The Manufacturing Economy: Ethnic and Gender Divisions of Labor." In *Ethnic Los Angeles*, edited by Roger Waldinger and Mehdi Bozorgmehr. New York: Russell Sage Foundation.

———. 2002. "Industrial Urbanism in Late–Twentieth–Century Southern California." In *From Chicago to L.A.: Making Sense of Urban Theory*, edited by Michael J. Dear with J. Dallas Dishman. Thousand Oaks, Calif.: Sage Publications.

Scott, Allen J., and Michael Storper. 1993. "Industrialization and Regional Development." Chapter 1 in *Pathways to Industrialization and Regional Development*, edited by Michael Storper and Allen J. Scott. London: Routledge.

Sell, Ted. 1972. "The Corner–Street Agency for Job Hunters." *Los Angeles Times*, June 26, 1972, p. B1.

Sequeira, Jennifer, and Abdul M. Rasheed. 2004. "The Role of Social and Human Capital in the Start–Up and Growth of Immigrant Businesses." In *Ethnic Entrepreneurship: Structure and Process*, edited by Curt H. Stiles and Craig S. Galbraith. Amsterdam: Elsevier.

Shackelford, Alison. 2004. "Day Worker Arrests are Halted in Redondo Beach." *The Daily Breeze* [Torrance, Calif.], December 8, 2004.

Shergold, P. R. 1976. "Relative Skill and Income Levels of Native and Foreign Born Workers: A Re-Examination." *Explorations in Economic History* 13: 451–61.

Sherman, Diana. 1979. "Korean Town's Extent, Population Grows Daily." *Los Angeles Times*, February 25, 1979, p. H1.

Shields, Nicholas. 2005. "Glendale Laborer Restriction Struck Down." *Los Angeles Times*, May 19, 2005, p. B1.

Shutika, Debra Lattanzi. 2005. "Bridging the Community: Nativism, Activism, and the Politics of Inclusion in Mexican Settlement in Pennsylvania." In *New Destinations: Mexican Immigration in the United States*, edited by Rubén Hernández-León and Victor Zúñiga. New York: Russell Sage Foundation.

Sik, Endre. 1995. *Measuring the Unregistered Economy in Post-Communist Transformation*. Vienna: European Centre for Social Welfare Policy and Research.

Silverstein, Stuart, and Don Lee. 1996. "Sweatshop Task Force Makes Biggest Sweep Ever." *Los Angeles Times*, August 23, 1996, p. D1.

Silverstein, Stuart, and George White. 1996. "Hazards Found in Nearly 75% of Garment Shops." *Los Angeles Times*, May 8, 1996, p. A1.

Simon, Gildas. 1995. *Géodynamique des Migration Internationales dans le Monde*. Paris: Presses Universitaires de France.

Skejskal, Leigh. 2003. "State Troopers Commended for Completing ICE Program." *The Auburn Plainsman* [Alabama], October 16, 2003.

Skelton, George. 1999. "Prop. 187 Decision Puts Governor to No-win Test." *Los Angeles Times,* March 29, 1999, p. A3.

Smith, Jack. 1976. "L.A. with a Korean Accent." *Westways* 68: 33–37.

Smith, James P., and Barry Edmonston. 1997. *The New Americans: Economic, Demographic, and Fiscal Effects of Immigration.* Washington, D.C.: National Academy Press. Available at: http://www.nap.edu/books/0309063566/html/index.html.

Smith, Kolin. 2000. "Gujarat Goes to Jersey." *Preservation* 52: 34–38.

Smith, Sandra Susan. 2003. "Exploring the Efficacy of African–Americans' Job Referral Networks: A Study of the Obligations of Exchange around Job Information and Influence." *Ethnic and Racial Studies* 26(6): 1029–45.

Soja, Edward W. 1989. *Postmodern Geographies.* London: Verso.

———. 1996. "Los Angeles, 1965–1992." In *The City: Los Angeles and Urban Theory at the End of the Twentieth Century,* edited by Allen J. Scott and Edward W. Soja. Los Angeles: University of California Press.

Soja, Edward, Rebecca Morales, and Goetz Wolff. 1983. "Urban Restructuring: An Analysis of Social and Spatial Change in Los Angeles." *Economic Geography* 59: 195–230.

Soja, Edward W., and Allen J. Scott. 1996. "Introduction to Los Angeles: City and Region." In *The City: Los Angeles and Urban Theory at the End of the Twentieth Century.* Berkeley: University of California Press.

Southern California Association of Governments. 2000. "2000 Census Data for Regional Cities." Available at: www.scag.ca.gov/census/index.htm (accessed December 28, 2005).

Stahl, Charles W. 1995. "Theories of International Labor Migration: An Overview." *Asian and Pacific Migration Journal* 4(2–3): 211–32.

Stalker, Peter. 2000. *Workers Without Frontiers.* Boulder, Colo.: Lynne Rienner.

Stark, Oded. 1991. *The Migration of Labor.* Cambridge: Basil Blackwell.

Statistics Norway. 2003. "Subject 03." Available at: http://www.ssb/no/english/subjects (accessed December 28, 2005).

Stein, Walter J. 1973. *California and the Dust Bowl Migration.* Westport, Conn.: Greenwood Press.

Stemfel, Michael. 1992. "Developers Move Ahead on 2 Giant Koreatown Projects." *Los Angeles Business Journal,* July 20.

Stewart, Jocelyn Y. 2001a. "Being Forced Out by Low Incomes, Rising Rents." *Los Angeles Times,* September 29, 2001, p. B1.

———. 2001b. "Crackdown on Unsafe Housing has Downside for Many Tenants." *Los Angeles Times,* December 19, 2001, p. B1.

———. 2001c. "L.A. becoming a City of Renters." *Los Angeles Times,* November 29, 2001, p. B1.

———. 2003. "Ex-landlords to Pay Millions to 19 Tenants." *Los Angeles Times,* August 6, 2003, p. B1.

Strickland, Daryl. 1999. "Rising Rents Squeeze Area's Working Poor." *Los Angeles Times,* September 10, 1999, p. C1.

———. 2001. "Residents Rally to Prevent Sprawl." *Los Angeles Times.* May 21, 2001, p. C1.

Stromberg, Edwin. 2005. *Why Not in Our Community? Removing Barriers to Affordable Housing.* Washington: U.S. Department of Housing and Urban Development.

Suro, Roberto, and Audrey Singer. 2002. *Latino Growth in Metropolitan America: Changing Patterns, New Locations.* Washington, D.C.: Brookings Institution and Pew Hispanic Center.

Takahashi, Lois M. 1997. "The Socio–Spatial Stigmatization of Homelessness and HIV/Aids: Toward an Explanation of the NIMBY Syndrome." *Social Science and Medicine* 45(6): 903–14.

Talwar, Jennifer Parker. 2001. "Contradictory Assumptions in the Minimum-Wage Workplace." *Journal of Contemporary Ethnography* 30(1): 92–127.

Tamaki, Julie. 2003. "Activists Push their Agendas via the Internet." *Los Angeles Times,* September 15, 2003, p. B3.

Teixeira, Carlos. 1997. "The Role of Ethnic Real Estate Agents in the Residential Relocation Process: A Case Study of Portuguese Homebuyers in Suburban Toronto." *Urban Geography* 18: 497–520.

———. 1998. "Cultural Resources and Ethnic Entrepreneurship: A Case Study of the Portuguese Real Estate Industry in Toronto." *The Canadian Geographer* 41(3): 267–81.

Thermos, Wendy. 2005. "Immigration protest in Baldwin Park is Peaceful." *Los Angeles Times,* June 26, 2005, p. B3.

Tienda, Marta. 2002. "Comparative Perspectives on Ethnic and Immigrant Entrepreneurship and Business Development in Chicago." In *Immigrant Workers and Entrepreneurs,* vol. 2, edited by James Lewis. Chicago: Illinois Department of Human Services.

Tilly, Charles, and C. Harold Brown. 1967. "On Uprooting, Kinship, and the Auspices of Migration." *International Journal of Comparative Sociology* 8: 139–64.

Tobar, Hector. 1997. "Riordan Proposes Anti–Slum Plan." *Los Angeles Times,* July 29, 1997, p. B1.

Todaro, Michael P. 1969. "A Model of Labor Migration and Urban Unemployment in Less Developed Countries." *The American Economic Review* 59(1): 138–48.

———. 1984. "Urbanization in Developing Nations: Trends, Prospects, and Policies." In *Urban Development in the Third World,* edited by Pradip K. Ghosh. Westport, Conn.: Greenwood Press.

Trotter, J. W., and E. Lewis. 1996. *African Americans in the Industrial Age.* Boston, Mass.: Northeastern University.

Tseng, Chilla Bulbeck, Lan–Hung Nora Chiang, and Jung–Chung Hsu. Taipei: Interdisciplinary Group for Australian Studies of the National Taiwan University.

Tseng, Yen-Fen. 1994. "Chinese Ethnic Economy: San Gabriel Valley, Los Angeles County." *Journal of Urban Affairs* 16(2): 169–89.

U.S. Bureau of the Census. 1971. *Minority-Owned Businesses: 1969,* MB–1. Washington: U.S. Government Printing Office.

———. 1972. *County Business Patterns, California 1970.* Table 2. Washington: U.S. Bureau of the Census.

———. 1980a. Current Population Survey. Public Use Microdata File. Washington: U.S. Government Printing Office.

———. 1980b. *Statistical Abstract of the United States, 1980.* Washington: U.S. Government Printing Office.

———. 1983. *Census of the Population,* vol. 1, Characteristics of the Population. Chapter C, Pt. 1 U.S. Summary PC-80-1-C1. Washington: U.S. Government Printing Office.

———. 1990. Current Population Survey. Public Use Microdata File. Washington: U.S. Government Printing Office.

———. 2005. *County Business Patterns, California 2003.* Washington: U.S. Bureau of the Census.

U.S. Census Bureau. 1997. *Statistical Abstract of the United States, 1997.* Washington: U.S. Government Printing Office.

———. 2000a. Current Population Survey. Public Use Microdata File. Washington: U.S. Government Printing Office.

———. 2000b. Series 4, Table PCT47. Available at: www.census.gov.

———. 2000c. Summary File 3, Table PCT20. Available at: www.census.gov.

———. 2001. *Survey of Minority-Owned Business Enterprises, 1997.* Economic Censuses, EC97CS-4. Washington: U.S. Government Printing Office.

U.S. Census Bureau, American Fact Finder. 2000. *Census 2000, Demographic Profile Highlights, Los Angeles City, California.* Available at: http://factfinder.census.gov/home/saff/main.html?_lang=en (accessed January 6, 2006).

U.S. Department of Labor. 1997. "No Sweat Garment Enforcement Report, 1995–1996." Washington: U.S. Government Printing Office. Available at: http://www.dol.gov/opa/nosweat/gcover.htm.

Uzzi, Brian. 1996. "The Sources and Consequences of Embeddedness for the Economic Performance of Organizations: The Network Effect." *American Sociological Review* 61(4): 674–98.

Van Vliet, Willem. 2002. "Cities in a Globalizing World: From Engines of Growth to Agents of Change." *Environment and Urbanization* 14(1): 31–41.

Velez, Maria Luisa Penalva. 2003. "L'immigration Economique en Navarre." In *Les Migrations du Travail en Europe,* edited by Klaus Morgenroth, Paul Vaiss, and Joseph Farré. Bern: Peter Lang.

Vernez, Georges. 1993. "Mexican Labor in California's Economy." In *The California-Mexico Connection,* edited by Abraham F. Lowenthal and Katrina Burgess. Stanford, Calif.: Stanford University Press.

Villar, Maria De Lourdes. 1994. "Hindrances to the Development of an Ethnic Economy among Mexican Migrants." *Human Organization* 53(3): 263–68.

Villard, Henry. 1904/1999. "Memoirs of Henry Villard." In *Immigrant Voices: Twenty–Four Narratives on Becoming an American,* edited by Gordon Hutner. New York: Signet Classic.

Vincent, Roger. 2001. "Luxury Spa to Open its Doors to Wealthy in Koreatown." *Los Angeles Times,* June 18, 2001, p. C1.

Vincent, Roger, and Don Lee. 2004. "Home Prices in L.A. Soar at Record Rate." *Los Angles Times,* April 13, 2004, p. A1.

von Scheven, Elsa, and Ivan Light. 2005. "Maturation of Mexican Migration Networks in the U.S." Unpublished paper. Department of Urban Planning, University of California, Los Angeles.

Waldinger, Roger. 1995. "The Other Side of Embeddedness: A Case Study of the Interplay of Economy and Ethnicity." *Ethnic and Racial Studies* 18: 555–580.

———. 1996. *Still the Promised City? New Immigrants and African-Americans in Post-Industrial New York.* Cambridge, Mass.: Harvard University Press.

———. 1999. "Network, Bureaucracy, and Exclusion: Recruitment and Selection in an Immigrant Metropolis." In *Immigration and Opportunity: Race, Ethnicity, and Employment in the United States,* edited by Frank D. Bean and Stephanie Bell-Rose. New York: Russell Sage Foundation.

Waldinger, Roger, and Michael I. Lichter. 2003. *How the Other Half Works: Immigration and the Social Organization of Labor.* Berkeley: University of California Press.

Walker, Keith. 2004. "Meeting Split on Day Workers." *The Potomac News* [Woodbridge, Va.], November 21, 2004.

Walton, S. F., Jr. 1994. *A Geonomical Solution to the Problem of Haphazard Black Migration.* San Ramon, Calif.: San Ramon Valley Counseling, Consultation, and Education Services.

Wang, Shuguang. 1999. "Chinese Commercial Activity in Toronto CMA: New Development Patterns and Impacts." In *Asian Migration: Pacific Rim Dynamics,* edited by Yen–Fen Tseng, Chilla Bulbeck, Lan–Hung Nora Chiang, and Jung–Chung Hsu. Taipei: Interdisciplinary Group for Australian Studies of the National Taiwan University.

Ward, Peter M. 2004. "Mexico City in an Era of Globalization and Demographic Downturn." In *World Cities Beyond the West,* edited by Josef Gugler. Cambridge: Cambridge University Press.

Wedner, Diane. 2001a. "Education, Employment Gains Help More Latinos Become Homeowners." *Los Angeles Times,* August 27, 2001, p. B1.

———. 2001b. "Fewer New Homes Go on the Block Even as Demand Swells." *Los Angeles Times,* May 21, 2001, p. A1.

———. 2001c. "Incentives Proposed to Build Affordable Housing." *Los Angeles Times,* October 16, 2001, p. C2.

———. 2003. "Study finds Rent Burden Growing for Poor Families." *Los Angeles Times,* September 9, 2003, p. C2.

Weil, David. 2003. "Compliance with the Minimum Wage: Can Government Make a Difference?" (January 2003). Available at: http://ssrn.com/abstract=368340.

Wells, Miriam J. 2004. "The Grassroots Reconfiguration of U.S. Immigration Policy." *International Migration Review* 38(4): 1308–47.

White, George. 1996. "El Monte Case Sparked Efforts to Monitor, Root Out Sweatshops." *Los Angeles Times,* August 2, 1996, p. D1.

White, Paul, and Louise Hurdley. 2003. "International Migration and the Housing Market: Japanese Corporate Movers in London." *Urban Studies* 40(4): 687–706.

Williamson, Jeffrey, G. 1990. *Coping with City Growth During the British Industrial Revolution.* Cambridge: Cambridge University Press.

Wilpert, Czarina. 2003. "Germany: From Workers to Entrepreneurs." Chapter 12 in *Immigrant Entrepreneurs: Venturing Abroad in the Age of Globalization,* edited by Robert Kloosterman and Jan Rath. Oxford: Berg Publishers.

Wilson, Tamar D. 1998. "Weak Ties, Strong Ties." *Human Organization* 57(Winter): 393–403.

WMUR. 2005. "Illegal Immigrants Charged with Trespass Seek Dismissal," May 26, 2005. Available at: http://www.thewmurchannel.com/news/4535583/detail.html.

Wolff, Goetz. 1995. *California Community College Fashion Consortia 1995 Economic Report*. Los Angeles: Los Angeles Trade-Technical College.

Wong, Bernard. 1987. "The Role of Ethnicity in Enclave Enterprises: A Study of the Chinese Garment Factories in New York City." *Human Organization* 46: 120–30.

Wong, Charles Choy. 1979. "Ethnicity, Work and Community: The Case of Chinese in Los Angeles." Ph.D. diss., University of California, Los Angeles.

Wong, Linda. 1998. *The Los Angeles Apparel Industry: Wage and Occupational Survey 1998 Report*. Los Angeles: Community Development Trade-Technical Center.

Wrigley, Julia. 1997. "Immigrant Women as Child Care Providers." In *Immigrant Entrepreneurs and Immigrant Absorption in the United States and Israel*, edited by Ivan Light and Richard Isralowitz. Aldershot, UK: Ashgate Publishing.

Zavella, Patricia. 1997. "The Tables are Turned: Immigration, Poverty, and Social Conflict in California Communities." In *Immigrants Out!* edited by Juan F. Perea. New York: New York University Press.

Zeman, Roy. 1944. "City 'Smog' Laid to Dozen Causes." *Los Angeles Times,* September 18, 1944, p. B1.

Zentgraf, Kristine M. 2001. "Through Economic Restructuring, Recession, and Rebound." In *Asian and Latino Immigrants in a Restructuring Economy: The Metamorphosis of Southern California*, edited by Marta C. López-Garza and David R. Diaz. Stanford, Calif.: Stanford University Press.

Zhou, Min. 1992. *Chinatown: The Socioeconomic Potential of an Urban Enclave*. Philadelphia, Pa.: Temple University Press.

Zhou, Yu. 1998. "How Do Places Matter? A Comparative Study of Chinese Ethnic Economies in Los Angeles and New York City." *Urban Geography* 19(6): 531–55.

Zimmerman, Wendy, and Michael Fix. 1994. "Immigrant Policy in the States: A Wavering Welcome." In *Immigration and Ethnicity*, edited by Barry Edmonston and Jeffrey S. Passel. Washington, D.C.: Urban Institute.

Zolberg, Aristide R. 1991. "Bounded States in a Global Market: The Uses of International Labor Migrations." In *Social Theory for a Changing Society*, edited by Pierre Bourdieu and James S. Coleman. Boulder: Westview.

———. 2001. "Introduction: Beyond the Crisis." In *Global Migrants, Global Refugees: Problems and Solutions*, edited by Aristide R. Zolberg and Peter M. Benda. New York: Berghahn Books.

Zook, Kristal Brent. 2003. "Hog Tied: Battling it Out Again at Smithfield Foods." *Amnesty Now* 29: 17–20.

Zorbaugh, Harvey W. 1929. *The Gold Coast and the Slum*. Chicago: University of Chicago Press.

Zúñiga, Victor, and Rubén Hernández-León, eds. 2005. *New Destinations: Mexican Immigration in the United States*. New York: Russell Sage Foundation.

=== Index ===

Boldface numbers refer to figures and tables.

234   Index

Bogue, Donald, 25
bogus immigration documents, 33–34, 98
Bonacich, Edna, 88, 100, 101, 108
border control, 11, 12, 190*n*21, 202–3*n*24
Brackman, Harold, 136
bridging networks, 86–87
Bump, Micah, 26, 44
Bureau of Field Enforcement (BOFE), California's, 98, 103
Burgess, Ernest, 25

Caces, Fe, 53, 86
California: demographics of Mexican immigrants to, 44–46; foreign-born wages declines, **66**; housing value changes, **146**; restriction attitudes in, **153**; and state vs. federal role in immigration, 11; wage decline in, **32**. *See also* Los Angeles; states and localities; traditional immigrant destinations
California Look, 108–9, 111
Cal-OSHA (Occupational Safety and Health Administration, California), 98, 102, 107
Camarota, Steven A., 56
capital: Asian immigrants' resources, 95, 120, 122, 123, 125; and global restructuring theory, 48–49
Caribbean immigrants in garment industry, **91**
Carrillo, Deana, 99
cash wages and growth of informal sector, 49–50
Catanzarite, Lisa, 64
Central American immigrants, 62, 64, 65, 68–69, **91**
chain migration, 181*n*27. *See also* network-driven migration
Chavez, Leo, 155–56
Chen, Roger, 121
Chesapeake Bay area, poverty intolerance in, 165
Chicago School of urban sociology, 25, 114, 129, 137
Chinatown, Los Angeles, 120

Chinchilla, Norma, 64, 69
Chinese immigrants: in garment industry, 90; as place entrepreneurs, 113, 119–22, 195*n*51, 55, 196*n*58, 62
Cho, Edward, 123
cities. *See* metropolitan areas
Clark, William A. V., 65
Clinton, Bill, 102
clustering, initial immigrant, 17, 27
contractors in garment industry structure, 100, 101
control of immigration. *See* laws and regulations
Cornelius, Wayne, 85
cultural factors: acculturation and dispersion of immigrants, 43–46; and black migrations to North, 54; and folklore on black American work ethic, 52; and immigrant exaggeration of job opportunities, 52–53; and poverty tolerance variations, 158–59
cumulative causation, 2, 23–26, 53, 58, 175*n*14

Davis, Gary, 155
Davis, Gray, 103
Davis, Mike, 136
day laborers, 69, 171
Dear, Michael, 119, 136
decency, human, and poverty tolerance, 13, 17, 100, 161
deflection of immigrants: absorption-deflection process, 37–43, 157–58, 163–71, 176*n*27; and driver's license requirement, 77, 151; and governmental attempt to increase housing, 137–42; and housing code law enforcement, 77–78, 79, 129, 132–35; and housing cost reductions, 145–48; and industrial-labor law enforcement, 108, 110, 161, 165, 167; and internal migration to tolerant cities, 17; introduction, 129–30; and low-density housing ideology in LA, 130–32, 135–37, 166–67; and nim-